When I think of Roger Spradlin, words like integrity, passion and godliness immediately come to mind. I know of few men that I love, respect and admire as much as I do this man. He is a role model par excellence for those who serve the Lord Jesus in the high calling of pastor. I thank God for his life and ministry.

Dr. Daniel L. Akin, President
Southeastern Baptist Theological Seminary
Wake Forest, North Carolina

Roger Spradlin is one of America's great preachers and pastors. He is a man of deep biblical conviction and great Gospel passion. Valley Baptist Church is a dynamic and growing congregation filled with people who know Roger Spradlin as Pastor. I also know him as friend, and as one who served as Chairman of the Board of Trustees for The Southern Baptist Theological Seminary. Through his service, I came to know Roger Spradlin as a man of tremendous wisdom, genuine courage, and visionary leadership. He and his wonderful family are an inspiration to all who love the Gospel.

Dr. R. Albert Mohler, Jr., President
The Southern Baptist Theological Seminary
Louisville, Kentucky

"From the first day that I ever saw Roger Spradlin as a new student at the Criswell College, it was obvious that God's hand was uniquely upon this man. Herein you have testimonies to the grace of God in his life. Few men are ever found who are gracious pastors, fabulous preachers, and able scholars. Roger Spradlin is such a man and is a consummate blessing to my own life, as well as to many others."

Dr. Paige Patterson, President
Southwestern Baptist Theological Seminary
Fort Worth, Texas

"Whenever I am asked to name some of the great churches and great pastors in America, Valley Baptist Church in Bakersfield, California and her pastor, Roger Spradlin are among the few I mention. I have had the honor of knowing Dr. Spradlin for over a decade. His humble leadership and faithful preaching of God's Word are models for all of us in Christian ministry. This book of but a few of his great sermons will give the reader a glimpse into the God-given greatness of one of God's choice servants."

Dr. Thom Rainer, President-elect
LifeWay Christian Resources
Nashville, Tennessee

CELEBRATING
20 YEARS OF
CHANGED
Lives

ROGER L. SPRADLIN

ACW Press
Ozark, AL 36360

Celebrating 20 Years of Changed Lives
Copyright ©2005 Roger Spradlin
All rights reserved

Cover Design by Jennifer Gardiner
Photographs by Kelly Carter and Christolear Photography
Interior Design by Pine Hill Graphics

Packaged by ACW Press
1200 HWY 231 South #273
Ozark, AL 36360
www.acwpress.com
The views expressed or implied in this work do not necessarily reflect those of ACW Press. Ultimate design, content, and editorial accuracy of this work is the responsibility of the author(s).

Library of Congress Cataloging-in-Publication Data
(Provided by Cassidy Cataloguing Services, Inc.)

Spradlin, Roger L.

   Celebrating 20 years of changed lives / Roger L. Spradlin. -- 1st ed.
   -- Ozark, AL : ACW Press, 2005.

      p. ; cm.

      ISBN-13: 978-1-932124-71-2
      ISBN-10: 1-932124-71-3

      1. Spradlin, Roger L.--Sermons. 2. Valley Baptist Church
(Bakersfield, Calif.)--History. I. Title.

BX6333.S773 C45 2005
252/.06--dc22   0511

Printed in the United States of America.

This book is dedicated to my daughter,
Charity René Spradlin.

Charity René Spradlin, age 5

God gave us Charity for only six short years. Her
death broke my heart and left my soul in darkness.
God, in His greatness, has mended my heart and
filled my soul with the light of His presence.

Charity's life on earth was brief, but the lessons
from sorrow continue to linger. God has used her
tragic death to shape me and conform me to His
image.

Sermons are born not only out of study, but the
best ones come from brokenness. I cannot assess the
impact of Charity upon my life and my ministry. I
am who I am, in large part, because of the sorrow
that God has entrusted to me.

There was a time when I could not think of
Charity without being engulfed in sorrow. Now, I
look forward to seeing her again and sharing with
her the profound impact of her life upon me, and all
those who hear God's message from a man whom
God has broken.

PREFACE

Twenty-eight years old and full of passion for serving the Lord! That was me in August of 1983, when I moved my family to Bakersfield, California, thrilled at becoming the new pastor of the First Baptist Church of Oildale, California! The early days of my new ministry were full of excitement as we grew to know our new church family. But in the midst of God's blessing, tragedy came to our home with the death of our firstborn, our precious daughter, Charity. In the dark days of grief, a special friend, Mike Miller, proposed that the church he pastored, Hillcrest Baptist Church, merge with our congregation in order to form a new church. Such an audacious proposal only months before, would have been met with my resistance. However, living in the wake of grief had created within me a willingness to share the ministry with a co-pastor. In the providence of God, a third pastor, Phil Neighbors, was also called to serve the newly formed Valley Baptist Church. In a real sense, Valley was formed not out of ambition, but out of a broken heart and a sense of inadequacy on my part.

I have truly "grown up" with Valley Baptist Church. My family and I have been the recipients of their generous love and patience. The people of Valley have listened as I spoke, followed where I have led and forgiven me when I have failed. They are my people, and I am their pastor.

This book represents twenty years of preaching, with one sermon selected from each year. These sermons were not written—they were preached. Therefore, this book is a transcription of these messages. Writing is a very different genre than speaking. So as you read, keep in mind that you are reading transcriptions of spoken words, not written essays.

As a pastor, I am committed to expository preaching. That is, I believe it is my task to explain and apply what Scripture declares. I have, however, included a few messages that are topical rather than expository, because I want this book to be representative of the preaching ministry at Valley Baptist Church over the last twenty years. Some messages are instructional; others are inspirational. Some messages appeal to the mind while others appeal to the heart.

As I have read through these sermons myself, I have relived the moments they were preached. In my mind, I can see the altars filled during the invitation. And I can see the faces of those whose lives have been changed. As you read through these pages, I hope you will join with me in *celebrating twenty years of changed lives!*

December 5, 1999—First service in our new sanctuary.

ACKNOWLEDGMENTS

A book such as this one is a group effort. I am listed as the author, but actually I had little to do with the book, other than preaching the sermons.

The driving force behind publishing this book was Rose Ann Park. Rose Ann was in charge of editing, meeting deadlines, promotion of the book, selecting a publisher—well, everything related to the book. Rose Ann, thank you for your tireless work. Without you, this book certainly would never have been published.

Vicki Parsons transcribed the sermons from their original audio recordings. To me, that was an amazing feat, considering how fast I sometimes speak. Thank you, Vicki!

A wonderful group of volunteers put forth a great amount of hard work to bring this book to completion. They include: Pam Ashby, Mildred Buss, Rita Christolear, Brenda Collins, Teri Goree, Don Laity, Jason March, Susie Park, Elisha Rimestad, Roseanna Sanders, Karen Sherley, Jeanie Smith, Andrew Spradlin, Matthew Spradlin, Vivian Thompson, Monica Vendsel and Stacey Payne.

A sermon that is spoken takes a tremendous amount of editing before it is ready for print—at least mine do! The following volunteers contributed countless hours of work in the editing of this book: Mary Billingsley, Tom Good, Sally Laity, Barbara Schmidt and Pastor Larry Wood. A very special thanks goes to Marilyn Whygle, who spent many long hours proofreading the pages of this book.

Jennifer Gardiner designed the cover. The texture depicted on the cover was photographed by Jennifer in Israel at the traditional site where Jesus appeared before Pilate. Dave Kalahar helped select the photographs used in the book, as well as providing valuable help regarding the cover. Thanks!

This book would not have been possible without the twenty years of sermons.

The twenty years of ministry would not have been possible without the support of my wife, Ginger. Ginger, thank you for your love and example of how a true Christian lives.

CONTENTS

FOREWORD

I *am often asked, "How has Valley Baptist Church grown so
large?" There are actually many reasons for the Church's
growth and success in its twenty-year history. However, my
first response is always this: God blesses the preaching of His
Word. Pastor Roger Spradlin's preaching is the reason for this
blessing!*

*Through the years, he has faithfully preached God's Word
line upon line, precept upon precept. He is committed to
expository preaching, which has led him to preach book by
book through the Bible. Over the past twenty years, the congregation of Valley Baptist Church has eagerly awaited each
Sunday's message. As a result, the Church has heard the full
counsel of God.*

*This volume of sermons is a collection of some of the best
of Pastor Roger's preaching over the past twenty years.*

*These sermons have been used by God to change countless
lives. As you read this book, open your Bible and follow along,
just like thousands have done for the past twenty years.*

—Pastor Phil Neighbors
Co-Pastor, Valley Baptist Church

~ 1985 ~

Valley Baptist Church was born in the year 1985!

In the summer of 1985, Pastor Mike Miller approached me about the possibility of Hillcrest Baptist Church merging with First Baptist Church of Oildale. We decided to consult a mutual friend, Phil Neighbors. All three of our families spent three days together at Lake Tahoe in conversation and prayer about the two churches becoming one.

At that retreat, it was decided that the two churches should merge to form a brand new congregation. The new church would initially meet in the facilities of First Baptist Church of Oildale until land could be secured for relocation. Hillcrest Baptist Church's facility would be used to begin a Hispanic mission. A Hispanic pastor would be called, and his salary would be paid for five years by the new congregation, at which time the Hillcrest facilities would be given to the mission church.

It was also decided that all three pastors—Mike Miller, Phil Neighbors and myself—would serve as senior pastors with equal authority but different ministry assignments.

During the fall of 1985, both congregations voted separately to merge in order to form a new church. Nearly fifty names were nominated for the new church. The name Valley Baptist Church won by two votes over Metropolitan Baptist Church.

The new church met for the first time on the first Sunday of December, 1985. There were 365 people in attendance for that first historic service.

"Preaching Christ" was preached on that Sunday as the first message ever preached at Valley Baptist Church.

Preaching Christ

1 CORINTHIANS 2:1-5

"And I, brethren, when I came to you, came not with excellency of speech or of wisdom, declaring unto you the testimony of God. For I determined not to know any thing among you, save Jesus Christ, and him crucified. And I was with you in weakness, and in fear, and in much trembling. And my speech and my preaching was not with enticing words of man's wisdom, but in demonstration of the Spirit and of power: that your faith should not stand in the wisdom of men, but in the power of God." (KJV)

On the day that a new church is chartered, it is appropriate that we drop some anchors, that we draw the lines of parameters of what this ministry intends to be, that we sound the tone for the ministry. 1 Corinthians 2 does that! As the apostle Paul approaches a new ministry in the ancient pagan city of Corinth, he sets the parameters of what his ministry and message is to be. He drops an anchor and rivets to it what he intends to do in the ministry there.

The nineteenth century has been called the Golden Age of Preachers. It produced some of the greatest preachers that

Christianity has ever seen. Many of those preachers resided and ministered in England. Charles Haddon Spurgeon was said to be the prince of preachers in the south of England. As he approached the Metropolitan Tabernacle pulpit in London for the first time, on the inaugural day of that great ministry, he said, "I am not ashamed to be called a Calvinist, nor am I ashamed to be called a Baptist." I would concur with both of those statements. He went on though, to say, reflecting upon this passage of Scripture, "*For I determined not to know anything among you except Jesus Christ and Him crucified.*" If Charles Spurgeon was the prince of preachers in the south, then in the north the prince was Alexander Maclaren who was perhaps even a greater preacher than Charles Spurgeon. As he approached the pulpit for the first time, he preached from this passage of Scripture. Some forty years later when his ministry drew to a close in that great congregation, he once again preached from this passage and said, with Paul, "*And I, brethren, when I came to you, did not come with excellency of speech or of wisdom declaring to you the testimony of God. For I determined not to know anything among you except Jesus Christ and Him crucified. I was with you in weakness, in fear, and in much trembling. And my speech and my preaching were not with persuasive words of human wisdom, but in demonstration of the Spirit and of power, that your faith should not be in the wisdom of men but in the power of God.*"

The apostle Paul journeyed from Ephesus to the city of Corinth. Corinth was a pluralistic city, a thoroughly secular, materialistic metropolitan center. In the inaugural days of his ministry, he set the parameters and made some affirmations that are appropriate for the inauguration of a new ministry. In this passage, we see what he declared would be his method of ministry, his motive for ministry and his message.

The Method of Paul's Ministry

In 1 Corinthians 2:1, we see his method. He said, *"And I, brethren, when I came to you, did not come with excellency of speech or of wisdom declaring to you the testimony of God."* He made one negative statement and then one positive statement—one great refusal and one great affirmation. The refusal was when he said, *"...when I came to you, I did not come in excellency of speech..."* There are those who would tell you that the apostle Paul had failed in his ministry at Athens where he had preached on Mars' Hill to the great intellects of his day. He had tried to couch the Christian message in terms of Epicurean or stoic philosophic language. This failure caused him to declare at Corinth that he was going to just preach Christ. That is not the case. If you study his preaching at Athens, his ministry was anything but a failure. Dionysius the Areopagate, a Supreme Court justice, was converted along with others.

The apostle Paul did not say that he was going to preach Jesus out of ignorance. He was acquainted with the philosophers of his day. He was a schooled logician and rhetoritician who knew the oratory and eloquence of his day. He knew all of the logical systems of his day, all of the philosophies of the day. It was a definite decision as he approached a new ministry, to declare the parameters to be Jesus Christ and Him crucified.

The Corinthians were known in the ancient world for two things. They were known for their license and the immorality with which the people lived in an awful, pagan city. They were known, number two, for their addiction to persuasive, ornate argumentation. They had an affinity for logic, and an affinity for excellent speech. To be called a Corinthian meant that you were either guilty of gross immorality or it meant that you spoke with the studied embellishment of an orator, or that you used verbal gymnastics in argumentation and persuasion. In the Greek theater, a Corinthian character was often typecast as an immoral, verbose rhetoritician. The apostle Paul, as he approached that pulpit for the first time with the message of Christ, refused to do that for which the city had an affinity. He refused to give them that to which they were addicted. Not only would the apostle Paul not compromise the message of Christ, he would not conform his methods to the world. He came with a single message, the message of Christ. He determined that would be the only reverberation, the only echo heard from his ministry. He came to Corinth determined to build a church, a new church in a great metropolitan city, but the only hammer he desired to use was the upright beam of the cross of Christ against the will of pagan people. He said, "...I did not come with excellency of speech..." The word *excellency* could literally be translated an "overhang." It is the word that describes the eave of a house that overshadows. If you plant a garden or flowers under the eaves of the house, they do not get sun because they are overshadowed. That is the word *excellency* of speech. He determined not to do anything that puts the message of Christ in the shadow.

When King James I was the sovereign of England, he desired a portrait of himself. He searched all over the empire for the greatest artist alive and finally found a man who was world renowned for his paintings; however, he had never painted a portrait. Instead he'd always painted nature scenes and landscapes. King James I commissioned him to paint the portrait. When the portrait was finished, there was the king, the sovereign of England, King James I, but all around about him were ferns and bushes. He was obscured by the landscape. He was outraged and had the painting destroyed. That is the connotation of this word. It means not placing the content of the message of Christ in the shadow, not allowing anything to obscure the message of Christ.

In our new church, our ministries will take various forms. We will have Sunday School, Bible study, CBS or Church Bible studies on Wednesday night; we'll have AWANA and youth programs. We'll have Evangelism Explosion, missions—in fact, all kinds of ministries. But the forms of these ministries are never to obscure the centrality of the cross and of the message of Jesus Christ and Him crucified.

After Leonardo DaVinci painted the masterpiece, "The Last Supper," he invited a friend to preview it before it was released to the public. The friend came in and looked at the painting of Jesus in the center, with His disciples reclined eating. As he looked, he became enamored with the cup that was being passed—the communion cup—and he remarked that he had never seen such detail as in the cup. He said, "It looks so real that you could reach out and touch it," and he continued, excitedly commenting on the cup. Finally, Leonardo DaVinci, with a stroke of his brush, painted through the cup and it was gone. His friend was shocked and appalled by his actions! Leonardo DaVinci said to him, "Christ is to be the center of the picture; He is to be the one that your eye is to be drawn to, not the cup. There is *nothing* that is to obscure Jesus in the center of the picture."

I hope we will never become enamored with the forms of ministry, whether it is Sunday School, AWANA, or youth programs. Whatever it is, I hope we will never become interested in simply perpetuating the status quo of a certain ministry method. I hope to God if we ever do, that those methods will be smashed by God and He will leave us with a single message—the message of Christ. Men and women across our city are famished for the Gospel of the Living Water. They do not care about the ornamentation, or the shape of the goblet from which they drink. They simply are thirsty, and we have the Living Water to give them.

The great refusal, I "...*did not come with excellency of speech...*" is followed by a great affirmation, when he said,

"But I came *'declaring unto you the testimony of God.'*" That word *declaring* is one of the strongest words he could have used. It means to clearly announce. It is a word that was not used very often because it was laden with such authority. It is a word that was used by the emperor to declare war against another nation. It is a word that was used when a new emperor was inaugurated in office. Paul was saying that when he came, his methodology was with strong authority. He was to stand forth and declare the testimony of God as revealed in Scripture.

Paul did not preach speculation; he preached revelation. He did not bolster his message with man's opinions and the fancy interpretations of his day. When Paul referred to the testimony of God, he meant God's testimony concerning the Son, Jesus Christ. What was the testimony of the Father concerning the Son? One day when Jesus went to the Jordan River to be baptized, John the Baptist lifted his hand and pointed to Him and said, *"Behold the Lamb of God that taketh away the sin of the world."* Jesus was baptized by John, and as He was being baptized, heaven split open. *"He saw the Spirit of God descending like a dove and alighting upon Him. And suddenly a voice came from heaven, saying, 'This is My beloved Son, in whom I am well pleased.' "* That is the testimony of the Father.

On another occasion, Jesus stood on the Mount of Transfiguration with Peter, James and John, and they beheld Jesus in His divinity. Elijah was there, representing the prophets. Moses was there, representing the law, and the voice of God thundered, "This one, Jesus, is my Son. You hear Him." That was the testimony of the Father concerning the Son.

The greatest testimony of the Father was the resurrection. The Father validated the work of Christ by raising Him from the dead. In the oriental market, a man would sit at a table with his goods and another man would come, and they would dicker and haggle back and forth over the price of the goods. Finally, the man who sat at the table with his goods, when the bidding was sufficient and the price was enough, would raise his hand sealing the transaction. By doing so, he was saying, "The price is sufficient. I accept the price that you offer." God the Father, when He raised Jesus from the dead was, in a sense validating Jesus, as in the oriental market. The price was sufficient, the price had been paid and God was satisfied in His justice.

My method, as your pastor, will be a singular method. The parameters of my method will be that I will simply point men to Jesus, not the philosophies of the day, not the argumentation of the day. I simply will be like a herald that points to another, that points to Jesus and Him crucified.

The story has been told that during the last century in London, a young boy about fourteen years old tried to make his way to church one Sunday during a fierce blizzard. The deep, icy snow prevented him from reaching his church, but there was a little primitive Methodist Church where he saw a light on and a fire, so he snuck into the back of the church. There a small congregation huddled around the potbellied stove. The pastor could not make it that day because of the weather. Finally after a few moments, a layman stood and began to speak about Jesus. He was totally unprepared; he spoke in broken English because he was an unlearned man. He spoke from a text that says, "Look to Jesus and be saved." He kept saying that over and over. He would talk about Jesus, His birth and His life, and then he'd say, "Look to Jesus and be saved." Finally, as the fourteen-year-old boy was sitting in the back, the story goes that this layman pointed to him and said, "Young man, look to Jesus and be saved." The young man looked to Jesus and was saved. His name was Charles Haddon Spurgeon, the greatest preacher of the last century. That is the message we need. We do not need the philosophy of the day, we do not need excellency in speech; we need those who will point to Jesus and say, "Look to Jesus and be saved." We cannot all be Corinthians with eloquence of speech; we cannot all be orators who are innately creative in our presentation of the Gospel, but the smallest and the youngest and the most unschooled of us can point to Jesus and say, "Look to Jesus and be saved."

We are to be careful that we not obscure Him, that we not put Him in the shadows. We are to be like the man at an art auction who holds the painting as people bid on it. He is careful that he does not stand in front of it or beside it; he stands well behind it, and he is careful so that his fingers do not wrap around the frame and obscure the smallest portion of the painting. He is careful that the painting is foremost as the bidding is being done. We, too, can be careful that nothing in our character, nothing in our conduct, nothing by life or by lip obscure and shadow the message of Christ.

If it was my business to establish a set of theological principles this morning, argumentation would be my weapon; logic would be my means. I would seek to win your intellectual assent. If I were here to proclaim simply an exemplary morality, I would point to the Mosaic Law with its stringent commands and say, "There, conform your life to it and be moral." Instead, my intent and my calling are to proclaim a living person, Jesus, and a historical fact, Him crucified. We are to stand as a herald in the marketplace with a trump in one hand and a message of the King in the other hand. We are not to prop up the message with our opinions and with speculation. Instead, we are to say, "Thus saith the Lord," declaring Jesus and Him crucified.

The Motive of Paul's Ministry

Now look at Paul's motive in 1 Corinthians 2:3. He said, *"I was with you in weakness, and fear, and much trembling,"* also *"...my preaching were not with persuasive words of human wisdom..."* but, *"in demonstration of the Spirit and of power…"* Here is his real motive. He said, "Your faith should not stand in the wisdom of men, but in the power of God." He said, "I was with you in weakness." I do not think that Paul is referring merely to physical weakness, although he evidently was weak. Instead, I think that Paul was aware of his own impotence to save anyone. Paul knew that in the final analysis, if he could talk someone into Christ, someone else could talk him out of it. He knew that it was not by argumentation, it was not by logical proof, it was not by the eloquence of his preaching or speaking, but it was by the power of God that people were saved. Paul knew that, unless the Father drew them by the power of the Holy Spirit and convicted them and made them aware of sin, he could not persuade them.

We can have all kinds of ministries of evangelism, youth ministries, Sunday School and AWANA. We can preach and teach, but in the final analysis we can save no one. He said, "It must be by the demonstration of the power of the Spirit. I was weak with you in weakness; I was impotent to do anything." He said, "I was with you in fear," which literally means "awe." He was in awe that he had the gospel within his hand.

Friend, I have learned that I can preach a clear message on salvation or talk about the new birth, and sometimes no one will be saved. There are other times that I can stutter and stammer, and people will come and give their life to Jesus. You see, it is not the persuasion of the pulpit; it is the conviction of the Holy Spirit. He said, "It was in demonstration of the Spirit and of power."

Once Charles Spurgeon was preaching in a great auditorium in which he had never preached before. It was, of course, before sound systems. He went in earlier that afternoon to check the acoustics and he lifted up his voice and said, "Jesus, behold the Lamb of God that taketh away the sin of the world." He said that two or three times and then he left. In the top of that building on scaffolding, doing some work on the ceiling, was a man that was stricken with conviction of the Holy Spirit. He gave his life to Christ simply with the reciting of those words. It is the demonstration of the Spirit and of power that converts men to Christ. Paul must have been tempted to dilute his message as he stood on Mars' Hill in Athens. As he looked off in the distance, there was the goddess of wisdom, Athenia. He must have been tempted to preach Christ *plus* Athenia, but he did not do it. He preached what he had learned, like the apostle John had learned. John said, speaking of Christ, *"...if I am lifted up from the earth, will draw all peoples to Myself."* Paul knew there was something magnetic about the life of Jesus; that if he could elevate Jesus in his preaching, and elevate Him in his ministry and point to the cross of Christ, He would be like a magnet through the ages that would reach out and draw men unto Himself. He said, "I preach Jesus and Him crucified."

In 1 Corinthians 2:5, Paul said that the goal of his ministry was that our faith should not stand in the wisdom of men, but in the power of God. He was saying that the reason he did not use fancy speech, the reason he did not use the dynamics of his personality, the reason he did not use the philosophy of the day, was because he did not want our faith resting in the personality or the persuasiveness of the pastor. He wanted our faith anchored in the power of God. If you come to church because of the personality of a preacher, then someone with more personality will lead you away someday. If you come because of the persuasiveness of the pastor, someone who is more persuasive will sway you away from Christ someday. If you come simply because of the logic of the presentation, a better logician will lead you and shake your faith someday. Paul believed that if he preached Jesus and Him crucified, then those who were converted would be anchored in Him. They would last. Paul was preaching to a church that was divided. Some said, "Oh, we are followers of Paul." Others said, "Well, we are followers of Peter," and others, "We are followers of Apollo." Paul said, "No, you are not to have your faith wrapped up in the ability and eloquence of a man. Your faith is not to be wrapped up in the following of a personality, but Christ is to be the anchor of your soul." The parameter of our message and of our motive is to be Jesus Christ and Him crucified.

The Message of Paul

Paul's message is in 1 Corinthians 2:2. He said, "...*For I determined not to know anything among you except Jesus Christ and Him crucified.*"

Friend, Christianity is Christ, and Christ is Christianity. They are inseparable. With other religions, you can accept the teachings and ignore the teacher, but in Christianity the teaching *is* the teacher. They are riveted together with steel bands that cannot be separated. Paul taught that the message of the New Testament is the person and the work of Jesus Christ. He viewed Christ with blinders on, or through a tunnel. He funneled the message down to one aspect— *"Jesus and Him crucified."* It was a bold decision. It was a decision to present the message of Christ and the message of Christianity to a pagan people in its least palatable form. There was no watering down of the gospel to fill the building. There was no "easy believism" so that the number of baptisms would be up. He said, "I preach Christ and in the least palatable form, Him crucified." He did not preach a gospel of health, he did not preach a gospel of wealth, he did not preach a gospel of positive thinking, or a gospel of good advice about your marriage, or even about your family. He believed that the good news is, first of all, a bloody message that Jesus Christ died in our place.

In chapter 1, he indicated that the Jews seek after signs and miracles; the Greeks seek after wisdom and logic. To the Jews the cross is a scandal, a stumbling block; to the Greeks it is foolishness, it is absurdity. But to those of us who believe, it is the power of God unto salvation.

Remember, what is food for our souls becomes "husks" for those who are perishing. What is "living water" that quenches our thirst is dry desert sand to the world. When we sing "Nothing But The Blood," which is music to our ears, it is discord and foolish babbling to those perishing. We still have the mentality of the Jews and the Greeks with us today. There are still those today who seek after logic; there are those like the Jews seeking after a sign. They like the sensuous things of religion, the sensuous things of Christianity. They love the healing lines and the health, they love the prosperity and the blessings of God, they love the idea of demons being subject to Christians. When the disciples who had been sent forth came back rejoicing, saying, "We can heal, we can even cast out demons," Jesus looked at them and said, *"Nevertheless do not rejoice in this, that the spirits are subject to you, but rather rejoice because your names are written in heaven."* The accent of Christianity is not on the physical things of health and wealth or the spiritual realm of demons; the accent is upon the fact that our sin has been forgiven.

We have the Greeks today who want rational proof; they want to argue systems and theology. Let the Jew who seeks after a sign see Jesus in the weakness of the cross; let the Greeks who seek after logic see Him in the absurdity and the foolishness of the cross. We preach Jesus and Him crucified.

There is much about Jesus' life that would have been impressive to the Jews. Paul could have appealed to the Jews by saying, "Jesus was one from your own nation. Jesus was a Hebrew of Hebrews. Jesus was a worker of signs and miracles." He could have talked about how Jesus reverenced the Mosaic Law, how He said, *"...I am not come to destroy, but to fulfill.*" He could have talked about how Jesus observed the Sabbath, or how Jesus fulfilled the minutia of the Old Testament prophets, but Paul knew something that we all need to know. He knew that it was not in the strength of miracles, but it was in the weakness of the cross that we are saved.

There was much about Jesus that would have appealed to the Greeks. He could have talked about God becoming man. That would have impressed them! He could have talked about the teachings of Christ, the resurrection of Christ and the witnesses and all the judicial proof.

The foolishness of the cross was a scandal to the Jews, the fact that their Messiah would come and be crucified. Paul said, *"Cursed is everyone who hangs on a tree."* The Greeks thought it was an absurdity and foolishness that someone crucified could affect us spiritually, but Paul said, *"It is the power of God."*

Friend, they were divided in that day—with followers of Peter, followers of Paul, followers of Apollo. They were a diverse people, like we are a diverse people. Do you know what the adhesive force was that pulled them together as a church? Do you know what the adhesive force is that will pull two congregations and three pastors together? That adhesive force is the preaching of the cross. That is the common denominator that will pull us together. I have never heard of a division in a church from an overemphasis on Jesus and the cross. I have heard of churches dividing because of an overemphasis on eschatology, or last things, or an overemphasis on creation, or first things; but I have never heard of division over an overemphasis on *"Jesus and Him crucified."* That is what bonds us together!

You have three pastors before you this morning, and we all emphasize different aspects of the Christian faith. We all place our accent in different places. Pastor Mike Miller will accent discipleship, nurturing and fellowship. Phil Neighbors will accent the work of the ministry of evangelism and youth.

I will accent worship, prayer, devotion, ethics both in our character and conduct. But that which is the unifying element among us three men and between two congregations is the cross of Christ. It is to be in the center of church life. Like centrifugal force, it will pull everything into its shadow. The cross of Christ is to be the fulcrum with which we move this city. It is to be the hinge upon which this ministry swings. Paul does not say, "I came not *saying* anything except Jesus Christ and Him crucified." He said, "I am determined not to *know* anything except Jesus and Him crucified." It was not simply the posture of the pulpit in preaching, but it was a desire to really know Christ.

If you want to pray for your three pastors, there are some ways you can pray for us. There are things we need to know. For example, we need to know everyone's name. We need to know about the needs of our community. There is an exhausting spectrum of things that we need to know. If you want to really pray for us, please pray that the hub of our desire, that the keystone of our lives will be a passion to know Jesus and Him crucified, that we might have an inward desire to be conformed to the image of Christ, to the fellowship of His suffering and the victory of His resurrection, to be crucified with Him. That is the only unique message that we have. That is it! Paul knew that he was going to Corinth, the "vanity fair" of the ancient world. He knew what I am learning, that the secular world can out-spend us, they can out-advertise us, they can out-build us. Friend, they can out-think us at times. Paul said, *"Not many wise are called, but God has chosen the foolish things of the world,"* and so they can out-spend us, out-think us, out-organize us, and out-advertise us. The only unique "thing" we have is *"Christ and Him crucified!"*

Let that be the anchor of this ministry, let the parameters of our message be Jesus Christ and Him crucified. We need to see Jesus in every aspect of His life. Let us view Him in eternity past in perfect harmony and fellowship with God the Father and God the Holy Spirit. Eons upon eons of time He was with the Father and the Spirit in perfect union. Let us view Him as the Creator, as Paul said, "That all things were created by Him." Let us view Him as He hung the earth in space. When there was nothing to stand upon, He stood upon His own omnipotent will and flung the earth into space. By His very thoughts and by His words, He scooped out the oceans and shoved up the mountains and laid the course of the rivers. He is not some kind of absentee God that wound the earth up like a clock and left it to run down. He is involved in human history and He can be involved in your life, too. Let us view Him as He was here on this earth as a great healer, as He spit in the dirt and made clay to anoint blind Bartemaes' eyes so he could see. Let us see Him as He reached out with compassion and touched the stench of the rotting of the leper's face. Let us view Him as He was teaching one day and His followers tore the roof apart and let a man down who was crippled, and He forgave his sin and healed him. Let us view Him in His compassion as a woman caught in the act of adultery was brought to Him, about to be stoned, and He compassionately said, *"He that is without sin among you, let him first cast a stone at her."* The greatest accusation the world could bring against this man of Nazareth was that He was a friend of sinners.

Let us preach every aspect of His life, from His birth in Bethlehem to His boyhood in Nazareth, to His baptism in the Jordan River, to His temptation in the desert, to His teachings on the seaside, to His transfiguration on the mountain, to His trial in Jerusalem, from His incarnation, to His intercession, from His vicarious death to His victorious resurrection, from His agony to His ascension, from His sermons to His second coming. We need to preach the life of Christ from the womb to the tomb, from the cradle to the cross. Let our message be from this pulpit, "*Jesus Christ and Him crucified.*" Let us speak of those hands that were never clenched in a fist against anyone, hands that never touched an unclean thing unless it was to make it clean. Let us speak of His feet that carried him on missions of mercy, let us speak of His beard that was plucked and pulled out for us. Let us speak of His face that was smitten for us and His back that was ripped for us, His brow that was pierced for us, His lips that spoke words of comfort and healing and yet were mute before His accusers. Let us speak of those eyes of compassion that felt the sting and the salt of His own tears as He beheld the ruins of humanity. *Let Jesus be our message!* Let Jesus and Him crucified be our message.

As you drive across this country today, you will see the landscape dotted with crosses rising from church buildings and cemeteries all over our nation. If you were to travel across the Roman Empire in the first century, that landscape, too, was dotted with crosses, but different from today's crosses. The crosses today are made out of gold or beautiful materials. Those crosses were made out of rough timber. The cross today is a symbol of hope. We have organizations named Red Cross and Blue Cross Insurance, emphasizing hope. The cross of the first century was an instrument of death and torture. Crosses today are used for décor. The Romans used them for torture. Today we wear crosses around our neck as jewelry. The people of the first century would no more wear a cross around their neck than we would wear a hangman's noose around ours today. The cross was an instrument of death. The cross for us has become appealing because of the hope that it represents and the message that we bear, but in the first century, crucifixion was anything but appealing. It was a ghastly sight. People would quicken their pace as they walked past the hillsides where men were crucified, as they were hanging there being eaten alive by birds and predators. Little children would hide behind the skirts of their mothers. Women who grew up in a harsh culture would be haunted by nightmares after seeing a crucifixion. Men who were used to the gore of war by a sword, shuddered at the foot of the cross. They lay in their beds at night in the city of Jerusalem and tossed and turned as they listened to the screams of those outside the city walls, dying of crucifixion.

That is **our message, the bloody message** of the cross. Let us see Jesus Christ this morning and Him crucified as they drive the nails into those hands and lift Him up and leave Him there to die. Let us see Jesus as the crowd gathers around. They gathered in silence, waiting to see what He would say. Usually a man crucified would curse those who crucified him. They waited to see what He would say, whether He would reveal His humanity apart from His divinity. He began to speak and silence fell over the crowd. Jesus looked down at the Roman soldier who crucified him—who still held the bloody mallet in his hands, He looked at the Pharisees with their robes of self-righteousness pulled about them. He looked at the angry mob and did the most natural thing He could have done. He said, *"Father, forgive them, for they know not what they do."* He turned the cross into a pulpit and preached a message on forgiveness. It is a continuous-tense verb meaning, "It is as if He is still saying it today—Father, forgive them, Father forgive them."

The road from Eden led straight to the cross. The Bible says that all have sinned and come short of the glory of God, and the wages of sin is death, so Jesus Christ died in our place. As He died, toward the end, He shattered the silence with a loud cry saying, *"Tetelisti,"* meaning, "It is finished." It is a word that means "Nothing else can be added." It is the word of an artist as he paints a picture and he is about to add another stroke, and then he thinks, "No, it does not need that, I am finished," and he says, *"Tetelisti,* nothing else can be added." Jesus said, *"Tetelisti."* It is finished; nothing else is needed. Not Jesus Christ and church membership, not Christ and baptism, not Christ and philosophy, only Christ and Him crucified—nothing else is needed. It is finished!

Today we live under the shadow of that cross. It is a symbol of grace, but it is also a symbol of judgment. That cross is God's great "yes" to those who believe, and it is God's great "no" to those who reject. Jesus Christ will either be your Savior, or He will be your Judge some day.

June 6, 1944 is a famous day. It is, of course, D-Day. It was a day of mourning for those who lost their sons and their loved ones in that great battle. As the battle was taking place, there was a young French girl that, inadvertently, was between the two lines. There were bullets flying everywhere as she was running, trying to escape. Suddenly, there was the thud of a bullet as it struck her chest. She fell, crumpled and limp to the ground. A young Canadian boy by the name of Al saw her fall. He, being moved with compassion, ran cutting and dodging through the line of fire, grabbed up her little limp body and took her back to safety, to a tent. He tried to bind up her wounds, but they were so serious that he took her back behind the lines to a medic, and there he left her. The little French girl lived. She never saw Al again. But every year on June 6, she would go to that place and look, hoping that some day, on the anniversary of the battle, Al would come back to the place of the battle. Every year she looked in vain. She grew into maturity and finally, last June in Normandy, as President Reagan was speaking, she was there. Now a mature woman standing in the crowd, she saw what she thought was a familiar face and thought, "No, it can not really be," and then she looked again. Yes, that is Al! He is more mature and he is much older now, but that is unmistakably Al. She ran up to him, the Canadian whom she knew simply by the name Al. Bridging the language barrier between the two, she threw her arms around him and said one word that he understood—"Savior! Savior! Savior!"

There are those who are like the Jews who require health, wealth, a sign, or a miracle to see the power of God. There are those who are like the Greeks requiring rational proof, argumentation and theological systems, but I for one, will fall at the foot of the cross and throw my arms around those bloody feet and say, *"Savior! Savior! Savior!"*

─◦ 1986 ◦─

In 1986, Valley Baptist Church began to search for land on which to relocate. Land was expensive and the church's budget for that year was only $265,480.

Valley owned a house on Niles Street that was used as a halfway house for men completing drug and alcohol rehabilitation. God used the home mightily in a number of individuals' lives.

In the fall of 1986, Charity Ministry was founded. It was named in honor of our daughter, Charity. A banquet was held at Hodel's, with Dr. Paige Patterson as the keynote speaker. Enough money was raised to launch our daily radio program, "A Time Of Charity." A new pastor was called to pastor our mission, Primera Iglesia Bautista. That year our church baptized 43 souls.

"How to Finish Well" was preached on August 10, 1986 as part of a series of messages called "Great Verses of the Bible." The series consists of sermons preached from a single verse from each of the sixty-six books of the Bible.

How to Finish Well

"For I am already being poured out as a drink offering, and the time of my departure is at hand. I have fought the good fight, I have finished the race, I have kept the faith. Finally, there is laid up for me the crown of righteousness, which the Lord, the righteous Judge, will give to me on that Day, and not to me only but also to all who have loved His appearing. Be diligent to come to me quickly; for Demas has forsaken me, having loved this present world, and has departed for Thessalonica— Crescens for Galatia, Titus for Dalmatia. Only Luke is with me. Get Mark and bring him with you, for he is useful to me for ministry. And Tychicus I have sent to Ephesus. Bring the cloak that I left with Carpus at Troas when you come— and the books, especially the parchments." (NKJV)

I once heard John Bisagno share, in a sermon, a personal illustration from his college days. That illustration became a haunting story for me. He said that, while attending Oklahoma Baptist University to prepare for the ministry, he met a girl there, and they were married. His father-in-law, who was also a pastor, said to him, "You had better be careful and guard your spiritual life because, out of twenty young men like you starting out in the ministry, *all but one* will not make it to the end." By "not make it," he meant that some kind of moral failure, discouragement, disillusionment, or bitterness would push them out of the ministry.

Bisagno said he did not believe that! So he wrote in the flyleaf of his Bible the names of twenty-four men who were on fire for God, just like he was. They were soul winners. The ambition of their lives was to serve God vocationally. He said that, one by one, through the years he has scratched names off the list because of failure, discouragement, or other reasons that have driven them from the ministry. He held up his Bible at the conference where I heard him speak and said, "There are only three names left on that list."

That was shocking to me, but I am not sure that it should have been. The fact is that beginners are a dime a dozen. It is terminators who are rare. We are good at starting things. If you do not believe that, just look in your garage! Most of our garages are filled with projects we have started but never completed. Our culture puts a premium on starting but not so much on finishing.

The sad illustration of this, culturally, is the breakdown of marriage. There is a jewelry store in Hollywood with a sign in the front window that reads, "We rent wedding rings." That is sad, isn't it? In our Baptist life, the emphasis today is almost exclusively on the initial step of Christianity. We speak in terms of how many people have accepted Jesus, or how many have walked down the aisle. We present the gospel of a good start. But the truth is, not all who start well finish well!

Chapter 4 of 2 Timothy is about *finishing well.* When the apostle Paul wrote these words, he was in prison in Rome for the second time. He was not under house arrest this time. He was in a dark, dank dungeon—literally a hole in the ground—under the sentence of death, waiting each day for his execution. He wrote to his young associate, Timothy, and sought to motivate him to persevere. He said, in essence, "I am going to disappear from this earth. I am going to be with God. *Don't you give up!*"

Paul pulled out all the stops to motivate Timothy. He used every metaphor he could about serving God. He challenged Timothy to be a *steward*—that is, to guard the gospel as a treasure. He told him to be a *soldier* and fight the battle, to be an *athlete* who strives for victory. He compared him to a *student* who gives himself to a lifetime of study and to a *servant who serves his master.*

Paul motivated Timothy not only with his words but also with his life. He became retrospective as he looked back over his life and then prospective as he looked beyond death to the crown that was awaiting him. By the world's standards, Paul's life had been a dismal failure. As a young man, he had thrown away the prospects of a bright future. He had jettisoned the prestige of being a renowned rabbi. He had often been beaten throughout his life. He had labored to the point of exhaustion. He had been hunted, despised, derided, ridiculed and laughed at. Now he was cast into prison awaiting execution.

In verse 6, Paul gives two images—one of *pouring out* and one of *packing up.* He said, *"For I am already being poured out as a drink offering,"* a reference to the libation offering where pagans would pour wine on the animal sacrifice, or to the Hebrews who would pour out the drink offering alongside the sacrifice. Maybe he was referring to the violent nature of his own impending death by being beheaded. That was an awful death! The executioners would take a man who was struggling and fighting and tie him down. Then they would take a double-bladed axe and sever his head. His body, limp and trembling, would spray out blood. Maybe Paul was thinking about his own death and the literal pouring out of his life. Perhaps he was thinking about the nature of his entire life—that his whole life had been like a libation offering, poured out to God as a living sacrifice of service to Him.

Paul said, "...the time of my departure is at hand." We could translate the word time as "season"—"the season of my departure is at hand." In the spring of his life, Paul met Jesus on the road to Damascus. He had experienced that long summer run of ministry. Then in the fall of his life, he had been arrested and taken from court to court. Now the winter of his life was before him. He said, "The season of my **departure** is at hand." The word he used means "to loose," like unfastening the moorings of a ship. It means to cut its tethers so it is free to sail. It was a word that was used of soldiers breaking camp, as they would loosen the tent stakes. He is saying, "I am ready to be loosed. I am ready to pack up. I am being poured out." These are the valedictory words of Paul's life, the benediction of a life well lived, as he motivates Timothy.

Paul began to reminisce about his own life. It is in this reminiscing that we see the principles that enabled Paul to finish well. The spiritual landscape today is littered with the broken lives of ministers who had great talents but ruined their ministries. Maybe there is a personal word of application for us as we look at the life of Paul and how he finished.

In Order to Finish Well, We Need to Fight for the Faith

The first principle that enabled Paul to finish well is that he *"fought for the faith."* Do not misunderstand Paul's statement as egotistical. It is not braggadocio. It is not *I* have fought the good fight, or *I* have finished the race, or *I* have kept the faith. In fact, the personal pronoun is not only *not* emphatic; *it is not even there!* It is simply understood. Paul is not bragging. He is emphasizing the nature of the Christian life and ministry. When we look at Paul's life, we see a life of maturity. We are spiritually envious of this man who has weathered the storms. He is like "spiritual leather." There is toughness about his life. We want Paul's maturity that speaks of unspeakable joy and peace that passes understanding. We want the ability to be content in whatever state we find ourselves. We look at his ministry that is expansive and pervasive, and we want to be like Paul. We want his maturity. We want his ministry. We want the product of his life.

But this passage is not a description of the product of his life. He is speaking of the process that produced such maturity. He is saying that the nature of the Christian life is a fight. The nature of the Christian life is not an invitation to prosperity and health. It is not an invitation to a life of ease that is free from struggle and pain. He says, "It is a fight." We get our word *agony* from the word that is translated "fight." It is an athletic word. Paul says that we have to be tough to finish. There is, of course, the constant battle against the temptation of Satan. Paul is also the one who said, "*For the good that I will to do, I do not do; but the evil I will not to do, that I practice*" (Romans 7:19). He constantly fought a battle with the flesh. Then there is the battle against culture. All of his life he was out of step with culture. If we are to live for God, we will be out of step with the world. There will be no end to the line of people who will try to talk us out of doing what we should do.

Paul said, "*I have finished the race.*" Paul is like a marathon runner who has run through the streets, and now he is entering the stadium for the final lap. Every muscle is being strained. His lungs are burning, but he refuses to quit.

The most enduring image, I suppose, from the Barcelona Olympics was that of the young British sprinter, Derek Redmond, who, in the midst of the race, pulled a hamstring and began to limp toward the finish line. The camera was on his face as he grimaced in pain. His father crawled over the railing onto the track and put his arms around his young son, and together they limped toward the finish line. The security guards came, but Derek's father waved them off. Together, as the world cheered, the two of them crossed the finish line.

Sometimes that is what the Christian life is about. It is not always about soaring like an eagle, or running and not being weary. Sometimes it is walking and simply not fainting. The ministry is not about how fast we run or about the size of the crowds to whom we minister. It is about *perseverance,* about enduring to the end.

Fighting the fight and running the race were Paul's illustrations for what he declared next. In verse 7, Paul says, *"I have kept the faith."* The word *kept* means "to guard as a sacred deposit." The faith had been entrusted to him, and he had carefully guarded it. Life had been full of voices urging him to give up the faith. There had been the bribes and threats of the old nature and the constant whispers of the world, but he had kept the faith. Paul uses "faith" in the sense of the message of the gospel or the doctrine that had been entrusted to him.

If Paul had not "kept the faith," maybe there would be no faith for us to keep. We are only one generation away from the faith becoming extinct. That is why we are to guard it like a treasure. We are in this long relay race, and the baton has now been handed to us. We hold it in our hands as a sacred treasure that we are to guard, and we are to be careful that it is still intact as we hand it on to the next generation.

This is why we need to be willing to fight for the inerrancy and authority of Scripture. We are to be willing to fight for the fundamentals of the faith because the nature of the Christian life is that it is a fight or a race. Alexander Maclaren said, "The Christian life is not a garden of ease, nor is it a desert devoid of joy. But it is a gymnasium—a place of struggle." We look at Paul's life, and we like the product of his life, but we are not so eager to welcome the process of sanctification that was in Paul's life.

I have often visited the giant sequoia redwood trees located about seventy miles north of where I live. I cannot even begin to describe how large they are. It is an amazing experience to stand at the foot of one of these massive trees, look up, and realize that it has been growing for hundreds of years! If God wants to grow a giant sequoia tree, it takes hundreds of years. If He wants to grow a daisy or a pansy, it takes just a few days. The problem is that we are content to be "daisy" or "pansy" Christians, rather than being spiritual giants. We want the product of spiritual maturity, but we do not want the process that produces that maturity within our lives. Paul describes the process that produces maturity as being a fight and a race!

In Order to Finish Well, We Need to Focus on the Future

In verse 8, Paul speaks of focusing on the future as the motivation of the Christian life. He said, *"Finally, there is laid up for me the crown of righteousness which the Lord, the righteous Judge, will give to me on that Day."* The word *crown* does not refer to the emblem of a king but rather to the emblem of a victor. It is the laurel wreath that was to be placed upon the heads of those who won the race. It was the most prized possession in the ancient athletic world. As the runners ran the marathon, they would run through the streets and then enter the coliseum for the final lap. The crown was always placed in a prominent place so the runners could see it. In a sprint, it was at the end of the race. For a marathon, it was placed up high so as they entered the stadium they could see the crown before them. Paul is like a runner whose legs are aching, his side is splitting, and his lungs are burning. But he thought, **"I will not quit because the motivation of service to God is yet ahead in the future. There is a crown laid up for me."**

As good as the Christian life is, as profitable as it is to serve God; our motivation at the end of the race ultimately is the Lord Jesus and the crown He has reserved for us. The crown was not placed at mile fifteen or twenty; instead it was at the *end* of the race. Paul tells Timothy, "I see the tape. I see the finish line, and there is a crown waiting for me." He is motivating Timothy by saying, "Do not get bogged down in the fight and the hassle of the race. The reward is at the *end.*"

In Order To Finish Well, We Need The Fellowship Of Friends

Not only did Paul focus on the future; he also maintained a fellowship of friends. He said in verse 9, this crown is to be given *"...not to me only but also to all who have loved His appearing."* Immediately he began to think about his companions. He said to Timothy, *"Be diligent to come to me quickly; for Demas has forsaken me, having loved this present world, and has departed for Thessalonica—Crescens for Galatia, Titus for Dalmatia. Only Luke is with me. Get Mark and bring him with you, for he is useful to me for ministry. And Tychicus I have sent to Ephesus" (verses 9-12).*

The word translated "come" that Paul uses means "come with velocity." It is a picture of a lonely old man in prison, desiring the fellowship of his friends. You will not likely finish well alone. When we look at Paul's life, we see that there was always an entourage of people around him. There were the "Timothys" in whom he was investing, but they were investing in return. There was a kind of mutual accountability.

God has designed us to serve Him in concert and coordination with one another. We *need* one another! We are too weak to go it alone. There are those who want to be "Lone Ranger Christians." They want to serve God alone. They do not want to let anyone into their lives because they have been hurt or wounded. The fact is that the church is full of people with imperfections. Even leaders are sometimes weak and immature, not to mention those whose lifestyles betray their confession.

In spite of the differences, in spite of the irritations, the imperfections and the hurts, we will not make it to the end alone. All of us need the fellowship of kindred spirits. We need to be open and honest with others. We need other people to hold us accountable.

In Order to Finish Well, We Need to Forget the Failures of Others

One last principle in Paul's life that enabled him to finish well is that he forgot the failures of others. He said to Timothy, "*Only Luke is with me. Get Mark and bring him with you, for he is useful to me for ministry.*" We know the story of Mark on that first missionary journey. When Paul and Barnabas started out from Antioch with the call of God in their hearts, and the message of the gospel on their lips, they took a young man, John Mark, with them. But along the way, John Mark quit and went home. We do not know if he was sick. We do not know what happened, but he turned back. As Paul and Barnabas planned the second missionary journey, Barnabas suggested that they take Mark with them, but Paul refused. Barnabas pleaded with Paul to give him another chance, but Paul considered him a quitter. A disagreement broke up the gospel team, so Paul took Silas, and Barnabas took Mark.

As the months stretched into years, and the years into decades, we find Paul, now an old man, writing to Timothy. He said, "*Get Mark and bring him with you, for he is useful to me for ministry.*" Somehow in the expanse of those years, Paul had forgotten, or at least forgiven Mark's failures.

Some people live their lives as though no slight will ever escape them. No injury is ever forgotten. They move from place to place in ministry, but tucked away within their hearts is a long list of everyone who has ever wronged them. If you want a formula for absolute misery, just try to settle every score in the ministry. Bitterness comes from unhealed wounds. Bitterness produces a critical or caustic spirit that eventually becomes a cynical spirit. It poisons your prayer life. It ruins your home life. It wrecks your ministry and destroys your spiritual life. If the nature of the Christian life is a fight, then you will get hurt. If it is a race, you will, at some point, be bumped in the race.

In the Los Angeles Olympics, Mary Decker was favored to win the women's eight hundred meters. As the race started, all of the commentators said that she was sure to win. As they came to the first curve, a girl from South Africa bumped Mary Decker, and she fell. As the camera focused on Mary's face, you could see the hurt of the injury of falling, and the hope of winning the race suddenly drained from her face. She sat there and cried.

It reminded me of another Olympic runner, the great Presbyterian missionary Eric Liddell. In the movie about his life, *Chariots of Fire,* he, too, was bumped during a race, and fell. For a moment he sat on the track. Then he got up and began running in his unorthodox style, arms flailing and his face pointed toward Heaven. He ran and ran—and he not only finished the race, but he actually won! Do you know why? Because he did not stay down. The fact is, you are going to get hurt in ministry. Those in whom you invest the most will sometimes yield a paltry return. There will be people who will turn on you—those you never expected to hurt you. You will be hurt! You will be bumped! Not everyone will love you! Sometimes you have to go where the band does not play, but the key is to get back up!

I remember when my first child was born. I had never thought that babies were all that pretty, that is, until we had *our* first baby. We named her Charity—a little girl with blonde hair and blue eyes! She brought so much joy into our hearts. She reminded me of a doll that my sister had when she was a kid. When Charity was in first grade, her school had an open house. It was a time when students could take their parents to school in order to show off all the little things they were doing and to meet their teacher. I was preaching across town in a revival meeting that week. At dinner, I sat down with Charity and explained to her that I wasn't going to be able to go that night. I told her that her mom would go, and that I would love to be there more than anything, but I was going to be telling people about Jesus. She seemed to understand.

As I was preaching in the little church, toward the end of the message, a phone began ringing in the back of the church. An usher went to answer the phone. As I was extending the invitation, he stepped in the back door and waved at me, indicating the phone was for me. I finished the invitation and went to pick up the phone. A voice said, "Your little girl, Charity, has been hit by a car." I rushed to the hospital, arriving ahead of the ambulance.

The ambulance came to a halt at the emergency entrance. When the ambulance doors opened, I could clearly see an attractive woman in a black dress leaning over a child. She was well dressed, but her hair was disheveled, and there was a smudge of blood on her face. Later I found out that she had given Charity CPR. As they brought the patient out, she appeared pale. She had a tube in her mouth and an IV in her hand. She was wearing a tattered red dress. It was Charity.

She is dead, was my first thought. Then, just as quickly, I thought, *Charity is really going to be upset when she finds out that her favorite red dress was torn from the neck to the waist so CPR could be administered.*

Charity was taken to an emergency room while my wife and I were ushered into a waiting room. A young doctor entered our room with a nurse. The doctor was Asian and spoke in broken English. It was obvious that he was extremely uncomfortable with his duty. He said, "I am sorry, but your daughter didn't make it." He droned on about doing all that they could but how nothing could be done.

Ironically, I remember feeling sorry for him. I thought how much I would hate to tell anyone such awful news. She was dead. Those words, even now, are difficult to write, and it turns my stomach to say them. The truth is often painful. This time the truth was *devastating*. There is perhaps no more wrenching word that can be said than *dead*. I cannot explain to you the pain of losing a child. It is difficult to hold the broken body of a little blond-haired, blue-eyed girl and to close the casket on your first child.

A few days later there was a knock at my door. I opened the door and a woman was standing there—the woman who had been driving recklessly that night, the woman who was a hit-and-run driver and who later turned herself in. She introduced herself and said to me, "Will you forgive me?" Under my breath I asked the Lord, "Give me grace." Somehow I found the strength to say, "I forgive you."

Looking back on that day, I know now that if I had not forgiven her, someone, somewhere would have scratched my name off a list, as *my* life would have devolved into bitterness.

The fact is that people are going to fail you. There are going to be hurts and bruises in life. The apostle Paul forgot those things. His final day on earth came perhaps a few days after he wrote these words to young Timothy—or maybe it was weeks or months. I do not know if Mark got there. I do not know if Timothy was there. But there was a day when the soldiers came and pulled the apostle out of that hole in the ground. He probably covered his face from the sun, which he had not seen for some time. In his shackles he walked between two soldiers to the south of Rome. There was a chopping block. He said a few words to his close friends— Mark, Luke, and Timothy, or whoever was there. He was strapped down, and then a burly soldier raised the two-bladed axe above his head. Perhaps Paul, for a moment, thought he saw the glint of the sun upon the axe. Then he realized in the next moment that it was the sheen on Jesus' face when the Master said, *"Well done, thou good and faithful servant."*

Paul had finished well!

1987

By 1987, the growth of Valley Baptist Church had slowed due to limited space. This problem was solved by creating a second Sunday School. That year we averaged 454 people in Sunday School attendance.

We finally found fifteen acres of land on Fruitvale Avenue for $675,000. The only problem was a lack of funds! We secured two loans for $150,000 and $125,000 respectively and decided to try to raise the rest. We asked our people to give over a six-month period in order to buy as much land as possible for $1 per square foot. A chart of our progress was kept at the back of the sanctuary. We called this first capital funds campaign "Sod for God." Enough money was raised that we turned back the $125,000 loan.

Charity Ministry expanded to two local radio stations, as well as one in Washington State and one in the Caribbean. An orphanage in India was built called Charity Home. The church is still supporting girls in the Indian orphanage.

"Everyone On the Wall" was preached on a Wednesday evening, March 18, 1987. Valley Baptist Church was hosting a conference on church growth, so there were a number of pastors and lay leaders in the service from across the state of California.

Everyone on the Wall

"From above the horse gate repaired the priests, every one over against his house." (KJV)

Although it is a rather obscure verse, and perhaps somewhat strange for a sermon, Nehemiah 3:28 represents a vital principle in the book of Nehemiah. I hope you will see the truth of this one verse.

In order to understand the meaning of this verse, we need to go back to the beginning pages of Nehemiah. As the book opens, we meet Nehemiah, the cupbearer to King Artaxerxes. As the cupbearer, he held a very prestigious, elevated position, since he was the man who not only served the king, but the man who would first taste the wine or the food, in case the king had an enemy. Of course, the cupbearer would die if he drank poison—but long live the king! The cupbearer was always with the king if there was food involved, whether at a state dinner, a cabinet meeting or in meetings with ambassadors and other kings. Nehemiah was a Jew in exile. In essence, he was a slave, even though he was the cupbearer to King Artaxerxes.

The drama opens in this great book as Nehemiah's brother came to the winter palace of the king and brought news of the homeland. Nehemiah was born, and had lived all of his life as a Jew in exile. He had never been to the Holy Land. If you have ever been away from home, you know how exciting news from home can be. Nehemiah's excitement gave way to despair. Chapter 1, verse 3 says, *"And they said unto me, 'the remnant that are left of the captivity there in the province are in great affliction and reproach: the wall of Jerusalem also is broken down and the gates thereof are burned with fire.' And it came to pass when I heard these words that I sat down and wept, and mourned certain days, and fasted, and prayed before the God of Heaven".* In despair, he wept, prayed and fasted because of the news that the walls of Jerusalem had been torn down and had not been rebuilt, and the houses were burned. It is hard for us to grasp the reason for his despair, but in the Old Testament, Jerusalem was crucial to the Jews. After all, it was the City of David. In the New Testament, we have the commission to "go and tell," but in the Old Testament it was "come and see"—come and see a theocracy at work, see the people of God in Jerusalem. The temple gave them their identity as a nation, as well as their religious identity. The temple represented the continuity of the Jewish people. The fact that the walls were broken down symbolized that their security was gone. If the walls of an ancient city were torn down, then any nomadic tribe could come in and plunder the city. With the walls down, they were vulnerable to attack, and to losing their continuity as a people, as a religion and as a nation.

Nehemiah was upset, and he prayed and fasted before God. His prayer was not a formal prayer. In fact, it is one of the greatest heart cries of the Old Testament. When he heard about the ruins of the city of Jerusalem, he did not go and buy the latest scroll on building walls, nor did he go to the latest conference on how to build walls. He went before God in prayer. It is not a "Santa Claus" type prayer of "give me this and give me that." It is the heart cry of a man who is broken before God. In his prayer, we have a glimpse into his heart.

In verse 5, we hear Nehemiah's view of God as he addresses Him, *"Oh, great and awesome God"*(NKJV). In verse 6, we hear Nehemiah's confession of sin. Nehemiah knows that because of Judah's spiritual declension, God has taken them to the woodshed. He blames the people, not God.

When Adam was caught in sin, he said to God, *"The woman whom You gave to be with me, she gave me of the tree, and I ate"* (NKJV). He was saying that it is either her fault, or perhaps Yours, God, since *You* gave her to me.

Habakkuk, the prophet, interrogates God, asking Him why He allowed His people to be conquered by the Chaldeans. Nehemiah, on the other hand, does not blame God, or even others. He confesses his sin.

Chapter 2, verse 1 says, *"It came to pass in the month of Nisan in the twentieth year of Artaxerxes, the King, when wine was before him, and I took of the wine and gave it to the king."* It is significant that he mentions the month of Nisan. Four months had passed since he had first heard the report of the walls being torn down. For those four months, he had been giving himself to prayer, fasting and weeping before God. At the end of the verse it says, *"Now I had never been sad in his presence before."* (NKJV) It was a capital crime for the cup-bearer or anyone else to be sad in the presence of the king. Persian kings were such egotists that they believed they were deity. Their reasoning went something like this: "No matter how bad the personal problems of your life, just to be in my presence should make you want to smile. All your problems should melt away by being in my presence. So if you are sad in my presence, then you do not really believe that I am deity and you do not believe that I am who I say I am." If you had a sad face, you were in danger of having no face; they lifted your head off. Nehemiah prayed for four months. He fasted and wept before God during the nighttime, but he put on his happy face to go in before the king and serve him. On that particular day, though, his heart shone through his countenance and he was sad. Verse 2 says, *"Wherefore the king said unto me, 'Why is thy countenance sad, seeing thou art not sick?'"* You could be sad if you were sick, but you'd better make sure you had a temperature, buddy, because the king was going to check you out. The king said, *"This is nothing else but sorrow of heart. Then I was very sore afraid."* That is probably an understatement. He was terrified because he thought that he was going to lose his job, be flogged and maybe even lose his life. Verse 3 says, *"And he said unto the king, 'let the king live forever.'"* That is a good thing to say in that kind of circumstance. He said, *"Why should not my countenance be sad when the city, the place of my fathers' sepulchers, lieth waste and the gates thereof are consumed with fire? Then the king said unto me, 'For what does thou make request?' So I prayed to the God of heaven.'"* In between these two verses, he sent a prayer up real quick, because the king had asked what he wanted. He boldly told him in verse 5, *"If it please the king, and if thy servant has found favor in thy sight, that thou would send me unto Judah, unto the city of my fathers' sepulchers, that I may build it."*

The Risk of Faith

It is at this point in the drama of Nehemiah that we see the risk of his faith. He could have been killed or flogged; certainly it looked like he would lose his prestigious position. But he did something. Nehemiah was concerned. For four months he prayed and fasted before God, but his concern did not end with merely concern. It led to commitment. Many times we become concerned about the world, we become concerned about our family or we become concerned about our church, but sadly often that concern does not lead to commitment. There was a point in Nehemiah's life when he was concerned, and then he got off his knees and did something. Most of us have that backwards. Most of us try to do something without being on our knees. Both are deadly—the activist who is "all work and no worship," or the pacifist who is "all worship and no work." There should be a balance between work and worship. Nehemiah was so concerned that he prayed for four months. He wept before God and then he risked everything to do what God had put in his heart to do.

Martin Luther spawned the Great Reformation beginning in Germany. He was living in a monastery before he was converted to Christ. The story has been told about a friend of his by the name of Myconias, who also lived in the monastery. He was saved about the same time Martin Luther was saved. Myconias told Martin Luther, "You leave the monastery and preach the gospel, and I will stay behind and pray for you every day." That sounds like a pretty good deal. I'd like it if people were in a monastery somewhere praying for me. Myconias prayed for Luther. Martin Luther began to light the fires of the Reformation, and also to suffer persecution. Myconias stayed in the monastery, faithfully praying for Martin Luther. One night, Myconias said he dreamed that he was standing on the crest of a hill. Looking in one direction as far as he could see, there were literally thousands of sheep, but only one lone shepherd—Martin Luther. Looking as far as he could see in the other direction, there were thousands of acres of wheat, ready for harvest, the gentle breeze causing the grain to move like the waves of the ocean, but he saw only one reaper—Martin Luther. When he awoke, he said to his friend, Martin Luther, "It is not enough that I should stay and pray, I too must be thrust into the harvest, I must go to the lost sheep."

Nehemiah reached a point in his life when he got off his knees and thought, "I am going to do something for God. If it costs me everything, if it costs me my life, I am going to risk something for God."

The Ruins

Chapter 2 is the second act of this great drama as Nehemiah goes to Jerusalem. He tells us nothing of the hardship of his journey of hundreds of miles across a barren desert by camelback. I think if I had made that journey I would have written a book about my experiences in the wilderness, but in verse 11 he simply said, *"So I came to Jerusalem and was there three days."* No trumpet sounded. He did not arrive riding on a white horse, although he was going to be the governor. He did not arrive announcing, "I have all the answers," but rather stayed there three days unannounced. He did not utter a word. Nehemiah had heard of the ruins from his brother, of the disgrace of Jerusalem. He wanted to take a personal assessment of the situation. As he entered the city, he could feel the discouragement and the pessimism, the depressiveness of a conquered people. On the third day, he mounted his horse late that night and rode through the streets of Jerusalem looking at the broken down walls and the burned out houses. Traveling as far as he could by horseback, and blocked by the rubble, he trudged his way by foot, probably crawling over the rubble. It is one thing to hear about the ruins, but now for the first time, he saw for himself—the fearful people, the jobless, the starving, the hopeless stare of orphans and the pathetic expressions of pain in a city that was paralyzed with apathy.

We need to see the ruins of our culture. For eighty years, the people had lived with broken down walls. They were so accustomed to the ruins that they hardly noticed them any more. Our culture has been on such a long, slow slide into spiritual declension that we hardly notice the ruins.

Nehemiah was fortunate. The ruins of Jerusalem were *physical*, brick and mortar. All around us are *human* ruins. Christians tend to see the world through the eyes of a Sunday morning. Often we know nothing of the ruins of a Saturday night.

Living in the comfort of our air-conditioned homes with the sound of Christian music filtering through each room, we enjoy the luxury of Christian fellowship. Every day we get into our cars and are unaffected, untouched as we drive past the human ruins. I am not just talking about poverty and social ruins. I am talking about the spiritual ruins all around us in this great city.

Our first child was a precious little girl with blonde hair and beautiful blue eyes, who we named *Charity*, meaning "love." She reminded me so much of a "Chatty Cathy" doll the first time I saw her. Charity loved school! Two weeks into her first grade, she was so excited about attending her Open House. That evening I was preaching a revival meeting across the city. Since I was unable to attend, Charity went with my wife, Ginger. As they arrived at the school and parked and exited the car, another car that was speeding down the street struck my little girl and killed her instantly.

I can not explain the devastation of losing my child. I remember as though it were yesterday, after all these years, the day that we attended Charity's memorial service. Our family was picked up by the church van, and I sat in the back of the vehicle while my family was sitting toward the front. Driving through the familiar streets of our neighborhood where I was a pastor, something struck me. I will never forget as I rode in that van and I looked out the window. I saw a man mowing his lawn, some little children playing in their front yard, and I saw teenagers riding bicycles. People were jogging and others were walking on that Saturday morning. I will never forget the thought I had: *"Lord, how many times have I driven these streets and there has been someone right over there who had the kind of pain that I have now—and I was untouched by it? How many times have people with the kind of pain that I have now, sat in a pew where I have preached, yet I was untouched and unmoved by the pain of their life?"* The fact is, there are ruins all around us. Many times we are untouched by the ruins because we will not allow ourselves to feel someone else's awful pain.

Every afternoon across this city and across this nation, there are people wiping the tears from their eyes because they've been watching "As The World Turns," or some other soap opera on television. They are sad because someone's home is breaking up, someone is getting an abortion, or someone is addicted to drugs. Maybe you will watch the movie of the week on television and wipe the tears from your eyes after seeing awful pain depicted in people's lives. We are able to feel the pain of divorce through a movie, or the pain of child abuse, or see the pain of alcoholism or drug addiction. Weeping and wiping tears from our eyes over what is not real, we sit untouched, dry eyed at that which is real. The fact of the matter is, all around us are people whose homes are breaking up from drug addiction and alcoholism, yet, for the most part, we are unmoved by the ruins. No, the houses are not burned and the walls are not torn down, but the *homes* are burned. The walls of protection around children are burned. Our culture is producing human ruins on a massive scale.

More than 25,000 runaways end up in Los Angeles each year. Children by the thousands, in our state, are forced into prostitution on our streets. Gangs have become a substitute for families. Broken homes are now the norm in our culture. Children are being killed by other children in our schools. Girls murder their own babies, with impunity, through abortion. We are producing human ruins on an unparalleled basis.

I realize that statistics can be cold and barren. But the fact is, where you live, and blocks from the church where we worship, right now as we sit in the comfort of this building, there are those with trembling hands tonight plunging a needle into their arms, trying to find an answer to life. When we gather to worship every Sunday, we sit shoulder to shoulder with people whose lives are in rubble and ruins. Maybe some are contemplating suicide, others are living in despair, or their marriages are being ripped apart. I drive the streets of this city just like you do. Sometimes I see little children playing in their front yards, splashing in their little pools. I see "little bitty" guys riding their tricycles and I have thought, "Chances are, they'll never have a Sunday School teacher ever visit their home. Chances are strong that they will never hear a clear presentation of the gospel." Those little children might as well grow up in a third world country, because they will grow up knowing nothing about God. They will become a statistic of human ruins some day!

In the face of those kinds of ruins, what is the church's strategy? Our strategy is to come! Come to us and hear what we are doing, rather than to go. On occasion, I preach in churches across our country, and my heart is broken when I hear about the fights and the divisions in churches. We can talk about charismatics, but we have a lot of schizmatics—a lot of schisms. At times the people of God in churches are introverted, cold and barren. The average church in America is running less than one hundred in attendance. I see the massive cities passing us by while we argue over carpet and personalities, money, buildings and budgets, while the people go on to become human ruins in this life and in the next.

Every month, I stand at Christ-less graves. Because I preach funerals of those in the community who do not have a pastor, I find myself standing at a Christ-less grave, trying to give a word of hope to the living. I see people sitting at a graveside, and their hearts are broken. They have absolutely no hope of eternity. There is no pastor who really knows them, and there is no godly deacon to put his arm around them; there is no Sunday School teacher to say, "I am praying for you." They weep as people without hope, absolutely without hope—*the ruins.*

Jeremiah prophesied for the people of Israel to turn back to God. He lived to see God's judgment. Jeremiah wrote the book of Lamentations after Jerusalem fell to the Babylonians. He was like a war correspondent stepping over the bloated bodies of the dead. Jerusalem was like a ghost town with empty streets. He declared that "the gold has lost its luster; the crown has fallen from our heads." He saw what he called the end of it. He saw the full consequence of sin. That is what we see as pastors. That is what I see—I see the end of it!

- I have never had a man or woman come into my office and talk to me about the exhilaration of drugs. But I have had the addict come because he has lost everything, and needs help.
- I have never had anyone come to my office to tell me how much fun it is to party and to drink. But I have had people come to me after they've lost their wife and their job and they are destitute.
- I have never had any young people come and talk to me about the exhilaration of promiscuity, and yet I have listened to the brokenness of divorce that promiscuity caused—the ruins that it caused.

We see the end of it. In the face of that, I am not satisfied with Sunday School campaigns, and I am not satisfied with bigger budgets and constructing more buildings. I am not satisfied until we impact the ruins of our city, our state and our nation. We have to impact the ruins!

Responsibility

In the third act of this drama, we see the responsibility. Chapter 2 is a tremendous chapter as Nehemiah crawls over the rubble of the city. Chapter 3 is one of the driest and deadest chapters in the entire Bible, with a list of unpronounceable names that reads like a Hebrew phone book. Yet, it is in chapter 3 that we find a wonderful principle. For eighty years, since the captivity, they had lived with the rubble and the ruins. Then in fifty-two days they rebuilt the walls. Why? How did they do it? I will tell you how they did it. *Everyone got on the wall.* That is what verse 28 is about. It says, *"From above the horse gate repaired the priest everyone against his house."* This verse is like a recurring refrain throughout the chapter:

- In chapter 3, verse 2 it says, *"And next unto him built it;"*
- In verse 4, *"and next unto them;"*
- In verse 5, *"and next unto them;"*
- In verse 7, *"and next unto them;"*
- In verse 8, *"and next unto him;"*
- In verse 9, *"and next unto them;"*
- In verse 10, *"and next unto them;"*
- In verse 12, *"and next unto them;"*
- In verse 16, *"and after him repaired;"*
- In verse 17, *"and after him repaired;"*
- In verse 18, *"and after him repaired;"*
- In verse 19, *"and next to him;"*
- In verse 20, *"and after him;"*
- In verse 21, *"after him;"*
- In verse 22, *"and after him;"*
- In verse 23, *"after him;"*
- In verse 24, *"and after him repaired."*

All through the chapter is *"after him"* or *"next to him repaired."* This chapter is about the division of labor. It is about *everyone* being on the wall. That is my challenge to you—to go and find some rubble, some ruins; and get on the wall!

There is a record of some who built nearly a quarter of a mile of wall. There is also a record of a man who built a small portion of the wall that was outside his bedroom window, probably only about three feet long. Someone else built a portion of the wall behind his house. That is how the work of God is done. That is what the body of Christ is about. That is what the Kingdom of God is about. It is not about a few mega churches; it is not about a few super saints. It is about everyone finding a piece of rubble, getting on the wall and doing something for God. It may be in a great church or in a big cathedral somewhere, it may be in a little country town, or it may be in a village somewhere. *Everyone on the wall, everyone on the wall!*

Nineteen hundred years ago, a lone figure traveling across the barren landscape in Asia Minor had tucked within his toga one of the greatest treasures of the ages, known to us today as the book of Ephesians. Who was this man? Was he a prophet or one of the apostles, maybe Paul or Peter or John? Was he one of the missionaries, Barnabas or Silas, or perhaps one of the young "preacher boys," Timothy or Titus? No, actually, he was an obscure man about whom little is known, named Tychicus. He traveled from village to village and city to city reading that parchment, one of the high-water marks of Biblical revelation that touched the ages. Did he know he was touching the ages? No. That is my point! You never know when what you do will have an impact upon the ages. You might think that you cannot do much, but building on a little piece of wall may touch the ages.

There was a group of Moravians on a ship crossing the Atlantic. During a storm, they were singing praises to God. Do you think they knew the significance of a young man, John Wesley, who was smitten by the conviction of God? He left that boat a changed man, though they never knew how their singing had impacted the ages. You will never know when what you do that is *ordinary*, all of a sudden becomes *extraordinary* in the Kingdom of God. Why not find some ruins, find some wall, and get on it when you leave here?

I love to read about World War II. One of my favorite stories is the Battle of Dunkirk, where the Germans trapped

390,000 British and French soldiers. German U-boats came in droves in the English Channel and, using mortar and launches, they pounded those who were involved in the rescue. The German infantry assaulted them day and night, cutting off their supply lines. It seemed that they could last for only four, maybe five days. It appeared that the entire British Expeditionary Army would be lost. But twenty-three miles across the English Channel, a man by the name of Churchill took the microphone. Making an impassioned appeal on the radio, he, in essence, said we have to do something. Those men across the channel must be rescued. Do what you can to rescue them! Hurriedly responding to his appeal, the people of England rallied, crossing the English Channel in all kinds of boats. There were dinghies, motorboats, rowboats, yachts, pleasure steamers and merchant ships. People from all walks of life, from Navy men to taxi drivers and yachtsmen, crossed the English Channel to rescue those men. Two hundred and twenty war vessels and 650 other vessels faced the cruel weather and choppy waves of the English Channel, weaving among the floating mines and the debris of sunken ships, as planes dove at them. Churchill thought that perhaps 30,000 of those 390,000 men could be rescued, but when that weekend was over they had rescued 338,226 men. Appropriately called the "miracle of Dunkirk," some say it was the turning point of the war for the morale of the English people.

A part of that story, unknown to many, is that of a small, aging man who wore thick glasses. He worked down the street from Whitehall in the area of government bureaucracy. Huddling around a radio with the rest of the employees in that office building, he listened eagerly to the impassioned words of Churchill. Not uttering a word to anyone that Friday, he left work and went home to his storage shed. Pulling out his little two-man canoe, and dragging it down to the beach, he launched it into the choppy waters of the English Channel. Determined, this one frail man paddled all the way across the Channel, among floating mines, in the wake of huge passing ships. Soaked and tired, he found a wounded soldier, loaded him in his two-man canoe and pulled all the way back across the English Channel to the beach of Dover. Upon unloading that man, though exhausted, he did not stop! By now it was night, but once again he launched that little canoe into the English Channel. Now spent, with aching muscles, he pulled all the way across the English Channel in the darkness and found another wounded man. Loading him into the canoe, he brought him back across and dumped him on the beach of Dover. Daylight approached but he did not stop! Now stumbling and dragging the canoe to the edge of the water, he paddled the twenty-three miles across, found another wounded soldier, loaded him and brought him back. By then the entire weekend was gone. He went back to work on Monday and though he never told anyone what he had done, it was later found out by someone that he had rescued those men.

That is what I am talking about—*getting on the wall!* This man did not look at the big ships that passed and say, "Well, I can't carry a hundred men so I just won't do anything." He didn't look at a yacht and say, "Well, I can't carry half a dozen like that guy in the yacht." Instead, he said, "I have a canoe and I can get *one*." He got one and said, "I am going to get another one." Then he said, "I have two, I will get another one." He did not say, "I can't do what the big ships can do," but instead he said, "I will do what I can do." And he did it! That's what it is about! That is how this city will be reached for Christ. It is not a matter of saying, "I can't do what *they* can do. I wish I could do what *they* can do." It is doing what *you* can do. It is getting on the wall for God and finding some ruins.

A couple of years ago, I was preaching on the East Coast and went into New York City. Driving through those crowded streets, it broke my heart to see so many homeless people huddled around vents, trying to stay warm in the brisk cold of that autumn day. I saw the teeming masses of people in Times Square, thousands everywhere. I drove past 42nd Street and was offended by the huge pornographic billboards, prostitutes walking the streets selling themselves, drug addicts stumbling, and drunks lying in the gutter. My heart was broken for the lostness of that great city. Sitting in the back of a taxi, heading down 42nd Street toward the Lincoln Tunnel, I thought, *"God, how could anyone ever reach this city for Christ? Ten thousand preachers couldn't reach this city. Lord, this city is on its way to Hell. How can this city ever be reached for Jesus?"* Then I heard a familiar sound, a familiar name. I quickly rolled down my window, because it was the name of *Jesus* that I had heard. There on the street corner, I saw a black man whose hair was white from age. He had a little guitar amplifier with a microphone plugged into it. That man was preaching about Jesus! There were a few policemen making fun of him and some prostitutes standing in the distance, but they were listening. There were also some businessmen who had wandered down that way, dressed in fine suits, probably from the Wall Street district. They were listening, and I could not help but say, *"God bless that man, God bless that man!"* There was a man who said, "I cannot do everything. I cannot preach to thousands of people in those skyscrapers, but I am going to find a little piece of wall, find a corner and preach about Jesus. I am going to preach so that someone will be impacted." That is what I am talking about!

Why not find some ruins when you go home, and *get on the wall for God?*

~ 1988 ~

Valley Baptist church participated in its first foreign mission trip in 1988. A pastor in Trinidad heard me preaching on the radio and invited me to come to Trinidad to establish a new church. My wife Ginger and I, along with Del and Dora Griffin, went to the Indian people of Trinidad. A number of Hindu people were saved. The next year, Pastor Phil, Del and I returned and baptized approximately thirty converts.

There was an amendment proposed to our by-laws in 1988 that would either remove our church covenant or change it in such a way that a person who either smoked or drank socially could be considered for a leadership role in the church. Some people thought such restrictions were legalistic. The people of the congregation were asked to write their opinions and a special document was published. The church voted not to change the covenant. Years later, separate membership and leadership covenants were adopted.

A banquet was held at the Civic Auditorium for the purpose of beginning a capital funds campaign entitled "Building for Tomorrow." Our people pledged $1.5 million for our building fund in order to relocate. We actually raised a little over $2 million over the next four years.

"A Matter of Perspective" was preached on Sunday morning, April 24, 1988, as part of a verse-by-verse series of messages through the book of James.

A Matter of Perspective

"What does it profit, my brethren, if someone says he has faith but does not have works? Can faith save him? If a brother or sister is naked and destitute of daily food, and one of you says to them, 'Depart in peace, be warmed and filled,' but you do not give them the things which are needed for the body, what does it profit? Thus also faith by itself, if it does not have works, is dead. But someone will say, 'You have faith, and I have works.' Show me your faith without your works, and I will show you my faith by my works. You believe that there is one God. You do well. Even the demons believe—and tremble! But do you want to know, O foolish man, that faith without works is dead? Was not Abraham our father justified by works when he offered Isaac his son on the altar? Do you see that faith was working together with his works, and by works faith was made perfect? And the Scripture was fulfilled which says, 'Abraham believed God, and it was accounted to him for righteousness.' And he was called the friend of God. You see then that a man is justified by works, and not by faith only. Likewise, was not Rahab the harlot also justified by works when she received the messengers and sent them out another way? For as the body without the spirit is dead, so faith without works is dead also." (NKJV)

James, chapter 2, verses 14-26 is one of the most misunderstood passages in all of the New Testament, and yet it is the thesis statement of the book of James. It is the apex of everything he wrote before this paragraph, and everything that he wrote after it is controlled by this paragraph of Scripture.

In the dark ages, there was a monk by the name of Martin Luther, who was trying to achieve his salvation. He was trying by religious rituals to earn favor with God. On one occasion, he climbed some stairs that were said to be holy steps. As he climbed each step, he would kiss the step in front of him and say a prayer. It was thought that by going through this laborious, religious ritual, a person would earn favor with God. It was in the midst of this process, that some say Luther began to think about Romans, chapter 1, verse 17, which declares, *"The just shall live by faith."* Continuing to climb those stairs, kissing each one and saying prayers, that Scripture kept flooding his mind, *"The just shall live by faith."* Suddenly, the truth of that Scripture impacted upon the life of Martin Luther. Luther came to realize that salvation is not by religious ritual, that it is not by achievement of works or anything we do. Instead, salvation is a matter of faith as the Bible says in Romans, *"The just shall live by faith."* Consequently, Luther was converted to Christ.

Martin Luther, of course, began the Great Reformation. The cry of the Reformation was *sola fide*—which, translated, means "faith alone," or "faith only." In other words, nothing else is needed regarding salvation other than faith. We are saved by grace through faith. That is what Paul said throughout the book of Romans, and that is what he said in Ephesians 2:8-9: *"For by grace are ye saved through faith; and that not of yourselves: it is the gift of God: Not of works, lest any man should boast."*

- We are not saved by faith *plus* good works, as some people think.
- We are not saved by faith *plus* joining the church.
- We are not saved by faith *plus* religious rituals.

We are saved by *faith alone!* If your salvation is dependent upon works, then you can never have the full assurance of your salvation. You can never really know for certain that you are saved. If salvation is dependent upon works, then everyone must survey their lives and determine whether they are really saved, based upon whether they have lost their temper recently or have had an evil thought.

The New Testament teaches that we are saved by faith alone, by God's grace. Martin Luther realized that and began preaching all over Germany. But when he read the book of James, it seemed to be saying to him that we are saved not by faith, but that we are justified by works. This caused Martin Luther to declare that the epistle of James is an "epistle of straw." In other words, it is not good for very much! In fact, he argued that the book of James should not even be in the New Testament, that it should not be considered part of Biblical revelation. There are others who have held that position through the ages. It is the apparent contradiction between the teachings of Paul and James that I want to address in this critical passage of Scripture.

The ironic thing about the conflict, or the apparent conflict, between Paul and James is that they used the same man, Abraham, as their illustration. Paul said, "Abraham was justified by faith." James, also using Abraham, said, "We know that Abraham was justified by works." In Romans 4, verse 2, Paul teaches, *"For if Abraham were justified by works, he hath whereof to glory; but not before God. For what saith the Scripture? Abraham believed God, and it was counted unto him for righteousness. Now to him that worketh is the reward not reckoned of grace, but of debt."* He goes on to say,

"But to him that worketh not, but believeth on him that justifieth the ungodly, his faith is counted for righteousness." Continuing in the book of Romans, Paul developed that thought. In fact, in the books of Ephesians, Titus, and 1Timothy, we find the recurring theme that we are not saved by the works of the law. He continues that we do not earn favor with God by keeping the commandments or the minutia of the ceremonial Jewish law, nor do we earn favor with God by our good deeds. Paul said, *"Knowing that a man is not justified by the works of the law, but by the faith of Jesus Christ, even we have believed in Jesus Christ, that we might be justified by the faith of Christ, and not by the works of the law: for by the works of the law shall no flesh be justified."* Now listen to the words of James again in chapter 2, verse 21: *"Was not Abraham our father justified by works when he offered Isaac, his son, upon the altar?"* Verse 24 says, *"Ye see then how that by works a man is justified, and not by faith only."*

What's going on? Paul said that we are justified by faith, and James apparently said that we are justified by works. I think what is happening between Paul and James is that they are giving the heads and tails of the same truth. They are approaching it from two different directions because they had two different purposes in mind. Paul, writing to those who were strict legalists, combated legalism in much of his teaching. The legalists or the Judaizers, in the day of Paul, thought that in order to be a Christian you must first become a Jew. You must keep the ceremonial law and be initiated into Judaism through circumcision. Then you must keep the minutia of the law, and the Sabbath—and somehow *that, plus faith,* will achieve salvation. Paul was saying that to be a Christian, you do not have to become a Jew first, or be circumcised, or keep the ceremonies, the dietary laws or the Sabbath law. You do not have to keep any of those things as far as salvation is concerned. It is by faith! You come to the

Lord Jesus Christ in faith, and by faith God justifies you. He declares you righteous.

That was Paul's purpose, but James' purpose was a little different. He was writing to Jews and Jewish Christians who had been under the bondage and the yoke of the law of God. Now, for the first time, they understood the liberation of grace. They understood that they were saved by faith, not by works of achievement. They realized that God saved them by grace through faith. So some of them said, "Hey, if we are not saved by our lifestyle, if we are not kept saved by our lifestyle, then let's go and live it up—it is party time! If we are saved by grace, then it does not matter how we live. We can go out and live in sin, immorality and do whatever we want. If we are saved by faith and not by works, then our lifestyle does not matter." James is writing this book to say your lifestyle does matter because your works are what prove that you really have faith. You are saved by faith, but it is your works that validate or justify your faith.

Paul and James are writing from two different perspectives. When you read the writings of Paul, he is always looking at things from God's perspective. From God's perspective, we are justified by faith. James is writing, not from God's perspective, but from man's perspective of what man can see. One man cannot see faith in another man. When you look at me as a pastor, you cannot see my faith. The only thing that you can observe in my life is the result of my faith, hopefully, or the evidence of my faith. Faith is like calories—you cannot see them, but you can see the result of consuming them. That is what James is saying, that if there is really faith, then we ought to be able to see the results. Paul is talking about what God sees on the inside, which is faith, and James is talking about what man sees on the outside, which is works, a lifestyle that is distinctively Christian.

Let me illustrate it to you this way: Suppose you are driving in a neighborhood and you drive past a house where there is a fire burning in the fireplace. No one can see that fire except the people inside the house. Driving by the house, you cannot see the fire on the inside, but you can see smoke coming out of the chimney on the outside. When you see the smoke, you assume that there is a fire in the fireplace. Therein lies the difference between Paul and James. Paul is looking on the inside and seeing faith, the fire that is in the fireplace. James, on the other hand, is saying that if there is a fire in the fireplace, there ought to be smoke in the chimney.

James is saying that if there is faith in the heart, there ought to be works in the life. There ought to be a lifestyle that is Christ-like. Paul is instructing us in how to be saved. We are saved by grace through faith. James is not instructing us, he is exhorting us—now that we are saved, there should be a lifestyle that is Christ-like. Paul is speaking of the *root* of salvation, which is faith. James is speaking of the *fruit* of salvation, which is works. Paul is talking about that which is *inward*, which is faith. James is talking about that which is *outward*, which is works. Same words—different meanings.

The problem between the two men is that they use the same terms in different ways. For instance, they both talk about works, but when they say the word *works*, they mean two different things. It is obvious that when Paul talks about works, he is speaking of works in the sense of keeping the commandments of God, trying to earn your way to God. He is speaking about the ceremonial law, because when he talks about works, he illustrates it with circumcision, which had to do with the ceremonial law. When James talks about works, he is not talking about the minutia of keeping this commandment or that commandment; he is talking about being Christ-like in your character, or living for Jesus. When he illustrates works, he does not do it with circumcision or the law. He illustrates it with being kind, loving your brother and meeting the needs of people around you.

Another word both men use interchangeably, and yet with a different definition is the word *justify*. Paul loves that word! Throughout the writings of Paul, he talks about "being justified by faith." For Paul, the definition of the word *justified* is the act whereby God declares you to be righteous. When a sinner comes to God, he asks forgiveness and the Lord Jesus Christ declares him to be righteous. It is simply an act of His sovereign grace! We are not righteous, but He *declares* us to be righteous. We are justified. James does not use the word in the same sense at all. He uses the word justified in its pristine or primary sense, which means "to be vindicated," or "to validate." For instance, if you do something wrong and try to weasel out of it, someone might say that you are just trying to *justify* your sin. What does that mean? It means you are trying to vindicate yourself, you are trying to validate that what you did is all right. This is how James uses the word *justify*. But Paul uses it in the sense of *God* declaring someone to be righteous. James uses the word in the sense of vindicating, that our works prove the fact that we have faith. Our works justify us in the sense that they prove that we really are Christians, and that we have faith on the inside.

When Paul speaks of being justified, he is talking about how we are justified before God. When James speaks of being justified, he is talking about how we are justified before men in our works. Paul's justification is a *declaration* of righteousness. When James speaks of justification, it is not a declaration of righteousness, but a *demonstration* of righteousness, or proper living.

- Paul speaks of the *provision* of salvation, that it is by faith.
- James speaks of the *proof* of salvation by works.
- Paul speaks of the *means* of salvation—it is by faith.
- James speaks of the *mark* of salvation—it is good works within your life.

What good is faith without works? In verse 14, there are two questions: *"What doth it profit, my brethren, though a man say he hath faith, and have not works?"* That is the first question. What good is the kind of faith that says, "Hey, I have faith, I believe in Jesus," and yet it does not affect my lifestyle? That is like saying, "What good is it if you carry a card in your billfold that says, 'Lifeguard,' if you do not know how to swim?" It does not do much good. What good does it do to carry a driver's license if you do not know how to drive? James was saying, "What good is it if you say that you have faith and it is not affecting your lifestyle?" Paul, in his writings, talks about the *cause* of salvation. But James is speaking about the *effect* of salvation.

Every Sunday afternoon or every Monday night during football season, there are a lot of "armchair quarterbacks." They sit in their easy chairs and second-guess the quarterback, saying, "Boy, he should have passed," or, "He shouldn't have done that, he should have handed off, he should have punted." Yet most of those who are armchair quarterbacks could not drop back and throw a pass within ten yards of the receiver. They are armchair quarterbacks! Some armchair Christians say they have faith—they have a profession, but they do not have any performance in their lives. They profess that they have faith, but their *performance* does not match their *profession*.

The second question in verse 14 asks, *"Can faith save him?"*. That is a poor translation in the King James Version. Maybe you have a different translation that renders it better. The reason it is a poor translation is because, in the original language, there is a definite article, *the*. Can *the* faith save me? Grammatically it can be understood as a demonstrative pronoun, "Can faith save him?" You can even translate it accurately as "Can *that* kind of faith save him?"

When James said, *"Yea, a man may say, Thou hast faith..."* he is not talking about the *real* believer. He is talking about the man who *says* that he has faith but does not have works. Can that kind of faith save him? So the question is not, "Can faith save?" The question is, "Can *that kind* of faith save?" It is a conditional sentence that anticipates a negative response. James is saying a certain man says he has faith, but he has no works. Can that kind of faith save? Of course not! That is not real faith.

Verses 15 and 16 contain the explanation to the two questions asked in verse 14. James said, *"If a brother or sister be naked,* [meaning to be ill clad, not literally naked, but poor clothing, not warm clothing], *and one of you say unto them, 'Depart in peace, be ye warmed and filled;' notwithstanding ye give them not those things which are needful to the body; what doth it profit?'"* Here's a poor, hungry person that needs shelter and you say, "Oh, bless you, brother, be warm, be filled, be clothed." James asked, "What kind of faith is that?" That is not real faith! It is like a man who has been stranded on the side of the freeway with a flat tire and obviously does not have a jack. He is waiting for someone to help him, and you drive by slowly and say, "Better get it fixed, buddy." That is a mockery! Those are good words, but they are without works. James asked, "What good is the kind of faith that has pious words that say, 'Oh, I love Jesus, and I love God and I have faith,' and then it does not produce good works?"

Listen to what John has to say in 1 John, chapter 3, verse 17. He said, *"But whoso hath this world's goods, and seeth his brother that has need, and shutteth up his bowels of compassion from him, how dwelleth the love of God in him?"* James is saying that if someone has a need and you have the ability to meet that need and minister to them, and you do not do it, how can you say that you have the love of God in you? John questions such faith as well. He said, *"My little children, let us not love in word, neither in tongue, but in deed and in truth."* James said, "If someone has a need, and you are unwilling to try to meet that need, then what kind of faith is that?" John seems to be saying, "Hey, I doubt that you even have the love of God in you if you do that."

That is basically what Jesus taught when He gave a parable of a man who was beaten and rolled into a ditch and left. The first man who came by was a priest. He did not have time to get involved. Another man came by, a Levite, the religious elite of his day, but he did not have time either. Finally, a despised Samaritan, known to us as the "Good Samaritan," came by and helped him. The priest and the Levite could have *defended* their faith, but they did not *demonstrate* their faith. James questioned the good of being able to defend your faith, of being orthodox in your mind, without good works in your lifestyle. John Calvin said, "Faith alone justifies, but faith that justifies is never alone." That is so true. Faith always produces good works. Faith without works is dead faith. Dead faith does not get involved in the needs of others. Now if that is true, the opposite of that must be true also—if you have real faith, then you must be a person that gets involved in the needs of others. Here's this poor person who needs clothes and food, and we say, "Go, be filled and be warm." James said, "That is not the way faith operates." We are tempted to say, "Well, there are so many poor people, so many needs around us; we cannot do everything," but that is no excuse for not doing *something*. We can get involved in some ministry. All around us people have desperate needs. Sometimes a person has a desperate need and we say to them, "Do not let it get you down. If you need anything, call me." Yet all the while, we know that they need something and we are unwilling to meet their need. As a matter of fact, we know very well they are not going to call us. In fact, we are hoping they won't call! James asks, "What kind of faith is that?" Lifeless faith!

He gave the question in verse 14 and the explanation in verses 15 and 16. He tells us what he thinks about it as he gives the conclusion of the argument in verse 17. "*Even so*

faith, if it hath not works, is dead, being alone." He said,
"That is not real faith at all; it is a phony faith." If you cut
the legs off the table, you do not have a table anymore. All
you have is a pile of wood sitting on the floor. You cannot
call it a table. James said, "If you take works away from
faith, then quit calling it faith, because it is not really faith."
If you do not have a lifestyle that is Christian, James is saying, "Quit calling yourself a Christian, because it is not real,
it is phony; it is dead. You may know all kinds of pious
words, you may quote Scripture that you have memorized,
you may be able to teach the Bible, you may know the divisions of theology, and you may sing the songs of Zion, but
at some point, your faith ought to affect the way you live. If
it is not affecting the way you live, then you have dead
faith."

After the conclusion, he anticipates that there is going to
be an objection. James knew that someone was going to say:
"Thou hast faith, and I have works..." James anticipates that
the pious person is going to say, "Look James, you have your
works; you get involved in social ministry, you get involved
in ministering to people. That is good for you, but that is
not my calling. My calling is to study and to teach the Word
of God, and I do not really want to help people or get
involved in the needs of other people. That is good for you,
but that is just not my thing, James." Look at how James
answers that person in verse 18. He seemed to be saying,
"Look, buddy, (that is my translation) show me thy faith
without works and I will show thee my faith *by* my works."
James said that we ought to have a show-me faith. We ought
to have a faith that displays itself prominently within our
life. If it is real faith, it will display itself.

Suppose you have two football teams and they are going
to play for the championship in the playoffs. Right before
the game, one football team goes to the locker room of the
other team. They have a spokesman who says, "Look, we are

here for the game, but we can tell you guys that we are the strongest team. We have been lifting weights and we are strong. We have the best players in all the positions, as well as the greatest skill and agility. We are definitely the best team! There is no doubt about it. We know that, everyone knows that, but we just do not want to display it! We do not want to show off, so we really do not want to play today, but we are the strongest team!" The other team is going to say, "Look, you *say* that you have the strength, but we are going to *show* you *our* strength. Get out on the field because we are going to show it to you." The nature of football is that you prove your strength and skill on the field. With a team that says it has strength, yet is unwilling to display it, you have got to wonder and question if they really have it. James is saying that the Christian who says, "Oh, I have faith," but is unwilling to display it in his lifestyle, or is unwilling to get involved in the lives of others, is one whom you begin to question as to whether he really has faith. If there is no smoke in the chimney, you have to wonder if there is a fire in the fireplace! If there are no works in your life, you have to wonder about your salvation. James taught that if you say that you love Jesus, *show me by the way you live.* Intellectual belief is not faith.

There is another objection that James anticipates. Listen to what he said in verse 19: *"Thou believest that there is one God; thou doest well."* He was writing to Jews, and the bottom line for a Jew was called the Shema, the ancient confession in the book of Deuteronomy, where they would say, *"The Lord our God is one God."* Every little Jewish boy and girl memorized the Shema; in fact, that was the first thing they learned religiously: "The Lord our God is one God." We, like Jews, are monotheistic. We believe in a Supreme Being and that there is only one God. James knew that there would be some who were going to say, "James, we believe in God. We do not have to do all this Christian living. We believe in the existence of God." Just like people today will say, "Hey, I believe in God. That is enough! I do not have to live like Jesus."

Look at the sarcasm of James in verse 19: *"Thou believest that there is one God; thou doest well: the devils also believe, and tremble."* What he is saying is that there are no atheistic demons. There is not even an agnostic demon. They all believe. James is asking, "What good is it that you just believe in the existence of God intellectually? Did you know that the demons even believe in the deity of Christ?" On one occasion, as Jesus was casting out some demons, they said, *"What have we to do with You, Jesus of Nazareth? Did You come to destroy us? I know who You are—the Holy One of God!"* On another occasion, they called Him, "Christ the Messiah." On another occasion, they indicated that they believed in Hell. In fact, the devil is probably more orthodox than most people in our society. James is saying that it is not a matter of intellectual belief, it is not a matter of fact, it is a matter of faith. The demons believe and they tremble. It is the word for "shudder." It is literally the word to "stand up," for your hair to "stand on end." They believe, but they do not have faith. They do not have a relationship with God.

Let's suppose that the devil wanted to join a church. Let's say he is in a nice suit and looks like a great prospect for the church. So we ask him a few questions, not knowing who he is. Do you believe that Jesus is the Son of God? He responds, "Oh, yes, I believe! Absolutely! I am convinced that Jesus is the Son of God!" Do you believe that Jesus died on the cross? Again he responds, "Yes, I believe! In fact, I saw Him! I know that He died on the cross!" Do you believe that Jesus was raised from the dead? "Yes! Absolutely! I know beyond any shadow of a doubt that Jesus Christ was raised from the dead!" Do you believe that Jesus is coming again? "Yes! I am convinced that He is going to come again!" Are you willing to be baptized? "Oh, certainly! That is no problem! I'd love to be baptized!" Are you going to attend the church faithfully? "Yes! As a matter of fact, I will probably be here more than any member you have! I will be here every time the door opens." Do you love Jesus? There is silence! Are you willing to say that Jesus is Lord of your life? "No, *never!*" You see, the devil believes intellectually, but he has no relationship with God. It is no feather in anyone's hat that they believe in the existence of God, or that they believe the *plan* of salvation. It is the *Man* of salvation that saves, the Lord Jesus Christ. It is not what we believe, but in whom we believe. Faith involves not just the mind, but at some point, the heart. If the heart is involved, it involves the lifestyle.

Look at the conclusion in verse 20. Though he has already told us the conclusion in verse 17, he gives the conclusion again, repeating it like a song. It is time for the chorus again. "Do not you know, vain man, that faith without works is dead?" He repeats it again, "...*faith without works is dead.*" That word *dead* does not just mean lifeless, it is the idea of "being barren" or "being idle." It is a word that was used in the financial world in Greek times, of money that was not drawing interest, money that was just lying around and was not in the bank. It was not doing any good; it was idle, barren. James was saying, "Look, your faith needs to be put in the bank, it needs to be doing something, it needs to be working. Faith that is not working, that is not producing works, is barren. It is lifeless! It is dead!"

I think James had no time for those who wanted to talk about the minutia of theology. I love to talk about theology; I love to discuss it with people who are hungry to learn about the Bible and the things of God—if they are trying to live right. But James had no time for those people who wanted to study and study and study the Word of God and yet never let it affect their lifestyle. Some view the Bible as something to be prodded, explained and outlined. James is saying that at some point, all that study and knowledge need to produce Christian living.

He moves from the conclusion to the illustration in verse 21. Abraham's faith worked. He asked, *"Was not Abraham our father justified by works, when he had offered Isaac his son upon the altar?"* Notice he uses the same illustration as Paul. Paul said, "Abraham was justified by faith." Now James comes along and says, "He is justified by works." They were talking about the same man, but about two different times in his life. When Paul talks about Abraham being justified by faith, he is referring to Genesis 15, where God told Abraham to leave Ur of the Chaldeans and go to the Promised Land, a land about which he knew nothing. By faith he obeyed. He loaded up all of his goods, took his family and went to a land, not knowing where it was. God said, "Because of your faith, it is going to be counted to you as righteousness. I declare you to be a righteous man because you have faith." When James illustrates from Abraham's life, he refers to a time thirty years later when God told Abraham to take his only son, Isaac, and offer him as a sacrifice. You remember the story of how God ultimately provided a ram as a sacrifice instead of his boy. God was putting Abraham to a test when he said, "Offer your son as a sacrifice." James is saying, "In the act of being willing to do that, Abraham was justified in the sense that it confirmed his faith. It proved his faith!" He was saved in Genesis 15, but in Genesis 22 he *proved* that he was saved, that he had faith. It was like the fire was put in the fireplace in Genesis 15, but the smoke was coming out of the chimney in Genesis 22. It was the proof validating that he had faith!

In verse 22, he moves from the illustration to the confirmation. He said, *"Seest thou how faith wrought with his works, and by works was faith made perfect?"* He believed that it was his faith that was confirmed by his works, and it was made perfect. Faith is perfected in works in the same way a tree is perfected by fruit. Suppose you have an apple tree. It looks like an apple tree. It has the characteristics, the leaves, and the texture of an apple tree; in fact, everything about it looks like an apple tree! But what is the ultimate proof that it is an apple tree? It is when you pick the apple from the tree. You may say, "Hey, I know trees, and this looks like an apple tree!" Then one day you walk out and there is a lemon growing on it. You know what? You were wrong! You may have said that it was an apple tree and you may have thought it was an apple tree, but the fruit proved that it was a lemon tree.

Jesus said, "*Good trees do not bring forth bitter fruit and a bitter tree does not bring forth good fruit.*" He was saying the same thing as James said—that if you have faith, that faith is justified, or validated, by your good works. Your good works are the fruit produced in your life that validate the root of your faith. In verse 23, James talks about salvation. He does not want any misunderstanding. He does not want anyone to think that we are saved by works, so he said, "*And the Scripture was fulfilled which saith, Abraham believed God, and it was imputed unto him for righteousness: and he was called the Friend of God.*" James was saying, "Look, I know that Abraham was saved by faith. I know that, but his faith was vindicated by his works." He said, "I know the Scripture says that he believed God and it was imputed to him for right-eousness." The word *imputed* is a legal, or really a financial term. It means "to transfer money to another account." When you accept Christ into your life, your sin is transferred into the account of what Jesus did on the cross; and the righteousness of Jesus that He earned by living a sinless life is imputed or transferred to you.

James said, "Look, I know that when Abraham believed God, the righteousness of God was imputed or transferred into his account by his faith, not by anything he did, but simply by his faith." So he said, "I do not want any misunderstanding about how a man is saved," but then he immediately moves to verse 24, the validation of faith. He asked, *"You see then how that by works a man is justified, and not by faith only?"* Justified in the sense of vindicated. Salvation is a private thing between God and a man, that we cannot see. You cannot *see* a person's faith. It is very private. The only thing that you can see are the works, and so James said, "I know that Abraham was saved by faith, but I also know that it was by his works that his faith is vindicated, validated, proved to be real." He is not saying, "You are saved by faith, *plus* works." He is saying, "You are saved by faith that works," that affects your life.

He gives another illustration in verse 25. He asked, *"Likewise also was not Rahab, the harlot, justified by works, when she had received the messengers, and had sent them out another way?"* James thought everyone would be thinking, "Sure, Abraham had good works. He is the Father of Judaism! Of course he had good works, he was the varsity squad; he was different from everyone else." So James said, "Let me illustrate it to you in the life of one of the least believers, a woman by the name of Rahab, who was a harlot before she was saved." You could not find anyone more different from Abraham than Rahab. Abraham was a Jew, Rahab was a Gentile; Abraham was a godly man, Rahab was a prostitute. Abraham was called the "friend of God," Rahab was a Canaanite, the enemy of God who lived in the city of Jericho. Do you remember the story of how the spies went to the city and how Rahab protected and hid them? James is saying, "Look, one of the least of the saints, Rahab, when she believed God and was saved, did something in her life. She had works; she had something to show for it." James taught that there are no "secret saints," that if you are saved, it is going to be manifested in your life. And if it is not manifested in your life, then you are simply not saved!

Sometimes we sing a little chorus with our boys and girls in Vacation Bible School or in Children's Church. It goes, "If you are saved and you know it, then your life will surely show it." That is all that James is saying, that if you are saved and you know it, then your life ought to surely show it.

Three times he gives the conclusion. In verse 26 he says, *"For as the body without the spirit is dead, so faith without works is dead also."* Three times he said it: *"Faith without works is dead"* He said, "Just as the body without the spirit is dead." That is what death is. When the spirit leaves the body, we say that person is dead. The spirit and the body are separated in death. James teaches that, "When you take faith and you separate works from it, then you do not have faith anymore. When you separate works from it, then it is dead—just as when the spirit leaves the body, it is dead. When works are separated from faith, it is dead." Think of it this way: faith is like the heart of salvation, and works is the pulse. The pulse does not make the heart go, does it? It does not affect the heart; the heart affects the pulse. If faith is the heart of salvation, then it is faith that produces works. The works do not produce salvation and works do not produce faith, but they are evidence of real faith. If you do not have a pulse, then the heart is dead. If you do not have works in your life, if you are not living like Christ, then you do not have faith. Your faith is dead! James is saying that it really does not matter what you say with your lips, if your life does not match it. You may say, "Oh, I love Jesus" or, "I know the Bible, I have studied the Bible, I come to church all the time." Jesus said, *"Many will say to Me in that day, 'Lord, Lord, have we not prophesied in Your name, cast out demons in Your name, and done many wonders in Your name?*'" But His response will be, *"Depart from Me, I never knew you..."*

Abraham Lincoln met a little boy on the street one day, and this little boy had his dog with him. Abraham Lincoln was talking to him and he said, "Son, I notice your dog has four legs, just like most dogs have four legs. Son, let's suppose that we called his tail a leg, then how many legs would he have?" And the boy said, "He'd have five," and Abraham Lincoln said, "No, son, he'd still just have four. Calling the tail a leg does not make it a leg; it is still just a tail."

"Calling yourself a Christian," James said, "does not make you a Christian." It is more than profession; it is *possession!* He is saying that if there are no works in your life, then three times your faith is dead. He asks us the question, "What kind of faith is it that does not minister to people's needs?" He answers it by saying that it is *dead faith*, it is no faith at all. What kind of faith is it that has knowledge but does not live right? I will tell you what kind of faith it is—it is *dead faith.* It is no faith! What kind of faith is it that says, "I am a believer," and has no action in his life like Christ? I will tell you, it is *dead faith!* It is no faith at all."

First point of application: Faith is only as good as its object. Some people think, "Well, it does not matter what you believe, as long as you believe." It is kind of a "have faith in faith" type thing—positive thinking, just believe. It does not matter. It *does* matter, friend! Let's suppose that a man worships an idol. He carves it out of stone or wood and he bows down and worships it. Let's say he has a need in his life and prays and asks this idol to help him to do something; and he is sincere. With as much faith as he can generate, he believes with every fiber in his body. Is that idol going to help him? No, because faith is only as good as the object of that faith. That is why it is not enough to have positive thinking, or to have faith in faith, and believe whatever you want. You must place your faith in the Lord Jesus. The object of your faith must be Jesus.

Second point of application: Maybe you are a believer and you say, "I am not involved in ministry right now." There are needs all around you, and you are unwilling to meet those needs, physical needs, spiritual needs. You say, "I do not want to get involved because I am burnt out. I do not want to get involved in the church," or, "I do not want to get involved in ministry to anyone, I just want to come and worship and not be involved." You know what, friend? James is questioning your faith. It is not me! *James* is asking, "What kind of faith is that? Can that kind of faith save, the kind of faith that is willing to disinvolve itself from human need?" The anticipated response is, "No! It cannot save!"

Another point of application: Maybe you have knowledge. Maybe you know the Word of God, and maybe you can even teach the Word of God. But you are not living right:

- Maybe there is some habit in your life that you know is wrong, and you haven't taken care of it.
- Maybe there is something in your life that you are unwilling to even pray about and confess, unwilling to even try to repent.
- Maybe you have an unforgiving spirit.
- Perhaps there is a root of bitterness in your life, or an uncontrolled temper.
- Maybe there are things that are *obviously* wrong in your life, and yet you keep accumulating knowledge about the Bible, although you are not living it.

James said, "Look, the demons do that. What kind of faith is that?"

The last question: Is your faith just a shell; is there any sign of life? Do you want to take your pulse spiritually?

Then put your hand on your works, your lifestyle. Are you living like Jesus? Are you meeting the needs of people around you? Are you involved in ministry? That is your pulse, friend! If your lifestyle is not Christ-like, and if you are not ministering, then your pulse is real weak. That is a sign that something is wrong with your heart! James is saying, "You may not really have a heart, you may not really have faith if you do not have works!"

⟋ 1989 ⟍

A dance studio was rented across the street from the church in 1989, to be used for Sunday School space. When the church was founded, a church growth expert surveyed our buildings and reported that we would never sustain more than an average of 150 people in Sunday School. In 1989 we averaged 663 people. That same year, we added 315 new members, 105 of them by baptism!

Gary Mathena was called in 1989 to serve as our Minister of Music. Also, we supported a mission pastor in New Jersey by the name of Larry Wood, who years later would join our staff.

In 1989, sixty-five people serving on ten advisory committees helped to design our first building. The church voted that Curt Carter would serve as the general contractor.

"When God Benches You" was preached on Sunday morning, September 17, 1989, as part of a series of messages on the life of Elijah.

When God Benches You

"And Elijah the Tishbite, of the inhabitants of Gilead, said to Ahab, 'As the LORD God of Israel lives, before whom I stand, there shall not be dew nor rain these years, except at my word.' Then the word of the LORD came to him, saying, 'Get away from here and turn eastward, and hide by the Brook Cherith, which flows into the Jordan.'" (NKJV)

Suppose you were walking through a beautiful forest on a tropical island, and suddenly as you pushed through the dense foliage and came to an open clearing, you saw a large, grand Steinway piano, with a concert pianist playing a piece from Chopin! Startling? Certainly! The natural question might be, "Where did *he* come from?" In similar manner, the prophet Elijah burst onto the biblical scene, like lightning flashing across the sky. Suddenly, he is standing before King Ahab, a full-grown, full-blown prophet! Like the Steinway pianist, we want to ask the same question—where did *he* come from?

In the book of 1 Kings, chapter 17, there was a time of testing in the life of this great prophet, Elijah. It was an unusual type of test, different from what we would normally think, nevertheless, *a test of faith*.

Most Bible characters are like the rising sun. We can see the fingers of first light in their life:

- We can see the first halting steps of Abraham's faith that he took in the Ur of the Chaldees.
- We can look into the life of Moses and trace eighty years of preparation for his public ministry.
- We can look at the life of David and trace faith all the way back to his boyhood.

That is not the case with Elijah, however. In the very first biblical scene of his life, we see Elijah standing as a prophet before the king of Israel, declaring the Word of God. Chuck Swindoll said, "People of steel are forged on the anvil and hammer of their time." Elijah's arrival on the biblical scene came during a difficult time in the nation of Israel when Ahab was the king.

One of the most famous sermons ever preached was by a pastor in the early part of this century named R.G. Lee. "Payday Someday," the title of the sermon, is the story of Ahab, Elijah and Queen Jezebel. In introducing the characters, the pastor said, "Ahab squatted on the throne of Israel like a toad, and Jezebel, his queen, coiled beside him like an adder." That is eloquent! That is beyond simply saying that he was a wicked king. Ahab *was* a wicked king and Jezebel *was* a wicked queen and, together they introduced the fertility cult of Baal worship. One by one, they sought to put out the lights of godliness in Israel and plunge the whole nation into the darkness of idolatry. The hillsides were covered with groves that had been planted for worshiping Baal. Elijah, in verse 1 of chapter 17, said to Ahab, "*As the LORD God of Israel liveth, before whom I stand, there shall not be dew nor rain these years, but according to my word.*"

I do not know how Ahab reacted to Elijah's declaration. Maybe he was stunned, maybe he laughed at Elijah, maybe he was cynical. The key word in this verse is *years*. Elijah declared that it was not going to rain for *years*, until he said that it was going to rain—or more importantly, until *God* said that it was going to rain. Anyone can endure a drought for a few days. Even for weeks, you can get a few buckets and save up some water. But he said that it would be years. We know historically, from the rest of the account, that the drought lasted three years. A week went by and there was no rain, two weeks went by and still no rain, a month, then two months and the crops began to die. Six months went by and even the olive trees began to wither and die. The animals pawed in the dust for water, and children begged for water. A year went by and men cried out to their pagan gods for relief from the drought. No doubt by this time, Elijah had made it on the list of the ten most wanted men in Israel. Everyone was looking for Elijah. Elijah was the one who started the drought with his word, and he was the only one who could end it. They scoured the countryside for Elijah, but it was as though he had dropped off the map and disappeared. 1 Kings 17:2 says, *"The word of the LORD came to him saying, 'Get away from here and turn eastward and hide by the brook Cherith.'"* God told Elijah to go and *hide himself!*

When God Takes You Out of Circulation

Oliver Cromwell was a great Puritan leader who ruled during the days of the Commonwealth. There was a time when the government ran out of silver to mint the coinage of Great Britain. Cromwell sent his men to search the country-side to find silver. They came back and reported to him that there was no silver left in the land except in the cathedral in the statues of the saints. Oliver Cromwell thought for a moment and said, "I'll tell you what we'll do. We will melt down the saints and put them into circulation." That is exactly what they did! God has a way of melting us down, doesn't He? In fact, the story of Elijah is a story of "spiritual meltdown." However, God did not put Elijah into circulation, but rather He took him out of circulation. The test of his life was to hide himself. It's like when a coach benches you. If you commit a foul or you mess up, you expect the coach to take you out of the game. But what if you are the star player? What if you're doing everything right, and it's the critical point in the game, and the coach motions and says, "You're out of the game. You're on the bench!" You wouldn't understand that! I think maybe Elijah struggled with being hidden by God. It was difficult. He was ready to go through the streets like Jonah and declare the word of the Lord. Instead, in effect God said, "Hey, you are benched!" Similar to Jeremiah, there was a fire in Elijah's bones to declare God's Word, but he had been benched. If he were alive today, he would be ready for the talk show circuit. He is the guy who stopped the rain! Give him a pair of alligator shoes and a bright suit and call him a televangelist! This guy was popular! Elijah was at the zenith of his career and yet God said, "Hide yourself."

Someone has said that for every one of us who can handle success, there are a hundred people who can handle adversity. Maybe the hardest trial of all in our life is success. Sometimes a spiritual arrogance creeps into our lives with success and we become self-sufficient, feeling that we do not really need God, that we can do it on our own. Self-sufficiency was the first temptation! The devil tempted Eve and in effect said, "Eat this fruit and you will be like God. You will not need God any more. You will be in charge; you will be in control."

At times, success whispers in our ear, "You don't really need God any more." That is hard for some of us to understand. You might be questioning whether success is really a test of faith. In the famous musical, *Fiddler on the Roof,* one of the characters is talking about riches and says, "If having money is a curse, then may the Lord smite me with it!" Basically, he was saying, "I would like to try *that* test for a while!" Prosperity really is a test of our faith. In ancient Greek mythology, Midas requested from the gods that everything he touched turn to gold. The gods granted the request, and he went around touching everything. He touched the trees, and they turned to gold. He touched the chair and the table, and it all turned to gold. He was delirious with joy since he was going to be so wealthy. But eventually he touched his wife and his children. Suddenly they turned cold and metallic as they too were transformed to gold. Sometimes that is what success does to us! Success can reach into your heart and instead of leading you to God, it turns you away from God. Maybe that is what God perceived in the life of Elijah when God told him to go and hide himself. God was teaching Elijah that the public life of success is worth nothing if it is not balanced with the private life of spirituality.

In Gordon McDonald's book, *Ordering Your Private World*, he describes what he calls the "sinkhole syndrome." In certain parts of Florida, there are limestone caverns underneath the earth that, when the water table drops very low, just collapse. Occasionally you will see a story on the news about sinkholes. There have been times that a car has been swallowed up, or even a house. On occasion, an entire city block has disappeared into a giant sinkhole. In Southern California, we do not know much about sinkholes, although this may sound familiar if you were watching the news about a year ago when seventy feet of Hollywood Boulevard disappeared into a sinkhole. They were building a subterranean passageway, using inferior construction. Seventy feet of the street just disappeared! Cars dropped off into it and were gone! Sometimes in our spiritual life, we develop a "sinkhole syndrome" where everything seems fine in our *public* world. We're so careful with our work life, our social life, our church life, and the external areas of life. But we neglect the things that are on the inside. Our reputation, as to what people think about us, becomes more important to us than character, what we actually are on the inside.

I had a professor from Yazoo City, Mississippi, who said it this way: "Some folks put more in the showcase than they do in the warehouse." There is truth in that! For some, everything is external. Everything is reputation instead of character. Maybe that is what God was trying to teach Elijah. He said, "Hide yourself. I want to fill the warehouse for a few months." God was doing an "inside job" on Elijah. What better way to do it than to take him out of circulation!

F. B. Meyers, writing about Elijah nearly a hundred years ago, said, "And there is no better manner of bringing a man down than by suddenly dropping him out of the sphere to which he was beginning to think himself essential. Teaching him that he is not at all necessary to God's plan and compelling him to consider in the sequestered veil of some Cherith, how mixed are his motives and how insignificant his strengths."

That's exactly what God was doing—taking Elijah out of circulation! God put him on the bench so that He could spend months developing his inner life. Here is just a sampling of how God did that many times with other Bible characters:

- Joseph, before he was ever a prime minister, spent years in prison;
- Moses, before he ever led the people out of Egypt, spent forty years in the desert;
- David, before he became king, spent some time in the cave of Adullam.

It may be that is where you are. You may be a young mother, and your life is an endless routine of one feeding after another. In the providence of God, maybe you feel like He has hidden you. Or perhaps you feel like you have been "put on the shelf." At one time, you were active and now, because of health or other reasons, you feel hidden. Or maybe you feel that your talents are being overlooked and you are not being used. Perhaps you haven't excelled the way you think you should have in life. Or maybe you are getting older. Once you were active in every facet of church life. Now you are not, and you feel hidden by God.

There was a time in my life when I wanted, above all else, to be an evangelist. I thought that was God's calling upon my life. When I graduated from college, I thought I would become an evangelist, going from church to church and city to city. My great grandfather was a circuit-riding preacher. He rode on horseback from one Methodist Church to another, preaching the gospel. I thought I would be the modern equivalent of that, preaching crusades in different churches week by week. When I graduated from college, I lined up revival meetings in ten different churches, assuming that would thrust me into the area of evangelism. Then one night I went to hear a preacher by the name of Leonard Ravenhill, a very prophetic type of a minister. That evening, he happened to preach from this very same passage, "Go hide yourself." He was speaking to young ministers about how we sometimes are thrust into the public arena too quickly. He said that we needed time in our lives to build our private world, on the *inside*. He said, "My challenge to you if you are a young pastor," (and, of course he didn't know *I* was sitting out there), "is to go hide yourself." That message so moved me, that the next day I called and cancelled all ten revival meetings. I took a job of menial labor working from daylight to dark that summer, and I refused any preaching engagements for a period of three or four months. For those months, I hid myself and spent time with God. In those months, God did an "inside job" on me! I have found that if God is going to do anything with you in the long run, often He hides you in the short run.

That was Elijah's experience. He became God's first backpacker! He "camped out" beside the brook Cherith. He was all alone! There was no one to applaud his faith or tell him what a great prophet he was. Alone with God! The obscurity and hiddenness of our lives tests our faith.

I heard about a young man who visited a monastery and asked one of the older men in the monastery, "Do you wrestle with the devil here?" The man said, "No, I wrestle with God here." The younger man asked, "Well, do you think that you're going to win?" He said, "No, I want to lose." That is what happened with Elijah for months at the brook Cherith. He wrestled with God within his heart and he lost! He surrendered totally to God, in an utter dependence upon Him. That is what trials do! Trials bring us to the edge, where there's no self-sufficiency left.

I am not certain how many months went by, but in verse 7 it says, *"It happened after a while that the brook dried up, because there had been no rain in the land."* The brook dried up because it had not rained. Do you know why there had been no rain in the land? Because Elijah had said there would be no rain in the land! It reminds me of the saying, "hung by your own rope." The whole land was suffering, but Elijah's needs were being met. He was beside a little babbling brook, and the ravens came and fed him every day. You might say, "That is hard to believe, those ravens feeding him." Well, you had better settle in your mind about whether or not God is supernatural. If Jesus was raised from the dead, do you not think God could instruct a few crows on what to do? Elijah had water to drink, he didn't have to work, and the ravens fed him! His entire life was spent on the inner life with God. But then the water table began to drop. I think he became an expert, going out every day and measuring the brook to see how much water was left. Then one day he arrived at the brook and there was nothing but dry, parched, cracked ground.

Sometimes our own faithfulness brings trials in our life. Trying to live godly is like swimming upstream. Sometimes the brook dries up, and the dried brook becomes the test of our faith. I think that God delights in drying up various brooks in our life to bring us to a place of dependence upon Him. That is where we learn faith. You can not determine what a ship will do in the water when it is built in dry dock. It is suspect until it faces the high seas. You do not know what an army of trained men will do until they face the roar of the guns in the midst of a battle. You do not know how precious your faith is until your faith is tested, and yet stands.

There are all kinds of brooks that dry up in our lives:

- It may be a business, possibly a business that you started. Maybe you thought that God was in it. You even prayed about it before you started the business, but now God has dried up the brook, and you are on the edge of disaster.
- Maybe it is a marriage that was made in heaven, or so you thought! Now after a period of years, it is like two strangers living together, and the brook has dried up.
- Maybe you were once at the very heart and center of a local church, and now it is as if you are on the outside looking in. Or maybe you had a ministry of teaching the Bible, and instead of it getting bigger, God shrunk it. The brook has dried up.
- Maybe you had hopes and aspirations for your children. They took a wrong path and the brook has dried up.

If you want to build muscle, there are two ways to do it with weights. One is to lift something that is extremely heavy a few times. You strain all you can, and that will build muscle. But there is another way that you can build muscle with weights— that is to take a much smaller weight and, with repetition, lift it over and over again. That also will build muscle. God uses both of those plans in building "spiritual muscles." Sometimes the trial is all encompassing, so much that it is all we can think about, such as the loss of a loved one, or some other tremendous trial. It is like the rug being pulled out from under us. Or, like the weightlifter, it is all that we can do to bear up under the great load that God has placed upon us. At other times, though, it is a series of irritations, frustrations, or of one trial after another. Have you ever noticed how trouble comes? Sometimes problems come back-to-back-to-back-to-back-to-back.

Shakespeare said it very eloquently, "Trouble seldom comes as a single sentry man, but instead it comes in battalions." Isn't that eloquent? Back home we used to just say, "When it rains, it pours!" It was that way with Elijah. There was not any huge overarching trial in his life. It was a series of trials. He stood before the king and said, "It will not rain until I say so." Rather than being able to flaunt his success in the street, God said, "Go hide yourself." He lived in obscurity, and when he finally started to relax and enjoy the presence of God beside that babbling brook, God dried it up!

The word *Cherith* means, "to cut, or to cut off or to cut down." God was whittling away at Elijah. Have you ever felt like that, that God is cutting things out of your life? Sometimes God removes the crutches from our lives, the things upon which we are dependent and in the process we are driven to God.

Living in the Crucible

Look at verse 8. "*Then the word of the LORD came to him saying, 'Arise and go to Zarephath which belongs to Sidon and dwell there; see, I have commanded a widow there to provide for you.'*" Zarephath was about a hundred miles away across the desert. Remember, it was dry, Elijah was thirsty, the brook had dried up and yet God said that he wanted him to leave and walk a hundred miles across a desert in the midst of a drought! It was a test of his faith. (Incidentally, the word *Zarephath* means to "smelt" or to "melt." Maybe that is where they purified metal. The noun form of it, literally translated, could be "crucible.") God wanted Elijah to leave his comfort zone, the beautiful little brook where everything was provided for him. He wanted to deal with the slag, or the impurity of

Elijah's life. That is what God does with us sometimes! With metal, you turn up the heat and the flame so that the impurities come to the top; then you can skim them off. That's what God does! Sometimes He turns up the flame to burn away the dross and the impurity of our lives.

A trial is like a storm as it blows through your life! It may be grief, it may be terminal illness, it may be the loss of a loved one, or it may be a wayward child. When a storm blows through your life, everything that is not nailed down very tightly blows away. Have you ever noticed how trials have a way of focusing your life and your priorities? What you thought was important when the trial came is not important at all. It does not matter at all. The trial focuses you! That is what God was doing with Elijah. He was focusing his priorities. Sometimes we have our own Cherith Brook! We are nestled away safe in our comfort zone, and all of a sudden God moves us out. Maybe it is the loss of a job or some problem in your life, or a broken relationship. God moves us out of our comfort zone, and we shrink back. We don't want change, and we get hung between verses 7 and 8. In verse 7, the brook dried up, and in verse 8, God told Elijah what he was doing and where he was going. I do not know how much time went by, but maybe Elijah became real thirsty between verse 7 and verse 8. That is where we sometimes lose faith. God loves to disrupt us to drive us to Him.

God said, "Go to Zarephath and a widow there is going to take care of you." "Hey, I am Elijah," he must have thought, "I am the prophet, I am the guy who caused this drought, and now you are saying that a little pagan widow lady is going to meet my needs?" Maybe the very first bit of dross in his life was pride. God selects circumstances in our life that are the most likely to produce holiness. *Do not miss this!* He reaches into the bag, pulls out the circumstances that are the most likely to bring about holiness, and plants them in our lives. We have a totally different agenda. Our criteria is different. If we designed the circumstances of our life, we would choose those things that would produce happiness. But that is not the agenda of God. His agenda is to produce holiness; after a while the fruit of holiness eventually produces happiness within our life.

To God, the pain of the trials that we go through is like a mosquito bite on a soldier in the midst of a battle—it is totally insignificant to Him because He sees the bigger picture and has higher priorities. God sees the bigger picture, and the bigger picture is this: as a believer, you have within you an old nature, a propensity toward sin, and a new nature of Christ. There is a battle between these two natures. Because God wants the new nature to overwhelm the old nature, He selects circumstances that will help you to learn the lessons of life that will feed the new nature and deprive the old nature. That is what trials are about in our lives. God wants to fill us with His presence, but before He can fill us with Himself, He has to empty us of ourselves. What better way to empty us than through suffering? Suffering has an incredible emptying effect. Suffering and trials have an exhausting effect that brings us to the end of ourselves in frustration. Our private agendas are turned upside down and our pride is stripped away when suffering comes into our life.

Let me give you several points of application from Elijah's life and the brook Cherith:

Being made righteous happens in an instant, but becoming holy involves a process

You are made righteous in an instant! When you invite Jesus into your life, the righteousness of Jesus is imputed or transferred to you, and your sin is taken care of by Christ. It is a wonderful transaction that takes place! From that moment on, God views you positionally righteous before Him. God imputes, or transfers righteousness, into your account in the same way an accountant moves one figure from one side of the ledger to the other, from the debit to the credit side. In essence, God says, "Since you have called upon My name, and have asked for forgiveness, I have imputed the righteousness of My Son into your account." *That* is salvation! But the *living out* of that salvation is a process we call "sanctification." We are declared righteous by God, but we increasingly become holy in our lifestyle. That is what God was doing in Elijah.

I like the fact that God paints Elijah, "warts and all." We see his weaknesses as well as his strengths. Later in his life Elijah was depressed and ran from Jezebel. Elijah was feeling sorry for himself and wanted to die. The best of men are only men at best. Elijah was like a roller coaster! One time he was way up, and another time he was way down. Sometimes we are like that. We're way up for God and then we are way down. That is part of the frailty of the human condition. That is the way life is! If we step back and see the big picture of our lives, we will see that most of us learn more from adversity than we do from prosperity. I really believe that! Most of us learn more from failure than we do from success. Failure is a better teacher than success, and adversity is a better teacher than prosperity. Why, then, would we not realize that there is going to be pain involved in the process of making us holy?

When the brook dries up, it does not mean that God has forgotten you

Sometimes in life, everything may be going smoothly. Suddenly, God may jolt you out of your comfort zone. You begin to think that God has forsaken you, or that God is against you. That is not true! In Isaiah 49:14, it says, *"But Zion said, the Lord has forsaken me and my Lord has forgotten me."* Do you ever feel like that? Do you ever feel like God has forgotten you and forsaken you? Listen to God's answer: He said, *"Can a woman forget her nursing child and not have compassion on the son of her womb? Surely they may forget, yet I will not forget. See I have inscribed you on the palms of My hands."* God asks if a mother would forget her child. Sometimes they do, although it's rare. When our children were very small, my wife and I came to church separately in different cars because we came at different times. I remember, on one particular day, arriving home after church, I thought my wife had the children, and she thought I had the children. We hurried back to church. The building was already locked, but there were our children asleep on the pew! So the question is, can a mother forget her children? Yes! Can a father forget his children? It is rare but it is possible. God said, *"Surely they may forget, yet I will not forget. I have inscribed you on the palms of My hands."* Sometimes we use the expression, "We know something like the back of our hand." We say that because our hands are always before us; we see them constantly. God says that we have been inscribed in the palms of His hands, we are constantly before Him and He will not forget us.

You may be thinking that God has put you on the shelf, or that He has benched you. God has never misplaced anyone. He knows exactly where you are! He knows how long you have been there. Your brook may have dried up. It may be your marriage, it may be grief, it may be sickness, or it may be finances. Listen to what the hymn writer said: "When darkness seems to hide His face, I rest on His unchanging grace."

The brook, in this case, dried up as a result of Elijah's own prayer

Sometimes that happens! Sometimes someone else is praying for us, a prayer something like this: "God, whatever it takes to focus this person's priorities and to focus their attention, then do it." Believe me, God will answer that prayer! Sometimes we pray for ourselves, "Lord, make me a godly man; make me a good husband." Or perhaps you have prayed that God would make you a godly wife. How do you think you are ever going to learn longsuffering if you never fail? How will you ever develop a forgiving spirit unless someone hurts you? We pray, "Oh,

Lord, teach me faith." How do you think that God does that? Often times God teaches us faith by drying up the brook.

Where God guides, God provides

God led Elijah beside the brook Cherith and the ravens came and fed him. I think if Elijah had not shown up, there would have been stacks and stacks of lunchmeat at the brook because the ravens would not have disobeyed! Sometimes we worry about things that never happened and may never happen. Have you found yourself thinking, "I just do not know how I could face the news of terminal illness, or I don't know how I could deal with losing a child, or a mate, or my job."? What we do not understand is that *grace* comes with the *need*. It does not come before the need, lest we squander and waste it. It does not follow the need lest we despair. With bonds forged in Heaven, grace comes with the need. It is the idea of supply and demand. When the demand is placed upon your life, God supplies the grace. I am sure you've seen people who seem to die so graciously. That is God's grace in the life of a believer. You may be saying, "I could not do that." Of course you could not, because you have not been called on to do it yet. I believe that when the time comes, God gives you grace if you do not resist. In whatever the loss or whatever the trial, remember that where God guides, God provides. You are not alone, even in the darkest trial.

God leads one step at a time

As we thumb through the rest of the story of Elijah, we know how it all turned out. Elijah did not know! He did not know whether he might perish in the desert between Cherith and Zarephath. He did not know. He could not see the whole plan of God.

Let's say it is late at night and you decide to go to your friend's house. You do not have a panic attack and say, "Oh, I can't drive over there because it's so dark between here and there." Instead, you simply get in your car, start the motor and turn on the lights. As you are driving, your lights shine a little way in front of you. But by the time you drive a little further, they shine further. Finally, when you get to your friend's house, you realize that you have driven all the way in the light. That is the way the plan of God is. You can not see all the ramifications. Life does not come in thesis form. God does not say, "I am doing this in your life now so that I might do that later on, and ten years from now this is going to be the result of that." You have a little bit of light now. As you follow that little light, you will receive more light. When you look back over your life, your entire life will be lived in the light, not in the darkness, if you allow Him to lead you!

The brook dried up as a sign of God's pleasure, not His disappointment

Chuck Swindoll has said that sometimes when the brook dries up, and trials come, you tend to think that God is angry with you. You might think God is trying to zap you, or punish you for some wrong you have done. At the height of Abraham's faith career, God was pleased with him, and yet at that time, God instructed Abraham to kill his son! Suddenly the brook dried up for Abraham.

On his first missionary journey, Paul was preaching the gospel when he came to Lystra. He was stoned, but that does not mean that God was displeased with him. In the Old Testament, Joseph was faithful, fleeing fornication, and yet he was unjustly thrown into prison. God was pleased with both these men, not angry with them. God wants to teach us to trust not His gifts, but to trust *Him*.

God has a purpose in suffering

We cannot always see God's purpose, but by faith we know He does have a purpose. Romans 8:28 says, *"And we know that all things work together for good to those who love God, to those who are the called according to His purpose."* The good is not necessarily your pleasure, the good is *your holiness and conformity to the character of Christ.* If it is true that God has a purpose in suffering, then should we not be slow to call suffering bad if it drives us to God? And should we not be slow to call prosperity good if it leads us away from God? Maybe in the humdrum and the routine of life, some brook in your life has dried up. Maybe God has allowed that to jolt you. Maybe it is sickness, grief, finances, or a wayward child, but all of a sudden God has your attention. I want you to know God has a purpose in suffering. You may not always be able to see that purpose, but God, in fact, has a purpose.

Last week was Father's Day, and it started me thinking about Father's Day in the past. It brought back memories of my precious little girl, Charity, who was hit by a car and killed when she was in first grade. On the last Father's Day that she was alive, she made me a gift. It was a bookmark, one I never have been able to use because it's kind of big! I suppose you could use it if you had a large family Bible, but because she was just a kindergartener, she made it large so her little fingers would be able to do the detail. On one side of this bookmarker, you can see only knotted threads. It is jumbled and it makes absolutely no sense whatsoever. But when you turn it over, you can see the large letters of a kindergartener spelling out "Father." It is like that when we look at life—we see the underbelly of life and we do not always understand. From my experience of looking at life and seeing the knotted threads, I may have wondered what God was doing. I believe, though, that some day God, in eternity, will be able to turn our lives in such a way that we will be able to see "Father" written on every page. We will see that our Heavenly Father was in control, and that what seemed to be a mess, and knots to us, was, from God's perspective, a designed plan of a beautiful mosaic! He takes not only the bright threads of laughter and the light threads of success, but He sometimes takes the dark threads of sorrow and trials and weaves them all together into a beautiful tapestry called *holiness.*

~ 1990 ~

In the spring of 1990, Valley had a high attendance emphasis called "Victory Sunday." We had an all-time high Sunday School attendance of 947 people. That evening, the church worshipped together at the Civic Auditorium. It was the first time that the entire church gathered for a single service.

By 1990, the budget of the church had grown to $568,000 and Sunday School attendance averaged 684 people.

"The Cost of Discipleship" was preached on Sunday morning, April 1, 1990, as part of a verse-by-verse series of messages that Pastor Roger Spradlin and Pastor Phil Neighbors preached through the Gospel of Mark.

The Cost of Discipleship

MARK 8:36-38

"For what will it profit a man if he gains the whole world, and loses his own soul? Or what will a man give in exchange for his soul? For whoever is ashamed of Me and My words in this adulterous and sinful generation, of him the Son of Man also will be ashamed when He comes in the glory of His Father with the holy angels." (NKJV)

Some of the most powerful words that Jesus ever spoke are revealed to us in Mark chapter 8. Mark begins by referring to Jesus in verse 34 saying: *"When He had called the people to Himself, with His disciples also, He said to them, 'Whoever desires to come after Me, let him deny himself, and take up his cross, and follow Me. For whoever desires to save his life will lose it, but whoever loses his life for My sake and the gospel's will save it. For what will it profit a man if he gains the whole world, and loses his own soul? Or what will a man give in exchange for his soul? For whoever is ashamed of Me and My words in this adulterous and sinful generation, of him the Son of Man also will be ashamed when He comes in the glory of His Father with the holy angels.'"*

These appear to be very harsh words. Certainly they were shocking to the people who first heard them; but to really understand what Jesus is saying, we have to back up and set the context of what is going on. A few days before Jesus spoke these words, there was a great multitude of people following Him. Being late in the day, it was too far to send them away to a city for food. Someone brought some fish and bread, and He broke the bread and the fish and miraculously fed 4,000 that day. Just a few days before that, nearly the same thing had happened when He fed 5,000 men. A few days previous, He touched a blind man so he was able to see. And only a few weeks before, there was a crippled man in Capernaum whom He touched, who was able to walk again. Also, He touched a little girl who was demon possessed, and she was made well.

Jesus tried to get away from the press of the multitude. The crowd was always trying to cling to Him, clamoring for a miracle. Everywhere He went they begged for miracles. Jesus wanted to get alone with them and, finally, in chapter 8, verse 27, we find Him alone with His disciples for the first time in many days. It was during this time that He asked them the question, *"Who do men say that I am?"* They answered, *"John the Baptist; but some say, Elijah; and others, one of the prophets."* And Jesus said, *"But who do you say that I am?"* Peter turned to Him and said, *"You are the Christ."* That statement became known as the "Great Confession" in the New Testament. For the first time, someone finally understood who Jesus was— "You are the Messiah, the Son of the Living God."

Verse 31 says, *"And He began to teach them that the Son of Man must suffer many things."* As soon as Peter said, "You are the Christ," Jesus immediately began at that point to teach them how He was going to go to Jerusalem to suffer and ultimately be killed. They were stunned! They rebuked Him. In fact, Peter pulled Him aside and essentially said, "Listen, You are the Christ, You are the Son of the Living God. Now You are saying that You are going to Jerusalem and You are going to suffer and You are going to die?" They could not comprehend it. Up until this time, Jesus had been speaking privately to His disciples, but now in verse 34, we see Him speaking publicly: *"When He had called the people to Himself, with His disciples also."* It is as if the people are on the periphery, on the edge, so He called them *and* his disciples. He evidently wanted everyone to hear what He was about to say. He said to them, *"Whoever desires to come after Me, let him deny himself, and take up his cross, and follow Me."* For the very first time, Jesus spoke of the real cost involved in following Him. Jesus knew that many of the people were following Him simply for the miracles, some were hoping for a free meal, perhaps thinking that they would happen to be there on the day that He would break the bread and the fish again. Even the disciples were suspect in their motives. In fact, in the very next chapter, James and John argued about who would be the greatest in the kingdom, who was going to sit on His right hand? So even the disciples misunderstood. Like machine-gun fire in rapid succession, Jesus gives us a description of what true discipleship is all about.

Denying Self

Verse 34 is actually divided into three parts, or three aspects of discipleship. The first is this: He said, *"Whoever desires to come after Me, let him deny himself."* Through the ages this statement has been misunderstood. During the Middle Ages, monks read it and thought they were to deny themselves basic comforts, so they lived in cold, dark, damp monasteries. They ate bland food and took vows of poverty because that is what they thought it meant to deny themselves. William Barclay, a commentator on this passage, said that the little phrase "to deny your self" simply means "to say no to self." I guess the phrase, "Just say no," originated with Jesus, instead of with Nancy Reagan! That is literally, what it means. Fundamentally, discipleship is saying "No" to yourself and saying "Yes" to Jesus.

Imagine your Christian life like this: you are standing in a long corridor, a long hallway, and at the end of that hall is the Lord Jesus. He is the goal! He is whom you want to be like. On each side of the hall, there are many, many doorways. Now if you go in any one of those doors, then, by default, you are taking your eyes off Christ. By default you are choosing that door over the Lord Jesus Christ, and that's what some people do. There is the door of greed, the door of materialism, the door of laziness, maybe even the door of apathy. When we say, *yes* to those sins, we are really saying, *no* to Jesus. Denying yourself is when you say no to self, and at the same time you are saying yes to Jesus. When you sin, not only is it a choice to do wrong, it is a choice against the Lord Jesus Christ. Later on in the New Testament, Paul said that there is no temptation taken us except that God will make a way of escape. In other words, as a believer, when you are tempted, God always gives you the grace to be able to withstand that temptation. So, if you sin, not only have you chosen to do wrong, you have chosen to resist the grace of God within your life.

Take Up Your Cross

Jesus said, "Number one in discipleship is to deny yourself," and then He said, *"Take up your cross."* Understand, He is not speaking about your mother-in-law, that's *not* the cross that you have to bear! Sometimes people will misunderstand and say, "Oh, this trouble or this sickness in my life is just my cross I have to bear." Or they say, "Oh, my husband, you know how he is! He is my cross I have to bear," or, "My wife, you know how she is! She is my cross I have to bear." That is not what He is talking about at all! The cross is a symbol of *hope*. The Red Cross is an organization that has nothing to do with a cross; it is a relief organization. What does it have to do with the cross other than that the cross is a symbol of hope? Then there is Blue Cross and Blue Shield Insurance. What does the cross have to do with insurance except that in our society, it is a symbol of hope? But in the time of Jesus, it was not a symbol of hope; it was a symbol of death. In Roman times, if you said, "Take up your cross," that meant the end of your life. That is an imagery used a great deal in the New Testament by the apostle Paul. He talks about being crucified with Christ. Not in a literal way, of course. He is talking in a symbolic way that means death to our own will. A crucified man looks in only one direction. He clings to nothing. A crucified man has no further plans for his life. He knows his life is going to end that day. A crucified man knows one thing for certain—he is not coming back. A crucified man is not hanging on to part of his life. He is giving everything. It is not that he is giving 50 percent of his life and he is keeping 50 percent for himself, or he is giving 80 percent and he is keeping 20 percent for himself. He is totally committed in crucifixion, and that is what Jesus means when He says, *"Take up your cross and follow Me."* He means for us to involve all of our life in the process of discipleship.

A little boy stuck his hand in his mother's very expensive vase. When his hand became stuck in the vase, he frantically tried to pull it out as his mother walked into the room. She did not want to break the vase to get his hand out, so she put soap on his hand and tried to pull it out. As she pulled, his wrist began to swell and finally it seemed like she had no other choice but to break the vase. When she released his hand from the vase, she realized that his hand was clenched in a fist, and that is why she couldn't get it out. When she opened his fist, to her surprise, there was a penny in the palm of his hand. She had broken her expensive vase for a penny! She was upset, but to the little boy that penny was really big! He wanted it, so he hung on to it. To that little boy, the penny was of more value than the vase. To him, it was significant.

Many people are holding on to things in their lives that they think are so significant, and yet in light of eternity, it is like a penny. Jesus went on to say, *"For what will it profit a man if he gains the whole world, and loses his own soul."* People are holding on to things that, in light of their soul, are worth a penny in value.

Follow Jesus

The third thing that Jesus said was simply, *"Follow Me."* Notice, this is in the present tense. This means it is continuous, a continuous action of following Him. It is not just a one-time decision for Jesus. The Christian life is a "crisis followed by a process." By that I mean there is a crisis—a point in time when you accept Jesus and appropriate the forgiveness of God within your life, and the Holy Spirit indwells your life. You do not grow into salvation. You do not earn it. You do not merit it. You ask for forgiveness of sin and there is a point in time, if you are a believer, that that happens in your life. That is the crisis! But then there is a lifelong process of growth and maturity.

I like the honesty of verse 34. Jesus has just been declared the Messiah, *"You are the Christ,"* and Jesus gathers the crowd around. He does not say, "Hey, Peter, tell them what you just said a while ago. Man, that was good. Peter, tell them how I am the Christ." He does not do that at all. He does not bribe the people and say, "Hey, for every one of you that follows Me, I will feed you and I will break the fish and loaves every day. You will never be hungry." He does not say, "Follow Me, and you will have great wealth." He does not say, "Hey, follow Me, and I am going to set up the kingdom and you are going to be one of the great ones in the kingdom." He does not try to bribe them to follow Him. He does not even say that the way is easy. We live in a society where televangelists and others try to bribe people to be saved. They say, "Hey, if you will come to Jesus, you will be healthy; you will never get sick." Or they say, "If you will come to Jesus, your pockets will be lined with money;

you will have wealth." Jesus did not say, "Come to Me and you will be healthy, come to Me and you will be wealthy." He simply said, *"Come and follow Me."* The best description Jesus gave us of discipleship was that of crucifixion, or death to self. There is a danger today that we water down the demands of Jesus. We need to be honest about the message of Christ.

Do you know, the greatest leaders and motivators of men that have ever lived have been men who were honest about the cost of following. In 1849, after Rome had been under siege for some time, General Garibaldi stood before his soldiers and said, "All of our efforts against superior forces have been unavailing and I have nothing to offer you but hunger and thirst, hardship and death. But I call on all who love their country to join me." By the thousands, they joined him! Why? Because he was honest when he said, "I do not have anything to offer you but hunger and thirst, hardship and death." They followed him. They were motivated to fight for him because he was an honest man. That's the way the Lord Jesus is!

In the middle of the last century, after he took over the reins of leadership of England, Winston Churchill said, "All I have to offer is blood, sweat and tears." We need to have that kind of honesty in the proclamation of the gospel. Being saved is easy. Salvation is the easiest thing that can ever happen in your life. You accept the Lord Jesus Christ, you breathe a prayer asking for forgiveness and Jesus comes into your life. He takes up residence in your life. We need to be honest. From that point on, there is no such thing as "Disneyland Christianity." In the Christian life, at times, there are trials and there are tests. In fact, trying to live godly in an ungodly world is like a salmon swimming upstream. Jesus was honest. He did not bribe the people to follow Him. He taught, "If you follow Me, you are going to have to deny yourselves; you are going to have to die to self."

There is something else I like about verse 34. Jesus never asked us to do anything that He has not already done, or is not willing to do Himself. He spoke about His *own* Cross. He said, "I am going to Jerusalem and I am going to die." Then He spoke symbolically about *our* cross. He never asked us to do anything that He is not willing to do with us or ahead of us.

Historians say that when Alexander the Great was in pursuit of Darius, he and his soldiers marched across the desert for eleven days, making what has been called "the wonder march." Men were exhausted; they were about to give up because they were out of water. They were thirsty. In fact, they were so thirsty they thought they were dying of thirst. Finally, in the middle of the desert, Alexander the Great and his soldiers came across a small caravan of people who had a little bit of water. They obviously did not have enough water for thousands of soldiers to all get a drink. However, when they realized that it was their king, Alexander, they took all the water they had and put it in one soldier's helmet. The people in the caravan brought that helmet of water to Alexander the Great and said, "You are the king; you must drink." Alexander the Great took that helmet of water and was about to take a drink when he looked around. All of his officers and soldiers were straining their necks trying to catch a glimpse of the water because they were so thirsty. When he saw them staring he said, "If I alone drink, the rest of the men will lose heart," and he gave the water back. Historians tell us that those men defied weariness and thirst, and they pushed on as men immortal to follow such a king. That is the way the Lord Jesus Christ is. He does not ask us to do difficult things without Him being with us. He is not sitting up in Heaven watching us squirm when we go through grief, through difficulty or hardship. These are the words of Jesus: "Follow Me." The implication is that *He is in it with us.*

The famous Roman general by the name of Quintes was discussing a military strategy with his lieutenant, as to how to win a certain battle. One man finally came up with a plan. He said, "If we do this certain thing, then we can win the battle and only a few men will lose their lives." The general said, "You mean if we do this, we'll win and only a few men will lose their lives?" and he said, "That's right. The cost will be that only a *few* men will lose their lives." The wise general asked, "Are *you* willing to be one of the few?" That is a good question! It is not that Jesus asks us to bear a cross and go through suffering and difficulty alone. The words of Jesus are, *"Follow Me. I will never leave you or forsake you."*

Keeping Your Life

Look at the second statement of discipleship that He adds quickly behind the first in verse 35. It is a paradox! He said, *"For whoever desires to save his life will lose it, but whoever loses his life for My sake and the gospel's will save it."* The word *saved* is not being used in the sense of salvation. It is in the sense of "keeping." *Whoever keeps his life for himself shall lose it.* It is the very opposite of self-denial in verse 34. When I speak of self-denial in the Christian life, I do not mean some kind of legalism. Sometimes people get the idea that the Christian life is about a list of things you will not do and a list of things you will do. And how well you measure on those two lists proves how spiritual you are. Such lists sometimes indicate how moral you are, but never how spiritual. Notice the motivation He gives to us in verse 35, *"But whoever shall lose his life for My sake..."* The motivation in the Christian life is not legalism or keeping rules; the motivation of the Christian life is a love for Jesus. We love Him because He first loved us. *That* is our motive.

Hudson Taylor was one of the world's greatest missionaries who ever lived. Someone asked him, "What is the number one requirement to be a missionary? Is the number one requirement that you have got to love souls?" He thought for a moment and said, "No, that's not the number one requirement. The number one requirement is that you love God. If you love God, you will love souls." My friend, the key to the Christian life is not how strong your will is to be able to keep a legalistic list of "do's" and "do-nots!" The key to the Christian life is the love relationship that you develop for God. Paul, who had such a passion for souls, told us his motive. He said, "*The love of God constraineth us.*"

Charles Spurgeon, the great English preacher, said that he wanted to get to the place in his Christian life that when he looked up to Heaven and said, "Jesus, I love you," that Jesus would respond by saying, "Yes, Charles, I know." It would be so wonderful to have that kind of relationship with God. Jesus said, "*If you keep your life, you will lose it; and if you lose your life for My sake, then you will save it.*" There are certain things that you *keep* by using. For instance, if you have a talent and you do not use it, you lose it. You can keep your talent by using it and giving. It is the same way with our money, to a degree. By keeping it we lose it. We are supposed to give it! God has given us not only our talent and our money, but also our very life, in order to spend it. We either invest our life with God or we waste our life for God.

He gave us a second motive when He said, "For My sake," and then He said, "and for the gospel." Our motivation in the Christian life is our love for God and then our compassion for other people.

A story has been told of a monk by the name of Telemachus, who lived in the Far East in the late fourth century, who loved the Lord. He wanted to get away from the world and live his life in isolation, and he did so for many years as a hermit. A man of deep devotion, he would spend time alone with God praying. Finally one day, because of all the Biblical mandates to witness and to minister to other people, it dawned on him that his lifestyle was not a selfless love for God, but a very selfish kind of love for God. He came to realize that God wanted him to go to the great city of Rome, which was nearly on the other side of the world from where he was. Finally he made the long journey across the land and across the sea, and arrived in Rome. Rome, by the time of the fourth century, was officially Christian. The heathen temples were nearly empty. People were pressed into the churches of Rome, but there was one thing in this "supposedly Christian" city that still lingered from the past, that was a throwback to Roman heathenism. It was the arena. They still had gladiators who would fight there unto death. No longer were they throwing Christians into the arena. Instead they forced prisoners of war to fight unto their death on Roman holidays. It happened to be a Roman holiday when Telemachus, this holy man who wore the robes of a holy man or of a monk, arrived in Rome. He heard the crowd in the Coliseum. Historians tell us that there were about eighty thousand people present on that day. Telemachus watched the chariot races and he watched the parades and enjoyed the activities. Finally the gladiators came who were to fight unto their death. Telemachus, this holy, godly man, was appalled that men in a Christian city like Rome were fighting to the death for the sport of the people. He was so moved that he jumped over the banister into the arena himself and pushed two of these large gladiators apart. The crowd was stunned! They were silent as they saw this man wearing the robes of a monk pushing the gladiators apart, and then they began to boo him crying, "Let the games go on." As they cheered, finally the men started fighting again. Once again he stood, risking his own life between the two fighters, stopping the fight. By now, the people began to jeer. They were even throwing stones and various things into the arena at Telemachus. The commander of the games barked an order to a Roman soldier. He pulled his sword and with one motion, with one slash, he took the life of this godly man, Telemachus. As he fell to the ground, his blood ebbed into the dust of the arena and stained the robes that were worn only by a holy man of his time. The crowd was shocked into silence! Everyone was stunned to see how this godly man had died. Historians say the people were so shocked to see him die in the arena, that one by one, they left the Coliseum. The games ended that day. But the interesting thing, historically, is that not only did they end that day, but also they ended for all time! There was never another fight to the death in the Roman arena. Here was a man that, by losing his life, did more than he could have ever done by keeping his life. That's an extreme example, and Jesus is not just speaking about death; He is speaking about the kind of commitment, of discipleship, where you are willing to *lose* yourself for the gospel's sake and for His sake.

A Lost Soul

Let's look at the third thing that He says about discipleship in verse 36, *"For what will it profit a man if he gains the whole world, and loses his own soul?"* What a penetrating question! Verse 37, *"Or what will a man give in exchange for his soul?"* Did you know it is possible to be a huge success, from the world's point of view, and still have a life that's not worth living? We hear every day about someone of promise that commits suicide! The world thinks they are so successful, they have prestige, they have position, maybe they have fame, and money! They have all these things that the world says is success, yet they themselves do not view their own life worth living. Jesus said, *"What does it profit a man if he gain the whole world and lose his soul?"* Do you know what the real paradox of this verse is? It is that you cannot save your soul in the first place. No one can save his own soul. Only God can save your soul! You cannot merit salvation, you cannot earn it, and you cannot perform some religious ritual to save your own soul. You cannot *save* your soul, but you can *lose* your own soul.

Jesus spoke often in the New Testament about things that can be lost. He spoke about lost sheep. He said, "There were ninety-nine in the fold and there was one sheep that was lost." He spoke about a woman who lost a coin, and the whole household looked frantically for the lost coin. I think if Jesus were upon the earth today, and if He came to our household, He would probably speak about lost keys. I lose my keys about three or four times a day. I have three sets, so when I lose the first two sets, I will still have a key. Jesus spoke about things that are lost. When you think about the word *lost*, it really is an awful word.

We say a guy *lost* his family, that's tragic! Or we say:

- A man *lost* his mind
- A couple *lost* their marriage
- Someone *lost* her job
- Someone *lost* his retirement
- They *lost* their life savings
- Someone *lost* his health
- A man *lost* his arm or a limb in the war

Just to think of a *lost* child sends terror into every one of us!

A few years ago a child was lost in Texas. Her name was Jessica, and she was lost down a shaft of an abandoned well. Thousands of people came to help in that rescue. In fact, the whole world seemed to stand still for a day as little Jessica was being rescued. Her rescue was broadcast around the earth by satellite. When they showed it on television around the earth, people cheered as the child who was lost was rescued. It is always sad when a child is lost. It is sad when someone loses an arm or someone loses his money. But what about when a *soul* is lost? Jesus said that a soul is worth more than all the world. My friend, you can drive through this city and take all the wealth of the city. Or you could drive by a spacious, beautiful home and you could take it. It's yours! You could see a beautiful shiny new car, maybe a Cadillac, maybe a limousine, and take it. It's yours! You could drive through the oilfields and watch the pumps. Take it, all of it. It's yours! You can see a high-rise bank full of all kinds of assets. Take them. They're yours! You can see the cattle grazing on the hillside. Take them. They're yours! You can see a store, a jewelry store, with its trinkets of gold and silver. There are diamonds and rubies. Take it! They are yours! "Take all the wealth of the world," Jesus said, "and all of it together would not add up to the value of one soul." It is an awesome thing for a soul to be lost.

When I was growing up in the country, we did not have neighbors who lived close to us. In fact, our closest neighbors were about a mile away. One family that lived about a mile and a half from our house, the Allens, had a little boy named Terry who was several years younger than me. I remember a time when he was about two years old, or maybe even younger. It was a Sunday evening and everyone was gathered in the little country church. It was about twilight, right before dark, when all of a sudden Terry's mother burst through the back doors of the church building. Interrupting the service, she screamed, "He is lost! He is lost! He is lost!" We asked what was going on as Dorothy Allen, nearly hysterical, screamed, "Terry's lost and we do not know where he is." She and Terry's dad had been looking for Terry after he had apparently wandered off somewhere. They could not find him. Do you know what we did? We "turned out church" to look for the lost child. I remember that men walked down the creek looking for the lost child, some walked down in the ditches, some walked down the little country road, and some went out in the cotton fields close to their homes looking for the lost child. Darkness had settled in when, at the end of our farm, about a half-mile from where the Allens lived, we found little Terry. He was playing in the rows of trees, just as happy as could be, the little hyperactive guy. He is now a medical doctor, so I guess all that energy paid off for him! Do you know what I remember about that incident? I remember the frantic search, and I remember the mother crying, "He is lost! He is lost! He is lost!"

Did you know that all around us there are those who are lost? They are *lost!* Their souls are lost! There are people in this room who have children who are lost. They may be grown now. Their parents know their telephone number, they know their address and they know where they are physically, but spiritually they are lost without God. If they die, they will lose their soul. You may have a mate who is lost, or your parents may be lost, without God. Maybe you have a family member whom you love more than anything in your life, and they are lost without hope, if they are without God. Some friend, someone that lives next door to you, a family member, someone that you work with, is lost. Often we do not have a burden for the lost. Maybe it is time that we "turn out church" and look for those who are lost, without God. If we would "turn out church" and look for a little boy that's lost, what about the souls around this community that are without God? *Lost!* It is an awful word. It is an awful thing to lose your soul.

There is another word, though, in this text that's a wonderful word. It is used in another context many times in the Bible. It is the word *saved*. Someone who was drowning has been rescued, and we say they've been saved! Someone is about to step in front of a train and another person grabs him, pulls him away and we say he has been saved. That is what God wants to do. He wants to save those who are lost! He wants to rescue those who are lost. That is what the gospel is about.

There is one last thing that Jesus tells us about discipleship in verse 38. He said, *"For whoever is ashamed of Me and My words in this adulterous and sinful generation, of him the Son of Man also will be ashamed."* It would be terrible to be part of a family that was ashamed of you. Yet there are people today who say they are Christians who are ashamed of Jesus. They never introduce Him to others. They are *ashamed!* They say, "Oh yeah, He is the Son of God," but they've never really confessed Him publicly as their Savior.

Many years ago I heard the story of a little boy who, from the time he was small, was obsessed with the dream of being a doctor when he grew up. He did not ever want to be a fireman or policeman like other little boys. Instead, he always wanted to be a doctor. When he was a young man, his father died; and with his father's death, his dreams and expectations of being a doctor died as well, since they were a very poor family. His mother did not have an education. She had no work skills, so she went to work in a menial job, earning just enough to support the family. Finally, when he graduated from high school, the mom said, "Son, are you going to go to college? You want to be a doctor so badly, so why not go to college." He said, "Mom, even with me working, there is no way we can afford it." She said, "Listen, I am going to sell this big house and take the equity out of it. It is too big for me anyway; I will buy a smaller house. I will work and you can work, and you will be able to go to college." He went all the way through college and graduated with honors. Finally on graduation day, she said to her son, "Now it is time for you to go on to medical school. You are going to make such a fine doctor." He said, "Mom, it is impossible. Medical school is so expensive, and I did not receive the scholarship I wanted. There is no way we can afford for me to go to medical school." She said, "Son, you have got to go, it has been your dream all of your life." She said, "I will sell this house and rent a little apartment, I do not need to own a home." She got another job, working day and night at menial tasks, and finally he graduated. He was a doctor and, in the meantime, he had met a young woman that was kind of a "high society" woman. He was ashamed of his mother because she was illiterate, kind of simple and worked at a menial job. He did not tell his wife about his mother. In fact, his mother would visit occasionally and he told his wife that she was his aunt, that his mom and dad had been killed. He told his mom about the lie, and she went along with it because she was so proud of her son and she did not want to embarrass him in any way. After all, he was a doctor now.

Finally the day came when the mother was very ill. The young man took her into his home and made a room for her up in the attic where he could care for her. He never told anyone that she was his mom. He would say that she was his aunt. Finally the day came when the daughter-in-law was at home and the mother was very sick, and in her fever and delirium she slipped and said, "Oh, my son such a fine doctor." When the daughter-in-law realized what was going on, she moved the mother out of the attic into the finest room in the house. When the young man came home, she confronted him and asked, "How could you? How could you deny your mother who has given you so much? How could you be ashamed of her and not tell everyone that she is your mother?" The young man hung his head because he had no answer.

My friend, the Lord Jesus Christ has done so much for us. He saved our souls and yet, at times, we are ashamed to introduce Him to those whom we know. He has done so much for us. He gave His life, yet some are ashamed to confess Him before men. In essence, Jesus said, "If you are ashamed of Me now, there will be a day when I will hang my head and I will be ashamed of you."

～ 1991 ～

On a Sunday morning in February, 1991, Valley Baptist Church rented the Standard School Auditorium for a business meeting to consider whether we would borrow the $3.5 million necessary to build. More than 750 people attended the business meeting. The church voted to borrow the money, even though the entire budget for that year was only $568,000.

Five hundred people gathered at Fruitvale Avenue for the groundbreaking. The joy of the occasion was muted by the resignation of Pastor Mike Miller.

Pastor Mike left to work for the California Southern Baptist Convention. Later he worked for Life Way Christian Resources. He is presently the Executive Pastor at First Baptist Church of Dallas, Texas.

We said good-bye to Mike with a sense of loss. He had the original vision for Valley. Personally, he was of an incalculable comfort to me when I lost my daughter.

In the fall of 1991, the church called Sal Sberna as Associate Pastor. Sal was a tremendous blessing to Valley, even though he served with us only two years. He is presently the Pastor of the Metropolitan Baptist Church in Houston, Texas.

"The Problem of Authority" was preached on Sunday morning, August 4, 1991, as part of a verse-by-verse series of messages through the Book of Ecclesiastes.

The Problem of Authority

"Who is like a wise man? And who knows the interpretation of a thing? A man's wisdom makes his face shine, And the sternness of his face is changed. Obey authorities for God's sake. I say, 'Keep the king's commandment for the sake of your oath to God. Do not be hasty to go from his presence. Do not take your stand for an evil thing, for he does whatever pleases him.' Where the word of a king is, there is power; And who may say to him, 'What are you doing?' He who keeps his command will experience nothing harmful; And a wise man's heart discerns both time and judgment, Because for every matter there is a time and judgment, Though the misery of man increases greatly. For he does not know what will happen; So who can tell him when it will occur? No one has power over the spirit to retain the spirit, And no one has power in the day of death. There is no release from that war, And wickedness will not deliver those who are given to it. All this I have seen, and applied my heart to every work that is done under the sun: There is a time in which one man rules over another to his own hurt." (NKJV)

The book of Ecclesiastes is one of the most unusual books in all of the Bible. Ecclesiastes is the record of the struggle of Solomon, who was on a quest, trying to find the meaning to life. His search for significance was on a horizontal level with no thought of God, no thought of the Creator or of the Divine. Nor was there any thought of man's accountability or responsibility to God. Solomon wrote most of the book of Ecclesiastes from a horizontal plane, or what he terms "life under the sun." The theme of the early part of the book is found in chapter 1, verse 2, where he said, *"Vanity of vanities;... vanity of vanities, all is vanity."* In chapter 2, verse 17, he said, *"Therefore I hated life because the work that was done under the sun was distressing to me, for all is vanity and grasping for the wind."*

The word *vanity* means "meaninglessness or futility." In stating that life under the sun was like grasping the wind, he was saying that life really doesn't have meaning or significance. In the early part of the book, we find Solomon traveling down every conceivable path, trying to find the meaning of life.

Chapter 7 is like a hinge! As the book turns in a different direction, there is a new word introduced, the word *wisdom*. Wisdom occurs thirty-four times throughout the rest of the book. Many of the verses in chapter 7 are proverbs, or theoretical statements about how to live a wise life. Solomon records his thoughts like "machine gun fire." In chapter 7, he said:

- *"A good name is better than precious ointment,"*
- *"And the day of death is better than the day of one's birth,"*
- *"It is better to go to the house of mourning than to go to the house of feasting,"*
- *"Sorrow is better than laughter,"*

- *"It is better to hear the rebuke of the wise than for a man to hear the song of fools,"*
- *"The end of a thing is better than its beginning."*

In these proverbs, Solomon paints in broad strokes what it means to have wisdom.

In chapter 8, he moves from looking at wisdom from a distance, as though through a telescope, and zeros in as if through a microscope, giving us a practical lesson on a wise life. He addresses one of the most critical, and yet one of the most difficult details of human life—that is our relationship to authority. Mankind's relationship to authority is the basis of most of the social, political, spiritual and personal problems of life.

Think about the social problems of our world today and how they relate to the issue of authority. Throughout our world, the big problem of today is that of human rights. In many ways, our country has become the watchdog of the world. We are always snooping around, trying to expose human rights violations. Within our own country, we constantly debate the rights of minorities, the rights of women or the rights of the unborn. At the crux of the issue of rights is the problem of authority. Who gives human beings their rights? Does God give those rights? Are our rights granted by civil government; are they philosophical, moral, or religious? Throughout our world today, the whole issue of social injustice relates back to the issue of authority.

Think about the political problems in the world in which we live. Everything revolves around the idea of authority. Consider the problems in the Middle East, particularly the Palestinian problem. It's an issue of rights! The Palestinians say they have the right to the West Bank, the Golan Heights and the Gaza Strip because they have lived there for generations. The Israelis say, "We have the right to the land because in the Old Testament era, God set the borders of Israel." The issue becomes one of authority. Which authority do you believe? The issue that we are facing in the Middle East with Iraq is an issue of authority. Does the United States or the United Nations have the right to violate the sovereignty of another nation? Do we, because of fear or the threat of mass destruction, have a right to set aside the regime of another government? Who has the authority in such matters? That is the debate of our day! In fact, any time you hear the evening news concerning political issues, it is nearly always related to the issue of authority. Whether it is the Senate or the House, Congress is debating whether the President has overextended his rights. The President is taking to task the Congress, to do this or to do that, to exercise their authority; and the judicial system is setting aside laws or interpreting the Constitution. The genius of our political system is that it is a balance of competing authorities. Authority is the political issue of our day!

The social issues of our day relate to authority, and I think the spiritual issues of our day have to do with authority. Very few people I have met are honest, intellectual atheists. Basically, most atheists do not want God telling them what to do. They cannot find God for the same reason a criminal cannot find a policeman. They do not want to find God, because it's easier to discount the concept of God than it is to discount the commandments of God! Authority is the central spiritual issue of most peoples' lives.

Are you the highest authority for your life? That's post modernism! You govern your life, you determine right and wrong for yourself, not culture, certainly not biblical revelation; instead you determine your own truth, your own narrative, your own score concerning the path that you have decided to take.

Many problems in life have to do with authority, as well as all types of conflict:

- Conflict with the law or with the police,
- Conflict with a boss,
- Conflict at work as to whose job it is, or who is responsible,
- Conflict between husbands and wives who many times fight over the issue of control or authority,
- Conflict when children resist parents' authority,
- Conflict with financial authorities who are ignored as people allow bills to stack up, only to find themselves deep in debt.

Authority affects every area of life. Solomon could not have picked a better or more pertinent detail of life to address specifically than that of authority. He tells us three things about authority in this passage:

The Demands of Authority Are To Be Obeyed

Verse 2 says, *"I say, keep the king's commandment for the sake of your oath to God. Do not be hasty to go from his presence. Do not take your stand for an evil thing, for he does whatever pleases him."* Solomon uses the illustration of a king in regard to authority. He could have used the illustration of a parent, of a teacher or of a boss, but the most obvious illustration in his day regarding authority was that of a king. Solomon declared that wisdom submits itself to authority. In all of us, there is a streak of rebellion because we do not want anyone ruling over us! Particularly as Americans, we find the idea of a monarchy repugnant. We are free spirits, and that is wonderful politically, but it is very disastrous personally. The fact of the matter is that in the life of every human being, God has set authorities over us. Much of our happiness depends on how we relate to those authorities. Rebellion becomes a very ugly thing in our life. It makes us feel dirty inside.

Wisdom teaches us to submit, first of all, because authority is from God. In verse 2, Solomon said, *"Keep the king's commandment for the sake of your oath to God."* He does not merely say, "Keep the king's commandment because if you do not, he is going to lop off your head," although that might have happened in the ancient world. He taught instead that the issue of authority has to do with God. Whether it is a policeman, teacher, coach or parent, ultimately the principle of authority is given to us by God.

In the New Testament, it is spelled out even clearer. Romans chapter 13, verses 1 and 2 say, *"Let every soul be subject to the governing authority, for there is no authority except from God, and the authorities that exist are appointed by God, therefore, whoever resists the authority resists the ordinance of God, and those who resist will bring judgment on themselves."*

Verses 6 and 7 say, *"For because of this you also pay taxes, for they are God's ministers, attending continually to this very thing. Render therefore to all their due: taxes to whom taxes are due, customs to whom customs, fear to whom fear, honor to whom honor."* The governing authorities of life have to do with God. There might be a dictator or an imperfect government, but still the very principle of authority is given by God. That is why it's proper for us to pay our taxes, even though we may gripe about it!

In Ecclesiastes, chapter 8 verse 2, Solomon talks about obedience to the king, and in verse 3 he talks about respect for authority. *"Do not be hasty to go from his presence..."* In those days, if you had an audience with the king, you could not leave the king's presence until you were dismissed. You were not permitted to simply walk out of a meeting; you had to be dismissed by the king. Today, when the family has a meal together, all the children are seated at the table and as one little child finishes his meal, he turns to his father and asks, "Father, may I please be excused from the table?" Well, maybe that is *not* how it happens but perhaps that is how it should happen! We are not very good at dismissing each other out of our presence, but in Solomon's days, it was common respect that you stayed in the presence of the king until he dismissed you, because he was in charge. What Solomon was saying is that you are to obey and respect authority, even when you disagree with that authority. Later he teaches us what we are to do when authority is clearly wrong. However, generally the demands of authority are to be obeyed.

I grew up on a farm in Western Oklahoma. The nearest town to where I grew up was ten miles away. It was a town of less than 2,000 people, perhaps about 1,600, although 600 of those were inmates at the prison! In spite of their inmate status, we still counted them and listed that number on the sign coming into town. The total free population really was about a thousand people or so. The nearest town that had at least 5,000 population was about thirty-five miles away. As you can see, I grew up "way out in the country." I grew up on a dirt road. In fact, to this day where my folks live, the road is not paved. Needless to say, it's muddy in the winter time and dusty in the summer time. The amazing thing to me, growing up in the country with dirt roads everywhere, was there would be an occasional stop sign in the middle of nowhere. Usually the area was heavily weeded so you could not even *see* the stop sign. In fact, people forgot that a stop sign was there. No one paid any attention to the stop sign because, number one, there had not been a policeman on one of those roads since Oklahoma was Indian Territory. Number two, not only was there never a policeman on one of those roads the whole time I was growing up, but it was a silly place to have a stop sign! But the fact of the matter is, it was there. I say it was silly because, after all, what makes one dirt road more important than another dirt road out in the middle of the country? However, the obligation was to stop. My point is, that even though it appeared foolish or silly, it is still our obligation to submit ourselves to authority.

We could work through the civil process and go before the county commissioners and have the stop sign removed, but unless it's removed, the obligation for us is to stop! We are to submit ourselves to it because of what it says in verse 3: "We are to obey because it pleases the king." It may not please us, but it pleases him. He is the authority that God has placed over our life. That is what we owe—submission, or obedience to the demands of authority.

The Decisions of Authority Are To Be Evaluated

Solomon writes, not only about the demands of authority being obeyed, but he goes on to teach that the decisions of authority are to be evaluated. Verse 5 says, *"He who keeps his command will experience nothing harmful; And a wise man's heart discerns both the time and judgment, Because for every matter there is a time and judgment;"* or literally, "There is a time and procedure."

Authority and rules in life are given to protect us. Whether it is a parent or the police, rules really are for our own good! For instance, when you were a little child, your mom and dad told you not to play with matches so that you would not burn your fingers. It is not that they were being mean to you. It was for your protection! When your parents told you not to play in the street, it was not because they did not want you to go where the best roller skating was. It, too, was for your protection, for your own good. It is much the same way with the Old Testament law. Even the dietary laws were given for mankind's good. The Bible said, for instance, that the Jews could not eat pork. Perhaps that is not a bad idea for today. Today we understand the implications of those health or dietary laws. Certainly the sanitary laws of the Old Testament were beneficial. In the New Testament, however, the Pharisees made rules as an end within themselves, and it became a great burden. The Pharisees did not present them as, "Hey, this is for your protection and for your health." Instead, they were simply presented as an end within themselves. Rules to keep! Such rules sometimes bring misery. Therefore, wisdom learns to appeal. There is a procedure for appealing to authority. If you disagree with some decision made by your boss, there is wisdom in appealing to him to reconsider.

One of the great illustrations of this principle in the Old Testament is in 1 Samuel, when Saul was the king and David was the would-be king. In fact, Samuel had anointed David to be the next king of Israel, and that galled Saul. Actually, Saul was so angry at David that he pursued him, trying to put him to death. But King Saul's son, Jonathan, who was David's best friend, appealed to Saul by saying, in effect, "Dad, David is a pretty good guy. Remember, he killed that giant, Goliath, for you when things were in a mess. Remember, Dad, everyone loves David, and if you kill him, you are going to be the 'bad guy' instead of the 'good guy'!" Jonathan appealed to the authority of the king, which is what we are to do.

Sometimes the decisions of authority by people over us are wrong, and they bring us misery. Solomon said that there is a way to appeal to authority. First, we can appeal any decision because authorities don't know the future. Verse 7 says, *"For he does not know what will happen so who can tell him when it will occur?"* He is basically saying, "Look, the king messes up sometimes because he does not know the future, and the government does not know the future." Right now our government is debating back and forth in the United Nations about what to do with Iraq, but the fact of the matter is that no one knows the future. We don't know what will unfold in the months ahead, and the wrong decision, quite possibly, could be made. Because authorities within our life are not sovereign or omniscient, sometimes the government makes wrong decisions. Police sometimes jump to conclusions and make the wrong decision. Sometimes parents make the wrong decisions concerning their children's lives. Solomon said, "Though the misery of man increases greatly," so there should be a mechanism for appealing to authority. Also in verse 8, he taught that not only do they not know the future, but no one has power over the spirit to retain the spirit. All authority is finite. That is why we should always evaluate the decisions of authority that are made concerning our lives. Otherwise, religiously we could end up with more incidents like Waco, Texas, and individuals like David Koresh, or Jim Jones, who led so many people to South America, where they died. We should learn to be discerning and evaluate authorities over us.

In Acts, chapter 5, the Roman government arrested some of the apostles for preaching. As the authorities were preparing to release them, the apostles were given a rather stern warning that, although they were free to go, they were not to preach the gospel any more. The law, of course, was an "authority" in their lives. On one hand, the law was forbidding them to preach the gospel, and the Bible clearly says that we are to obey the king, the authority over us. So what did they do? Peter said, "We will obey God rather than men!" There are times in all of our lives where there is conflicting authority, where the authority of God comes in conflict with the authority of our boss or the authority within the home. What are we to do? *We are to always obey the higher authority.* Suppose that in the office where you work, the phone rings and your boss instructs you to tell the caller he is not there. Your boss just asked you to lie, breaking one of the Ten Commandments. The Ten Commandments outrank your boss! They outrank you as a parent! If your phone rings and you instruct your child to tell the caller you are not there, you have just asked your child to violate a higher law than what you have the right to ask any child to do. At that point, your child does not owe you obedience, but rather owes it to God. Peter said that they would obey

God rather than men. In other words, there are limitations placed on human authority.

Solomon said, *"No one has the power in the day of death."* He taught that human authority is limited, because the authority does not know the future; the authority cannot control the wind, the circumstances of life, or death! Then he said that there is no relief from war, and wickedness will not deliver those who are given to it. In essence, he was saying that if you are a soldier in the army and there is a war declared, do not count on getting out. It may be the time for you to be released from the army, but if there is a war declared, you are probably going to serve more time in the army. You cannot be released from the battle; in the same way, human authorities cannot keep us from sin.

As parents, we tend to think that if we have enough rules, we can cover all the bases and keep our children from sin. No, we really cannot. When they are very young, we can control their actions, but we cannot control their attitudes. Sin has to do with the *heart.* That is the imperfection of legalism. Sometimes church leaders think that more rules, such as "You cannot do this," and "You cannot do that," will govern life in such a way that we will be kept from sin. Legalism is inherently flawed because sin is not merely borne in our actions; it is borne in the attitudes of life. So what does God say? The demands of authority are to be obeyed, the decisions of authority are always to be evaluated and then the dangers of authority are to be avoided.

The Dangers of Authority Are To Be Avoided

Verse 9 says, *"All this I have seen, and applied my heart to every work that is done under the sun: There is a time in which one man rules over another to his own hurt."* There is a built-in frustration with being a boss. In fact, there is a built-in frustration with being a leader, whether it is in the home or in the workplace. You have to understand that there are limitations upon your authority. Authority will only take you so far as a parent. Then, if you press that authority too hard, it is to your own hurt. God gave the Ten Commandments and the Old Testament law, but not with the expectation that the Ten Commandments would stop sin. Rather than stop sin, they were given simply to *define* sin. At times, we have unrealistic expectations of what rules will do in our children's lives. Ultimately when we hold too tightly, it is to our own hurt.

As an employee, we must learn to see our boss, whoever that might be, as a link in the chain of authority of which God is at the top. God has ordained the system of authority. You might be saying, "Well, you just do not know my boss!" The fact is, I do not know your boss, but God does! For some reason, in the providence of God, He allowed that person to be over your life. A person in authority may not be perfect but God allowed him to be over you. There is a word for bosses in verse 1, *"Who is like a wise man and who knows the interpretation of a thing? A man's wisdom makes his face shine and the sternness of his face is changed."* Sometimes authority has a pretty stern face, does it not? Sometimes, for the boss, it is all about rules and policies. When you acquire wisdom, it changes the hardness of your face. It changes the sternness of authority. Being a good boss, involves not flaunting authority, whether as a parent, in the workplace or in governing authorities. It is a very insecure leader who is always flaunting his authority, who has to remind you, "Hey, I am in charge, I am the authority in your life, I am your boss." That is a mark of insecurity. A boss allows wisdom to change his face of hardness to one of tact. Someone has said that tact is the ability to make someone feel at home when they wish they *were* at home. If you are in charge, if you are a boss, then the best advice that I can give you is to "lighten up." You do not have to be a hammer all the time. You do not always have to growl at people.

I grew up on a farm, and my Dad loved to hunt, so he always had a lot of hounds from the time I was little, to this very day. Usually they were in pens, but sometimes they were lying around the yard. Growing up, I remember that my mom always had a little dog, sort of like a watchdog, that would bark when people would drive up. If you drove into the driveway, you would see that little dog just lying under a tree; but when he saw you, he would get up and start barking and growling. If one of those hounds was anywhere close, that little dog would chase the hound, growling fiercely, nipping at him. He wanted you to know he was on the job, that he was taking care of business.

Sometimes people think that authority means that you growl a lot. Maybe you are a dad, and you think you have to growl and let everyone know you are in charge. Or maybe you are the boss at work and you think you have to growl, or you're the teacher or the coach and you think you've got to growl. Solomon taught that wisdom changes the hardness of your face. It makes you mellow regarding how you relate to other people in authority. There is some application, not only for the boss but for the parent and child as well. The Bible says to children simply, "Children obey your parents." As a young person, God has placed your parents over you, and God knew exactly how old your mom and dad would be, and how set in their ways they would be. He also knew how "cool" you would be as a child, and yet He still placed them over you as an authority. There is a place of appeal, and parents should always be willing to listen to their children. As a young person however, you are to obey your parents, unless they are clearly giving you a command that is morally against what God says.

I have noticed that there are some pastors who become dictators. They have a sense of spiritual authority in their life and they start thinking that they speak ex-cathedral, that is, when they speak, it is the voice of God speaking. There are some parents like that. They start thinking that they are God in their child's life. We need to understand the built-in limitations of authority. You are not God in your child's life. You can use your authority ultimately to your own hurt if you hold too tightly. When I was a little kid, right before my dad would spank me, he would say, "This is going to hurt me more than it hurts you." I think that is a universal statement that dads and moms make. I always thought, "Just go ahead and spank me, but do not insult my intelligence like that. It cannot possibly hurt you as bad as it hurts me." Solomon taught that it is to your own hurt when you use too much authority. Someone has said, "Authority is like perfume, when you have too much on, it stinks!" Have you ever noticed that when someone is wearing a little too much aftershave or too much perfume, all of a sudden what was supposed to smell good does not smell good any more? That's the way authority is! God has given authority within the home and within society. Sometimes, however, when you give people a little bit of authority, or you put them in charge of something, they become Adolph Hitler! It goes to their head!

Suppose that you buy a little puppy dog. Oh, it's such a cute little puppy! It plays, bites at your feet and your shoestrings, and it plays tug-of-war with you. You build a little pen in the backyard and your little puppy has a doghouse in which to live. At first, he hardly ventures out. Later he will go out a few feet and run back to the doghouse. Well, suppose he is one of the big breeds of dogs and very quickly he grows into a huge dog, but you keep him in the same little pen. After a while, he begins to pace back and forth along the fence, always testing the fence because it is such a small enclosure. Day after day he paces back and forth, and then one day he climbs over the fence. He runs and runs and runs and runs, because finally he has escaped! Would it not be better to expand that fence as the dog grows, to push the boundaries out so that he is comfortable living within the restrictions?

Sometimes as a parent, a child comes into our life and we build a little pen for that child. We set all kinds of rules for their own good: *Don't play with matches; don't play in the street, no, no, no, no, no!* At first, the child needs all those rules. But as he grows up, some parents keep the little fence. After a while that child begins to test the fence, and he begins to rebel. God has built into every child a desire for independence. With this growing independence, one day the child climbs over the fence, and there are no restrictions any more. He is out on his own, making decisions on his own. Would it not be better to have a growing sense of expansion of those rules, of that authority, so that the child is not always testing the limits? You can give your children more and more independence, and yet still have some restrictions upon their lives. I am convinced that some parents are too permissive. They need to stand in front of a mirror and practice saying the word, "No!" No, you cannot do that! No, you cannot go there! No, I am sorry, but no, no, no! I am also convinced that there are just as many parents who need to practice saying, "Yes. Yes, you are old enough! Yes, now you can do that! Yes, you can!"

Leadership has to do with expectations. I heard about a principal who was walking down the hall at school, and he heard a little fourth grader who was in an argument with his teacher. Finally, the little boy got loud and said, "I am not an underachiever, you're an 'over-expecter.'" Did you have a teacher like that? The problem was not that you were an underachiever; the problem was that your teacher was an "over-expecter." Sometimes parents are "over-expecters!" Some bosses are "over-expecters," sometimes coaches are "over-expecters," and sometimes preachers can be "over-expecters." I cannot tell you the number of people who have sat in my office over the years who have said to me, "I could never please my dad," or, "I could never please my mom." The sad thing is, in some of those cases, I knew their dad, and I knew their dad was extremely proud of them. But *they* never knew it!

One last insight: *Your example outlives your achievement!* Do you remember your favorite teacher from school? Do you remember your least favorite teacher from school? Most of us could probably easily name both. With those teachers you liked the most, did it have to do with the information, the data they imparted to you? Do you find yourself saying, "Oh, she really taught me algebra? I would not have learned it without her." On the other hand, with your least favorite teacher, what is it that you remember? Was it all the rules? No, sometimes your favorite teacher had more rules than your least favorite teacher. It did not have to do with rules—it had to do with the *spirit* of that teacher, of how that teacher made you feel. Sometimes as a boss, or a parent, we can get more interested in the product of achievement than in the process. We tend to think authority is all about keeping policies, or it is all about keeping rules, being home at a certain time—that kind of thing. Life is modeled for us. Sometimes we become merely goal oriented because, after all, there's a job to do! For example, it's Saturday morning and Mom wants the kids to get the dishes washed, and Dad wants to clean out the garage. We want the car washed and the lawn has to be mowed. What happens? We get in a "fizz" with all these things we want to do. What is really happening on that Saturday, is that a child is learning how to be a parent. They are watching Dad— "Well, that's how a dad should act." They are watching Mom's attitude, assuming that's how a mom should act.

Sometimes there is a conflict between a husband and wife and a big argument ensues. You both know you are going to get it resolved, and you are both going to continue to love one another. But the little children are listening! And they are learning! "Oh," they are saying, "that is how you act when you are a husband. That is how you act when you're a wife. That is what a daddy does. That is what a mommy does." We are modeling! In some ways we are modeling God because God is depicted as a Father. For so many people in our culture, their view of God is connected to their view of their parents. God is not all about rules! God is not carrying a big stick. He is a God of love and grace and acceptance. God has a perfect balance of authority, law and grace, justice and mercy. He is the Perfect Father!

～ 1992 ～

In April of 1992, Valley Baptist Church moved! It was a glorious day with over 2,000 people worshipping with us. From the very first Sunday, it was necessary to have two worship services at our new location, 4800 Fruitvale Avenue.

The week before we moved was the first time that we surpassed 1,000 people in Sunday School attendance. That was an amazing blessing from God, considering the church only owned 1.3 acres of land on Airport Drive! In 1992, we baptized over 200 people for the first time. We added 450 new members and averaged 973 people in Sunday School that year.

"Winning Over Bitterness" was preached on Sunday morning, May 31, 1992, as part of a series of messages entitled "Winning Attitudes."

Winning over Bitterness

HEBREWS 12:14-15

"Pursue peace with all people, and holiness, without which no one will see the Lord: looking carefully lest anyone fall short of the grace of God; lest any root of bitterness springing up cause trouble, and by this many become defiled..." (NKJV)

In surveying my preaching, I discovered that I have never preached an entire message on bitterness. Yet I do not know of anything that is more disabling in the believer's life than a root of bitterness. Bitterness can:

- Rob you of peace in your life
- Blow out the candle of joy in your life
- Cause barrenness in your spirit
- Place its tentacles in your marriage and ultimately cause divorce
- Cause brokenness in your life
- Keep you from understanding the Bible
- Keep you from being a soul winner
- Bitterness can even keep you from comprehending the grace and the forgiveness of God. All of us have known, or know someone who is bitter. Maybe there has been a

time in your own life when you have experienced bitterness. A bitter person can often be hostile, caustic, critical and cynical. Bitter people are often overloaded with resentment, fault finding and anger. Sometimes bitterness manifests itself with people who:

- Are the "crybaby" type: morose and sad
- Carry their feelings on their sleeve, offended by the least little provocation
- Are wounded, hurt and full of self-pity

On the other hand, sometimes bitterness manifests itself with a "coolness," or with an aloofness. Bitter people can become disinterested or non-participatory in family life, or life around them. This same person, however, can be a seething volcano of hostility, anger and bitterness.

The book of Hebrews is written to the believer. These words about *"looking carefully lest anyone fall short of the grace of God; lest any root of bitterness springing up cause trouble"* (NKJV) are for the Christian. We are not immune to bitterness simply because we are believers. In fact, I believe that God has many dysfunctional children in His family. There are many "sour saints," "caustic Christians," and "bitter brothers!"

The Root of Bitterness

Where does bitterness come from? It always comes from the same source. It comes from a hurt within your life that has not been dealt with, and that you have allowed to fester. It may even be that the hurt is perceived as being from God.

- Maybe life has not turned out the way you wanted, and you blame God.
- Maybe you are not the way you want to be; yet you know that is the way God has made you.
- Maybe God allowed adversity in your life, and now you are bitter against Him.

- Maybe you are bitter against society because of how you grew up, or because of the oppressiveness of some element of society.
- Maybe you are bitter against your family, or your parents because of the way they reared you; maybe it was a father who was angry or a mother who was disinterested in your life.
- Maybe you are bitter against a church. Maybe there has been a church in your past that you did not think treated you right, where the people weren't as compassionate as you thought they should be.
- Maybe a religious leader hurt you.

Maybe you are not bitter against God, the church, your family or society as a whole, but perhaps it is a specific individual. Maybe you are bitter at your husband or your wife. Sometimes the better half can become the bitter half! I do not know how many times in counseling I have discovered, and uncovered, a root of bitterness within a marriage. Bitterness comes from a hurt that is allowed to fester. It is like a boil that eventually erupts with anger and hostility within your life.

The hurt may have been *intentional,* possibly from your past when someone meant to hurt you. They said things or did things that were wrong. They were wrong before God, they hurt you, and they did it on purpose! Now you are bitter. Or maybe the hurt was unintentional. They did not mean to hurt you; they may not even know that they hurt you. Or maybe it is an *imagined* hurt. It is not even real. There is no substance to it. Maybe you *feel* like you were abused, or wounded. You *feel* like you were used and mistreated. And you are hurt!

All of us have been hurt by life. We have been hurt somewhere in our past, perhaps by someone who was a friend. Or we have been hurt by a family member, or perhaps in church. If you have been in church for very long, most likely you have been hurt somewhere along the way. It is natural to react to a hurt with anger. It is natural to feel resentful, or even to desire retaliation. As a believer, however, you recognize that getting even is wrong, and you confess those feelings to God. I am convinced that God gives grace for every hurt. I am convinced that for every demand that is placed on your life, there is the supply of grace. You may be saying, "You do not understand how badly I was hurt." My response is, "You do not understand how great the grace of God is." It does not matter how you have been hurt, or how severe a cut it is in your life. With the demand, I believe that God will give you the supply of grace to forgive, and to go on with your life.

Verse 15 of Hebrews 12 says, *"Looking diligently lest any man fail of the grace of God."* Literally that means, "go back" on the grace of God. This is not talking about falling from grace in the sense of your salvation. It is saying that when you are hurt in life, if you do not allow God's grace to heal your wounds, then you are going back on the concept of grace. When you do not release the anger created from life's hurts, a root of bitterness springs up. I know there are some awful hurts here today. Any time this many people are gathered together, there are bound to be some deep wounds—the loss of loved ones or disease, divorce or parents who physically or sexually abused or emotionally tortured their children. However, with every demand comes the supply of grace. Often a hurt is not taken care of because we fall back, or pull away from the grace of God. Then what happens? When you are hurt, if you allow God to give you the grace to forgive, you get over it. But the bitter person does not *deal* with the hurt. The bitter person takes the hurt into his heart and dwells on it. Bitter people mull it over in the night. They go over and over what a person said, or what happened. Like a recording over and over in his mind, the bitter person hears the words of his father who is already dead, or the words of an ex-mate who hurt him.

Bitterness starts with a hurt that is not dealt with. Someone hurt you, and you have feelings of resentment. You know it is wrong. So in order to justify it, you begin to scrutinize their life. You look critically at their life, trying to find something else that is wrong. What I have discovered is that if you look hard enough, you are going to find wrong in everyone's life.

If you come to this church, which I believe is a great church, or go to any church in America and look for something wrong, you are going to find it. It may be too hot, or too cold, or too loud, or not friendly enough. On the other hand, if you have come to this church looking for a blessing, you will find it. If you have come to this church looking for people who are friendly, you will find them. If you have come looking for those who care and will shoulder the burden with you, you will find them. Whatever you look for is what you tend to find in life. The bitter person begins to look for the negative. Someone has hurt them, so they begin to scrutinize that person's life in order to justify their feeling of resentment. They raise their expectations, and then the person who has hurt them simply says one thing, and wow! It is just terrible! Someone else could say it and it would not be that bad. Someone else could treat them the same way and it would not be that bad, but they have been hurt by this person, and they are bitter. If they are bitter at their mate, the smallest thing sets them off. Bitterness becomes a downward spiral. They are hurt, so they become negative and look for other wrongs. They find them and that feeds the negative, and it becomes a downward spiral until it blows out the candle of joy in their soul, leaving them in darkness.

In years of counseling, I have found that few people admit that they are bitter. This is an underground sin. Even God calls it a *root!* It is underneath the surface; it is not seen. Most people deny it, they disguise it, they disregard it, but they do not admit that they have a root of bitterness.

I have met few people who have said, "Preacher, I am just bitter!" If someone tells you they are bitter, I guarantee you have found a really bitter person, because most people will not admit it. Most of the time we justify our bitterness, saying, "It is not my fault. It is because of what they did to me. You do not understand how they hurt me." Anna Russell wrote a poem about a man:

> *"He said, 'I went to the psychiatrist to be psychoanalyzed,*
> *To find out why I killed my cat and blackened my wife's eyes.*
> *He put me on a downy couch to see what he could find.*
> *This is what he dredged up from my subconscious mind.*
> *When I was one, my Mommy hid my dolly in the trunk*
> *And so it follows naturally that I have always drunk.*
> *When I was two, I saw my father kiss the maid one day,*
> *That is why I suffer now from kleptomania.*
> *When I was three, I suffered ambivalence from my brothers,*
> *So it follows naturally that I poisoned all of my lovers.*
> *I am so glad that I have learned the lesson it has taught*
> *That everything that I do that is wrong is someone else's fault.'"*

We laugh at that, but that is the way the bitter person operates. They always blame someone else. Everyone knows that bitterness is wrong. Your conscience bears witness it is wrong. The Holy Spirit convicts you that it is wrong. You know that it is wrong to harbor feelings of resentment or revenge. But everyone thinks that they are the exception! People say, "Hey, I have the right. You do not understand. My husband left me. He left me with the children, saddled with all the bills. You do not understand how he treated me, how he abused me." Others say, "You do not understand how cold my wife is. You do not know what she has done," or "You do not understand my children. I tried to raise them with Christian values, but they rejected those values and threw them back in my face." Then there is the woman who says, "I have been passed over for another job simply because of being a woman," or the man who says, "I lost a promotion because of my color," or the couple planning to retire and enjoy life, when a disabling disease or terminal illness strikes their life and robs them of the anticipated joy of their golden years. Everyone feels justified, and feels they have the right to be bitter. Where does bitterness come from? The root of bitterness grows in the soil of a hurt that has not been properly taken care of.

The "Fruit" of Bitterness

Not only does bitterness have a root, but it also has *fruit.* Bitterness is never constructive. It is always destructive within your life. Verse 15 says, *"Looking diligently lest any man fail of the grace of God; lest any root of bitterness springing up trouble you, and thereby many be defiled."* Bitterness has both a personal and a social impact. First of all, it troubles you, and then it defiles many. It hurts *you!* Bitterness is a subtle form of revenge. Someone hurts you and you think, "Well, I cannot get them back." It is wrong to murder that person, so you decide to be angry with them on the inside and become bitter against them. Though it is a subtle form of revenge, the person who has hurt you cannot feel it. You are the one who feels it. It is like holding onto acid!

Bitterness Can Affect You Physically

Physically, bitterness will take a toll on your body. Dr. S.I. McMillan wrote a book called *None of These Diseases.* In his book, he said that at least fifty diseases could be traced to emotional causes. The stress of bitterness can cause sickness. I am not saying that every sick person is a bitter person, but bitterness will affect you *physically.* Bitterness is like a machine that is running all the time. It is like a motor that is always running. When you are asleep, it is running. When you are walking, it is running. When you are sitting and quietly talking, it is running because it is part of you. It is deep in your heart. Like a motor that is running all the time, bitterness is going to cause fatigue in your life. It is like a short circuit in an electrical current. Bitterness will short-circuit your body physically and will cause undue stress. Eventually it will make you sick—or at least it *can* make you sick.

Bitterness Can Affect You Emotionally

Not only will bitterness affect you physically, but it also affects you *emotionally*. If you are bitter against someone, you have become that person's "emotional slave"! Perhaps it is your ex-mate who has hurt you, and you are bitter against him. Maybe it is a former employer who has left you bitter because of some hurt. Often times the reason for your bitterness is because that ex-mate or employer was controlling and manipulating you. Reflecting back on your relationship, you might say, "They knew how to push my buttons and bring out the worst in me." If you are bitter, let me tell you something—they are *still* pushing your buttons! If you have bitterness in your heart, they are still in control of your life. You are their emotional slave!

Bitterness Can Affect You Spiritually

Physically, bitterness takes a toll. Emotionally, bitterness takes a toll. but it also affects you *spiritually*. In verse 14, it says, *"Follow peace with all men, and holiness without which no man shall see the Lord."* In this verse, there are two elements of the Christian life: vertical holiness with God and horizontal peace with all men. Did you know that you could not have hellishness in your heart towards others and have holiness toward God at the same time? Those two things cannot grow together in the same heart. A root of bitterness pushes your spiritual life out. For example, I have known bitter people who wanted to get involved in the Christian life. They began to grow, and then they came up against their bitterness. Perhaps they thought of a person they had never forgiven, or a person who hurt them deeply in their past. They refused to forgive the person who hurt them. This hurt became a cap on their Christian life. After a while, their bitterness caused them to regress spiritually. It became a cycle in their life. They would say, "I am going to try it again. I am going to go back to church, and begin to serve God again. I will read my Bible every day, and I am going to rededicate my life to God." They begin to grow and grow, and then they come up against the cap again. Their bitterness stops them in their Christian life. They begin to slide back, and it becomes a vicious cycle in their life. They ask, "Why can't I get victory, why am I up and then I am down? Why do I go through these cycles in my Christian life?" You have a cap in your life called bitterness, and until you deal with it, you will never be able to mature or grow further in your Christian life.

Bitterness has many sprouts! Years ago there was a fascinating story in the news. It was reported that they had discovered the largest living organism in the world at that time. In the forest of Northern Michigan, they found a huge fungus growing under some fern. I do not remember exactly how big it was, something like fifteen acres. They calculated the weight of it and said it was, by far, the largest living organism in the world today! Guess how they discovered it. Every once in a while, it would send up a sprout of little mushrooms growing here and there. Walking through the forest, you might think they were merely little mushrooms but what you would not know is that they were attached to a fifteen-acre fungus growing under the earth! That is how bitterness is in a person's life. You do not see it, and do not even realize that it is growing! But every once in a while, a little mushroom will pop up and you will ask, "Where did that come from?" I will tell you where it came from. It came from the root growing underneath the surface! Every once in a while, hostility spills out. Someone is angry and you say, "Where did that come from?" When all that anger spills out, you think, "I do not deserve that. Nothing that big happened. Where did that come from?" It came from the root that was growing. Bitterness is like an iceberg! Most of it is under the surface, and once in a while bitterness comes to the surface and sends up a sprout called insecurity. It may send up another sprout that is called distrust and another one that is called low self-esteem or poor self-worth; it sends up hostility, it sends up anger sometimes, and it sends up irritability most of the time. That is bitterness!

Perhaps worst of all, it sends up guilt. Bitterness can create doubts about your relationship with God. If you are bitter, you know in your heart that having those feelings toward someone else is wrong. Your reasoning on a subconscious level goes something like this: "This attitude I have is not pleasing to God. If God is not pleased with me, then God must not accept me. If God does not accept me, then how could I be His child?" So bitterness causes you to doubt the very core of your relationship with God, and it creates a cloak of guilt within your life that paralyzes you spiritually.

Bitterness and the Scapegoat!

There is a social fruit produced by bitterness. The Scripture says that many will be defiled. Bitterness always produces a chain reaction. In my years of counseling, I have found that every bitter person I have ever met has a scapegoat. What is a scapegoat? It is a Hebraism. It comes from the Old Testament. On the Day of Atonement, two goats were used. The High Priest would take one goat and slit its throat and shed its blood as a sacrifice. He would take the other goat that was called the scapegoat and pronounce all the sins on the head of this second goat. He loaded onto that goat all the failures, all the baggage, all the guilt of everything that anyone had done wrong. Then the goat was symbolically led out into the wilderness and released to wander. The goat symbolized carrying the people's sins away. Every bitter person that I have ever known has a scapegoat. They have someone they dump on, and, unfortunately, it is usually their mate. It is the person with whom they feel most secure. When bitterness develops in a teenager's heart, they often use their mother as a scapegoat. They vent all their hostility and rage on their mother because they feel the most secure with her. They think, "Mom is going to love me, no matter what." Sometimes a married person has a root of bitterness that has been growing for years in their life, and they do not know how to deal with it. So, from time to time, they dump it all on the scapegoat, their husband or their wife, the person with whom they feel the most secure. Unfortunately, we are not made to be scapegoats. After years of dumping all of that venom of bitterness on your mate, it is going to kill the love that you shared.

Bitterness always takes a toll. The best biblical illustration of bitterness is Saul, from the Old Testament. Saul became so embittered at young David that he almost went insane. David was his scapegoat! David was chosen by God and anointed by Samuel to be the next king over Israel. David was in Saul's army. He fought and killed the giant, Goliath, for Saul! The people were ecstatic as they made their way back to the city. Women sang, "Saul has killed his thousands, but David his ten thousands." The Bible says that it galled Saul in his heart, and made him bitter against young David. From that point on, David became the scapegoat of Saul's life, even though David had never done anything wrong. David tried to be a servant and a good soldier. Whatever Saul said to do, David did! In fact, as David played music to comfort Saul, Saul threw a spear at him, venting his hostility on David. Saul continued venting his rage to the point that he made David a fugitive. Saul tried to kill David. In fact, he hounded and hunted David down like a common criminal. Another time, Saul was spilling out all this bitterness about David, in essence saying, "We are going to get David; we are going to hunt him down and kill him." Jonathan, his son, simply asked Saul the question, "Dad, what has David ever done wrong?" Saul was so angry that he threw his javelin at Jonathan, his own son that he loved, and nearly took his life.

I have seen many fathers who threw verbal javelins at their sons, though their sons did not do anything to deserve the abuse. I have seen mothers who threw verbal javelins at their little children, who withered under their verbal assault as their self-esteem was shattered. Many times such hostility and bitterness comes from their own childhood, because of how they were raised. Bitterness is passed from generation to generation. If I, as a pastor, could tell you parents anything, it would be this:

- Dads, do not pass the bitterness of the past to the future!
- Do not take the baton that your father handed you, and the frustration and the anger in which he dealt with you, and hand it on to your son.
- Ladies, do not pass on to the next generation the frustration of your mom, or the bitterness she had over how she was raised.
- Mothers and fathers let the cycle of bitterness end with you!

Saul tried to kill his own son. There is a chain reaction of bitterness. In Ephesians, chapter 4, beginning in verse 26, you see the progression of what bitterness will do in your life.

Verse 26 says, *"Be ye angry and sin not; let not the sun go down upon your wrath."* God is saying to take care of the hurts, take care of the frustrations of the day when they happen. Do not allow them to accumulate. Deal with your anger. Do you know what's going to happen if you do not deal with anger, and if you allow a wound to fester? Verse 27 says, *"Neither give place to the devil."* When you are hurt, and you do not face the hurt, or the anger, then you give a beachhead to the devil in your life. He will use it! Verse 30 talks of "grieving the Holy Spirit of God." The next step is in verse 3—bitterness!

Bitterness begins with a hurt, a wound or anger. When that anger is not taken care of, it leads to bitterness in your life, and then it leads to wrath in your life. The word translated *wrath* means "hot" or "smoldering." That is what bitterness becomes!

Unresolved hurts are like taking oily rags and throwing them in a trashcan in the garage. Later, someone happens to toss a lit cigarette or match in the can. The lid is put on, and it does not immediately catch fire. It sort of smolders for a while until someone comes along and opens the lid. When the oily rags are exposed to oxygen, they suddenly burst into flames! That is what bitterness does! Bitterness becomes a wrath that smolders away inside your spirit. Then your wife, or your husband, irritates you in some small way and you explode with anger and hostility! They are shocked and ask, "Where did that come from? I didn't do that much wrong!" It is because the rags have been smoldering, and then suddenly they explode. Maybe a little child who has nothing to do with your bitterness, messes up and spills something, and the father explodes and spills out all of this smoldering fire that is inside of his spirit. The little child thinks, "It must be my fault, I must be a terrible person to deserve that kind of anger." Their little self-esteem and their self-worth is shattered, and they grow up being the same way as Daddy. They pass their bitterness on to their children. And so it goes from generation to generation.

Bitterness Leads to Clamor

Clamor means a "war of words"—verbal assault. Then it moves even beyond clamor to what is called "evil speaking." Evil speaking is not being argumentative. It is saying things that are intended to hurt and destroy. You know they are not true but you say them anyway. It is the bitterness speaking. You say, "I wish that we would have never met! I hate you! I wish that we were divorced, or I wish that we had not married." The next step is malice. That is the desire to actually do harm to someone. Where does it begin? It begins with a wound, a hurt that you did not face, that you did not take care of before the sun went down. Bitterness can become contagious. The writer of Hebrews said to watch it! Guard it! It becomes cancerous! It will tear a family apart, it will split a church, it will rip a business apart!

The root of bitterness grows in the soil of a hurt that is not taken care of. The fruit of bitterness is destructive, both personally and spiritually.

The "Pursuit" of Bitterness

Hebrews chapter 12, verse 15 says, *"Looking diligently lest any man fail of the grace of God; lest any root of bitterness springing up trouble you, and thereby many be defiled."* A root is underground. You have to search for it, seek it out and face it. You must become introspective. Right now you might be saying, "I wish all those bitter people I know were here to hear this." It may be that the Holy Spirit has *you* here to do some spiritual surgery. There may be some root of bitterness in you that has been growing since your childhood. Perhaps you have become calloused around some wound. You have never really faced it! Maybe you have never forgiven your parents for their verbal abuse, or maybe you have never forgiven your dad for his hostility, or maybe you have never forgiven your former mate for running out on you and wounding you. Perhaps you have never forgiven that church that did not treat you right, or that pastor who was immoral or failed you at a time when you needed help. Or maybe, if I can say it respectfully, you have never forgiven God for some perceived wrong. God has done no wrong! He needs no forgiveness, but you perceive somehow that He has done wrong and mistreated you, and you have never let go of that.

The first step of winning over bitterness is to recognize it, to face it. We hide behind a mask many times, and we do not face our bitterness. It is like the preacher and the deacon who were playing golf together, neither one of whom was a very good golfer. Slicing the ball, the deacon would become flustered and frustrated, and finally he said to the preacher, "You make as many bad shots as I do, and yet you do not throw your clubs. How do you do it?" He said, "I just keep everything inside. I have noticed, though, that everywhere I spit, the grass dies!" There are so many bitter people like that who keep it all inside. Their response is usually something like this: "I have been hurt, but I am tough, and I just keep it inside. I do not have to deal with it. I do not have to dialogue about it. I do not have to ask anyone to forgive me. I do not have to be reconciled to anyone." They keep it all inside, and everywhere they spit, the grass dies.

Bitterness will cause a caustic, cynical, critical spirit to develop in your life. Rather than hide from bitterness, rather than building a facade in our life, we should recognize bitterness and deal with it. I have seen a scenario over and over again, where a bitter person decides to come back to church. They join the church and even become a leader in church, but never deal with the bitterness in their life. That is the worst thing an individual can do! That is like pruning the limbs while you strengthen the root. That same person who has not dealt with his bitterness and is back in church, eventually says, "I am not right; I do not have peace and joy. So I am going to start serving the Lord." They get busy with all kinds of religious activity, but every time they prune the limbs, it just strengthens the root in their life.

Perhaps you have had a similar experience—before long, there are so many limbs that you cannot keep up with them.

Eventually, they overtake your life and you drop out of church again. Then you try again, saying, "I have got to get back in church." You start pruning limbs, saying, "I am going to serve the Lord." Before long, it overtakes you again, but you are not strong enough to keep up with the symptoms. You have got to get *under* the surface and get the root that is troubling you. It defiles many. I have seen in marriage counseling so many times, husbands who say, "I want to love my wife," and wives that say, "I want to love my husband." Many times, it is not a matter that they will not love—it is a matter that they *cannot* love. Why is that? It is because their life is so full of bitterness, that there is not room for anything else. Bitterness has shoved all the love out of their life. It is like a root under a sidewalk; after a while, it buckles the sidewalk. There is not room for the sidewalk any more because the root takes over. Roots have a way of doing that! They will ruin the foundations of buildings and they will cause skyscrapers to collapse, if left unattended. They shove everything else out, and after a while, it is not a matter that you will not love the person that you want to love, or that you will not love your children, or you will not love your wife. It is a matter that you cannot because there is not room in your heart for anything else. How can we win over bitterness?

Removing the Root of Bitterness

First of all you must recognize the bitterness, and second of all, you must remove it. In the last few weeks, I have prayed, "God, show me how to win over bitterness," because I see this as such a problem. I am convinced that there is only one way that you can win over bitterness—just one way, and that is, *you must forgive the person who wounded you, the one who caused the bitterness.* That is the only way! Whoever it is that wounded you, you must forgive them. It may be a parent who is dead, that you cannot call on the phone and say, "I forgive you," but in your heart you must forgive them. It may be an ex-mate. You are asking, "Are you sure that is the only way to do it? You do not know what they did to me. You do not know how bad they were." You are right! I do not know. You may have a wound so deep that there is not a psychologist or psychiatrist, pastoral counselor or human being on earth that can touch your wound. If it will ever be healed, it will be by God's grace. With the demand comes the supply. God will give you the grace to release the past and forgive that person, if you will allow Him. *You* may be saying, "Well that is not fair; they do not deserve it." You deserve it! You deserve to be able to release that person. They may not deserve your forgiveness, but you deserve to have joy and peace in your life, and you are not going to as long as you are bitter. You do not know enough to punish that individual. You may think you do, but you do not know enough. That is why God says, "Vengeance is mine. I will recompense." It is only God who has the will to mix justice and temper it with mercy.

You are probably asking, "Well, how do I do that?" God is our model! Forgive as God forgave! That is what it says in Ephesians. This is not new with me. I did not invent this solution. Ephesians, chapter 4, says, *"Be kind one to another, tenderhearted, forgiving one another, even as God for Christ's sake has forgiven you."* How do you forgive? The way God forgave you. Did you deserve God's forgiveness? "Oh no, theologically, I know that no one deserves God's forgiveness." We know that theologically, but in our hearts somehow we think, "Well if anyone deserves it, I guess I do. I am a pretty good guy, I deserve it." At times we have a theologically faulty view of ourselves. Whenever you view yourself as depraved and totally destitute without God, *then* you understand the enormous debt that was paid in your stead, and you understand the enormous grace gift that God has given you. Such understanding releases the grace in your life to forgive other people. You might say, "Well, I could never forget." I am not asking you to forget. You are still going to remember. There are hurts in your life that you will never forget, but I have found that there is a big difference between a scar and a sore! You will have scars in your life; everyone has scars from past hurts, but there is a big difference between a scar and a sore that is kept open and infected. Someone said it wisely, "The hornet of memory may fly again, but the sting of bitterness can be gone."

Replacing the Root of Bitterness

How do you win over bitterness? You recognize it, you remove it and then you replace it. Hebrews 12:14 says, *"Follow peace with all men and holiness, without which no man shall see the Lord."* That is how you do it. You let peace and holiness be your obsession. Peace with all men! Let that be the goal of your life. The intensity and energy that you used to fan and feed that bitterness for years—let that same intensity be directed toward holiness and peace.

Leonard Holt was a paragon of respectability. He was a middle-aged, hardworking lab technician who had worked at the same Pennsylvania paper mill for nineteen years. Having been a Boy Scout leader, an affectionate father, a member of the local fire brigade and a regular church attendee, he was admired as a model in his community—that was until that image exploded in a well-planned hour of bloodshed one brisk October morning. A proficient marksman, Leonard Holt, stuck two pistols in his coat pockets and drove to the mill. He stalked slowly into his shop and began shooting with a calculated frenzy. He filled several co-workers with two or three bullets apiece, firing more than thirty shots, killing some men that he'd known for more than fifteen years. When the posse found him standing defiantly in the doorway, he snarled, "Come and get me, you 'blank,' I am not taking anymore of your 'blank.'" Bewilderment swept the community.

Puzzled policemen and friends finally found a train of logic behind the brief reign of terror down deep within the heart of Leonard Holt. Inside, Leonard's heart rumbled the giant of resentment. His monk-like exterior concealed the seething hatred within. The investigation yielded the following facts: Several victims had been promoted over him while he remained in the same position. More than one in Holt's carpool had quit riding with him due to his reckless driving. The man was brimming with resentment and rage that could no longer be held. Beneath his picture in *Time Magazine,* the caption told the whole story, "Responsible, Respectful, Resentful."

Let me ask you. Does that sum up *your* life? Okay, maybe not to the degree of Leonard Holt—responsible, respectful, resentful. Bitterness is like an iceberg. All that the people around you see is the responsible and the respectful, but *God* sees the resentment!

~ 1993 ~

We grew so in 1993 that a third Sunday morning worship service was added. For the first time, we averaged over 1,000 people in Sunday School attendance for the year.

That year our choir performed a musical called "Jesus, the Heart of Christmas." Their performance was professionally filmed and aired on the local television station. Phones were manned at the church when it was aired. A number of people called, making life-changing decisions.

Also, 1993 was the first time that we had over 1,000 children in Vacation Bible School.

"Continuing—the Key to Life" was preached on Sunday morning, April 18, 1993. We had been in our building for a year. Our people had sacrificed and worked hard. They were tired! I thought what was needed was an inspirational message encouraging our people not to quit.

Continuing—The Key to Life

ACTS 1:14

"These all continued with one accord in prayer and supplication, with the women, and Mary, the mother of Jesus, and with His brothers." (NKJV)

After Jesus' death and resurrection, the disciples gathered in the upper room in Jerusalem, with about 120 other believers, to await the coming of the Holy Spirit. Acts 1: 14 says, *"These all continued with one accord in prayer and supplication, with the women, and Mary, the mother of Jesus, and with His brothers."*

This is not the only verse in the book of Acts that talks about the people continuing:

- Acts 2:42 says, *"And they continued steadfastly in the apostles' doctrine and fellowship, and in breaking of bread, and in prayers,"*
- Acts 2:46 says, *"And they, continuing daily with one accord in the temple, and breaking bread from house to house, did eat their meat with gladness and singleness of heart,"*
- Acts 6:4 says, *"But we will give ourselves continually to prayer, and to the ministry of the word,"*

- Acts 8:13 says, *"Then Simon himself believed also: and when he was baptized, he continued with Philip, and wondered, beholding the miracles and signs which were done,"*
- Acts 14:22 says, *"Confirming the souls of the disciples, and exhorting them to continue in the faith, and that we must through much tribulation enter into the kingdom of God,"*
- Acts 26:22 says, *"Having therefore obtained help of God, I continue unto this day, witnessing both to small and great, saying none other things than those which the prophets and Moses did say should come."*

Continuing seems to be one of the common themes of the New Testament, and in particular the Book of Acts. Evidently, God wants us to keep going! He wants us to continue and not quit. Yet we live in a society of quitters, where:

- If a marriage is not working out just right, then just quit the marriage!
- If a pregnancy is not convenient, then just quit the pregnancy!
- If you are too busy to come to church because your life is full of other activities, then just quit coming!
- If you get tired of serving the Lord, then just quit serving!

This passage occurs before Pentecost, as the disciples awaited the Holy Spirit. After the Holy Spirit came, however, it says, "They continued steadfastly." Later it says, "They all continued daily." When we look at Pentecost, we think about the great sermon that Peter preached and the 3,000 who were saved and baptized that day. Or we think about the rushing mighty wind, or speaking in tongues, or the coming of the Holy Spirit. But the Holy Spirit Himself, when He inspired the Word of God, thought in terms of the people continuing! He said, before and after the Holy Spirit came, "They continued." Maybe Pentecost is not so much about power as it is about persistence!

I believe that continuing is the key to life. It is the key to marriage, certainly. When you first fall in love, you are infatuated with one another, and you think, "We can not live without each other." You decide to get married, but then difficult days come. The bills stack up, the stress mounts, but you continue because of commitment. Commitment is the glue that holds the marriage together during difficult days. What is commitment? Commitment is continuing! Commitment is a determination and a will to continue. When you stand in front of a preacher and take your vows of marriage, they are not vows primarily of love. They are vows primarily of continuing. You say, "For better or for worse, we are going to continue." You say, "For richer or for poorer, in sickness and in health, we are going to continue." The key to a successful marriage is the spirit of continuing.

I believe persistence is, also, the key to being a good parent. Sometimes you are inspired to be a parent, and sometimes you are not. Sometimes you feel like it, and sometimes you don't. The key to being a good parent is discipline, particularly with small children. The key to discipline is consistency, and the key to consistency is continuing. I think children have a kind of built-in radar! They disobey at the most difficult times. They know when company is coming over, don't they? They know when they are in the grocery store, and they know when they are at church. It is like a little kid who is playing tag who has run breathlessly trying to get away. Then he grabs the pole, and says, "This is base; you can't get me here." Well, every church kid knows that the church parking lot is "base," especially preachers' kids, deacons' kids and Sunday School teachers' kids! They instinctively know that church is "base," and that Mommy and Daddy are not as likely to spank them there as they would be at home. They learn that very, very quickly. The key to being a good parent is to be consistent, no matter where you are.

Not only is perseverance the key to marriage and the key to good parenting, but also it is the key to success in other areas of life, including your work. It was Thomas Edison who said, "Success is two percent inspiration and ninety-eight percent perspiration." When you begin a new job you are excited about it, no matter how mundane the job might be. The first day of work, you get up early and go to work. But after a while, the job loses its edge for most people and things begin to change. Monday morning, when the alarm clock goes off, you drag yourself out of bed. You do not necessarily want to go to work, but you go because you have to continue in order to be successful. Those who do not continue in their work are not successful. We have a term for such people—unemployed!

I read recently of a study done by businessmen who discovered that eighty percent of sales are made after the *fifth* call. They also discovered that:

• Forty-eight percent of salesmen quit after the first call
• Twenty-five percent quit after the second call
• Twelve percent of the salesmen quit after the third call
• Five percent quit after the fourth call.

If eighty percent of the sales are made after the fifth call, that means that only ten percent of the salesmen are making most of the sales, because ninety percent have quit before the fifth call! Continuing is the key to success in our work life. It is certainly the key to success in advertising. When you turn on the television, you hear about Reeboks. When you turn the channel, it is Reeboks, Reeboks, Reeboks! We are bombarded with advertising. It is repetition that makes us go out and buy Reeboks! It is the repetition, the continuing, that grabs us. It is not the first commercial, but the hundredth commercial that grabs us, maybe even in our subconscious.

I read an article that claimed that when scientists looked at different jobs, they discovered that people who hold certain jobs live longer. They said of all the vocations, people who live the longest are lawyers, educators, scientists, engineers, philosophical and theological teachers and doctors. What do all those people have in common? What they have in common is that it takes persistent preparation in order to work in those occupations. It takes years of preparation to earn a theological degree or an educational degree, or to go into law, or to become a doctor or an engineer. Scientists have found that those who are the most persistent in preparing for their life's vocation are the people who live the longest.

Continuing is the key to character. I believe the mark of character is what it takes to make you quit. Character does not give up. The difference between a student who makes A's all the time and a student who makes C's all the time is not necessarily intelligence. Many times the difference is a spirit of perseverance. The "A" student is the one who continues.

I believe that continuing is also one of the keys to the Christian life. I ran across a quote by Calvin Coolidge some time ago where he said, "Nothing in the world can take the place of persistence. Talent will not. In fact, nothing is more common than unsuccessful men with talent. Genius will not. Unrewarded genius is almost a proverb. Education will not. The world is full of educated derelicts. Persistence and determination alone are omnipotent. The slogan 'press on' has solved, and will always solve the problems of the human race." There is a lot of wisdom in that quote. I believe it is true in the Christian life.

It is interesting to watch a marathon on television—perhaps the Boston, New York or Los Angeles Marathon. Before the gun sounds, as the cameras pan the crowd, you will see people pressed against people, elbow to elbow. At the sound of the gun, the runners begin to move slowly; they are jostling and bumping each other. Some people fall, and they are nearly trampled. The beginning of the race looks like a herd of cattle going through the streets. But if the same camera panned the same race at the ten-mile marker or the fifteen-mile marker, there is plenty of elbowroom! No one is jostling or bumping anyone, because so many people have quit by this time. There are many people who start the marathon, but there are fewer who finish. It is much the same way in the Christian life. There are many people who start, and yet they do not continue in the Christian life. Continuing is one of the keys to the Christian life.

Continuing is also one of the keys to Christian fellowship. Acts, chapter 1, says, *"They all continued with one accord..."* It says that after the Holy Spirit came, they continued in the apostles' doctrine and fellowship. Then in Acts 2:46, it says, *"...continuing daily with one accord in the temple and... from house to house."* They continued one with another. Folks, we are talking about basics here! We are talking about church attendance, about fellowshipping with one another. Although church attendance is not the highest mark of spirituality, it is a spiritual indicator in a believer's life. Sometimes people say they can be just as good a Christian and not go to church. It is true that you can be a Christian without going to church, but it is not true that you can be just as good a Christian without going to church. In fact, the very height of arrogance is to say that you can live just as good for God apart from the plan of God, as someone else can live fulfilling the plan of God.

It is God's plan that we serve Him in harmony, that we serve Him in orchestration with others. Our lives are to be intertwined with other believers. God does not want any "Lone Ranger Christians" riding off into the sunset by themselves. In fact, even the Lone Ranger had Tonto! There is strength in the fellowship of other believers. Some believers are "Alka-Seltzer" Christians! They "fizz" for a while, and then they're gone! Maybe they come when the church is having a high attendance emphasis, or on Easter. They attend once in a while on a Sunday morning, but they never come back on a

Sunday night, and they do not even know the church has a service on Wednesday night. I have noticed that, after a while, people who isolate themselves from other Christians begin having trouble in their Christian lives. Though they may start out fine, those who do not faithfully come to church eventually drift not only in their church commitment, but often in the spiritual commitments of their personal life. Theoretically, you could be just as good a Christian apart from the church, but that is only in theory. In practice, it does not work because you need the fellowship of other believers.

Back in the days of wooden bridges, if an army was marching in cadence with one another, when they came to a bridge, the sergeant would bark an order for them to fall out of step. If they walked in cadence, the continued rhythmic pounding of an entire army crossing a wooden bridge could cause a fault in the bridge or even collapse the bridge. The bridge was strong enough to hold up the weight of the entire army, but it was not strong enough to hold up an army that was marching in rhythm, or cadence one with another. There is power in fellowship one with another. There is power in being in harmony with other believers. When you get out of cadence or out of step with the church, you become vulnerable to collapse and to faults within your life. You need the fellowship; you need the mutual accountability that comes from serving God in harmony with other believers. No one is strong enough to serve God in isolation.

In Acts 6:4, the apostle said, *"We will give ourselves continually to prayer and to the ministry of the word."* They continued in the word and in prayer. This is what the Christian life is about—basics! Many times people want to get away from the basics. People are always looking for something new: a new Bible study, a new thought, a new truth. The priorities of the Christian life are measured in basics. The apostles said they were going to give themselves to prayer and to the study of the Word of God. Historically, we know that the people were hungry in Jerusalem. They needed food and clothing. The apostles declared these physical needs were important, but our priority is the Word of God and the basics.

Someone asked me some questions this week about the ministry of our church. That is not unusual; that happens every week. But they asked an unusual question that I haven't been asked in a long time. They said, "We know what the church is now, but what is the church going to be twenty years from now?" That is a good question. My answer: Same thing, just bigger! That is it! We are not going to change anything from the basics. Twenty years from now, when you come to church, you are going to hear the Word of God preached and expounded. It may not be by me, or it may be by me, but it will be preached in this place if the Lord has not come. Twenty years from now, this church is going to be about small group Bible study through Sunday School. It is going to be about personal commitment in discipleship, personal evangelism and soul winning. It is going to be the same thing, just bigger! That is what character is about. It is about being the same every time people see you. That is what makes a church great. It is not something new, not the "razzle dazzle," but the priorities of the basics within life.

God has blessed our church, but there is a danger inherently within that blessing. The first time people come to Valley Baptist Church, they are so excited! I hear the testimonies of people every week who are thrilled with the service and the invitation as they see people come and join the church. They cannot get over the fact that people are saved at nearly every invitation, and at nearly every service people are baptized. Those who are new at Valley Baptist are so excited to see what is happening here. But then after a while when they come Sunday after Sunday, it is the same thing! The message is preached, the invitation is given, people are saved, and people are baptized, Sunday after Sunday after Sunday.

The danger is that, after a while, you will get used to it and begin to take God's blessings for granted.

It is like the first time that you fly in an airplane. I remember the first time I flew on a plane. I was so excited at the take-off and the landing, and to look out the window. After you have flown for a while, it is not as exciting. In fact, tomorrow I will be boarding a plane early in the morning, and I am not excited about the trip whatsoever. I am going to try my best to be asleep by the time the plane takes off. If I am not asleep, I plan to be reading something. I am not excited about the take-off; I am not excited about the landing. As far as I am concerned, it is just a means of transportation. We need to experience fresh the blessings of God. The first time you go on a trip, or go to a certain place, or see new scenery, you are excited. There are people who live in the most beautiful place on earth, yet they do not even see it any more. Sometimes you will travel somewhere new, and you will be enamored with the beauty of the ocean, the mountains, or the trees. Yet people who live there kind of yawn and take for granted their surroundings. It is possible for that to happen in a church. We must learn to continue when we are satisfied with the blessings of God. We should not have to have something new to excite us. We need to be excited simply by the Word of God and by prayer, the basics of a church.

Acts 2:46 says, *"And they, continuing daily with one accord in the temple, and breaking bread from house to house, did eat their food with gladness and singleness of heart."* Continuing daily—I like that! That is how character should be measured, and that is how you should measure your spirituality—daily! So many Christians are up and they are down, they are up and they are down. They are either a fever or a chill. They are like a baseball player. They are either a home-run hitter or they strike out. They either hit the ball out of the park, or they fan it and completely miss. We need base hitters. We need people who will hit a single and get on base. That is what character is about. Character is about being the same every day. Character is about being the same every time someone sees you. I know many Christians who, in psychological terms, are spiritually manic-depressive. One day they are manic, they are so excited about God and serving Jesus. They want to tithe and teach Sunday School, and go soul winning. But the next time you see them, they are depressive. They are not in the manic stage now; they are in the depressive stage. They are just dragging. They want to give up, and they do not want to serve God any more. They are way up or they are way down. Character is about continuing, continuing, continuing!

Sometimes people will hear a message on tithing, or they hear about the financial needs of a ministry, and they say, "That's it! I'm going to start tithing." They do it for a week or two, or for a month or two, or even for a year or two. Then they stop. They do not continue! But there are other people who continue tithing, no matter what's going on in their life financially, or with their family. The whole world could fall down around them, and they would still give to God that which belongs to Him. They are going to continue. That is what character is about.

Do you realize that anybody can continue? Not everyone has the gift to be able to stand and preach, not everyone has the ability to teach a Sunday School class, not everyone has the talent to sing specials, sing in the choir or play in the orchestra. Not everyone has great abilities, but everybody and anybody can be faithful. Everybody can continue to do that which God has called him or her to do. Occasionally there are people who say, "You expect too much of people to come to church on Sunday morning, come back on Sunday night and to come on Wednesday night. People are too busy in this culture. It is too much to expect people to come for Tuesday night visitation, or a Saturday men's ministry event, or a women's ministry event or Bible study during the week. You expect too much of people."

Today the emphasis on church growth is toward the "user-friendly church." People are busy with their children playing soccer, baseball and other things, and they are busy with two jobs. They will come to church on Sunday morning but they are too busy to come on Sunday night—and they are certainly too busy to come on Wednesday night. Well, maybe they *are too busy!* God ought to be a priority in your life. I am sick of this idea of making the church user friendly, by lowering it to the least common denominator of people's spiritual commitment. I like what the sociologist, Tony Campolo, said, "It is not that we expect too much, it is that we expect too little in Christianity today." That is why the cults are growing. Cults expect people to give everything socially, culturally and spiritually, to merge their whole life into the cult. Cults are growing because people are hungry to have a defining force in every aspect of their life. Cults are outgrowing all the mainline denominations in America today, not because they expect too little, but because they expect so much! It is not that Valley expects too much, but we are expecting too little!

The Bible says that they were *daily* in the temple. Daily they were at the church; daily they were involved in the ministry of the church. They did not divide their life with their work life over here, their recreation life over here, their social life over here, and then over here is their church life. That is not the way it was. Everything in their life was given to the work and the ministry of the church! They did not have this big secular life over here and a little sacred life over here. Everything—culturally, socially, politically—everything revolved around the church, everything revolved around the mission of getting the gospel out and reaching their city for Christ. We do not expect too much. At times we expect, if anything, too little.

Valley Baptist Church is your home! It is not that you *go* to church. Actually, you *come* to church because when you are here you are coming home! You may go to work, you may go to school but you *come* to church because you are coming home. That big old patch of grass out there in front is *your* yard, so you ought to play in it. That fellowship hall is *your* fellowship hall, so you ought to eat in it. The kitchen is *yours*, so you ought to cook in it, the auditorium is *yours*, so you ought to sit in it, the classrooms are *yours*, so you ought to learn in them. This is *your* home and we are family! We are not asking you to go somewhere; we are asking you to come home! That is what the church is to be. It is to consume the very core of people's lives and their commitment to Christ. "They continued," it says, "daily."

Acts 14:22 says, *"...Exhorting them to continue in the faith, and that we must through much tribulation enter into the kingdom of God."* This verse teaches that we must continue in trials. It is not always easy to serve God. Sometimes we have trials, sometimes we have grief, sometimes we go through financial reversal, or sometimes there are relationships that go sour within families, or within the church family. The key to life is not to quit! The key to life is to continue in the dark until the light breaks through.

Bob Pettitt is a member of the Basketball Hall of Fame. He played years ago for Louisiana, and later he played professional basketball for St. Louis. When he was in high school, he went out for the basketball team. He attended a little rural high school where there were only twelve boys, and he still did not make the team. That is pretty bad, isn't it? I think even I could make a team if only twelve boys were in the high school, considering there are usually twelve on a team! Since he did not make the team, he decided to go out for the baseball team. He made the second string, playing second base. He played in a crucial game. A ground ball was hit that went between his legs, and the coach was so angry that he kicked him off the baseball team! Then he tried out for the football team, and they put him on the line, second team. In a crucial play during one of the games, because he was out of his position, the other team scored a touchdown. So the coach kicked him off the football team. He did not make the basketball team, he was kicked off the baseball team, and he was kicked off the football team. His church started a church basketball league. If you have ever seen a church basketball league, you know that pretty much anybody can play! So he did! By his junior year, Bob Pettitt made the high school basketball team; by his senior year he made All State, in college he was a great player at LSU, and he eventually became a professional basketball player and ultimately became a member of the Hall of Fame! Why? Because he would not quit! He did not make the basketball team, he was kicked off the baseball team and the football team, but he did not quit! He kept going, and because he *continued,* he eventually reached his goal.

One of the keys to victory is that you do not quit, that you do not quit, that you do not quit—that you keep going, that you continue, continue, continue. That is the key to life!

Every Sunday, I preach to more than a thousand people, and multiplied thousands by radio, but it has not always been like that. I remember times early in my ministry when fewer than ten people showed up to hear me preach on a Sunday. I remember some Sunday nights when no one came to hear me. It was just my wife and me, and I was not too sure she wanted to be there! No one came. There is something to be said for *continuing.* There were times I wanted to quit, in that little church my wife and I started. When no one would come, I thought, "Is it worth it? Why don't I just quit?"

Recently I was digging through a box of old stuff and found a financial statement for that church from the early days of my ministry there. Last week our entire offering was over $50,000. This old financial statement, for that particular month, showed that we had $26 in the bank and less than $500 offering for the entire month. Less than $500 for a month, and now we have over $50,000 in one week! Less than ten in attendance and now over a thousand in attendance and thousands by radio! You have to keep going! When things are tough, do not quit! That is what the Book of Acts is about. They continued steadfastly, they continued daily, they continued in the Word, they continued in prayer, they continued in trials. Do not quit!

In Acts 26, Paul said, *"Having therefore obtained help of God, I continue unto this day, witnessing both to small and great, saying none other things than those which the prophets and Moses did say should come."* Continuing to witness! I see so many people who, when they are first saved, start telling their friends about Jesus. They have tracts in their pockets; they tell their neighbors about Jesus, they tell their mom and dad about Jesus, they tell their family about Jesus. Yet after a while they kind of mellow out. They say, "Well, my ministry is to sing in the choir," or, "My ministry is to teach Sunday School," or, "I do something else in the church now." The apostle Paul had another ministry; it was called writing the Word of God. Yet he said, *"…I continue to this day witnessing both to small and great."* Paul never got over it! He wanted to tell people about Jesus.

- Everywhere he went, he must have said, "'I was on the road to Damascus one day, and I saw a light, and I heard a voice, and God changed my life."
- He went to Antioch and he said to the people, "I was on the road to Damascus one day, and I saw a light, and I heard a voice, and God changed my life."
- He went to the apostles in Jerusalem and he said, "Hey guys, I was on the road to Damascus one day and I saw a light, and I heard a voice, and God changed my life."
- He would go into the marketplace and find someone, pull him over to the side and say, "Hey, let me tell you, I was on the road to Damascus one day, and I saw a light, and I heard a voice, and God changed my life."

- He went to the intellectuals at Mars' Hill in Athens, and preached the same message to them. Everywhere he went, he told people about Jesus!
- Finally he was manacled to a soldier, and I think old Paul pulled on that chain and said, "Hey buddy, have you heard? I was on the road to Damascus one day, and I saw a light, and I heard a voice, and God changed my life."
- He appeared before the Emperor of Rome and he must have said, "I was on the road to Damascus one day, and I saw a light, and I heard a voice, and God changed my life."

He never got over it. He kept going; he continued and continued and continued. I somehow think that one day when they took the apostle Paul out of the dungeon to the edge of the city of Rome, as they laid him down on a big old stump and a soldier raised that double-bladed axe high over his head, Paul twisted his neck, looked up at him and said, "Hey, I was on the road to Damascus one day, and I saw a light, and I heard a voice, and God changed my life." He never got over it, and that is how we should be. You have got to continue! Some of you have husbands who are not saved; some of you have friends who are not saved, parents, moms, dads, and some of you have children who are not Christians. You do not know, but the very next time you tell them about Jesus may be the time they get saved. You have got to continue, you cannot give up, you cannot give up, you cannot give up!

Early in my ministry, I started a church south of here and there was a lady attending the church who is with the Lord now. Her husband was not a Christian, so I asked, "What if I go and visit him?" She said, "Oh, don't bother; he'll be hostile towards you. You do not need to go and see him. Every evangelist and every pastor who has been here for years has gone to see him. It is no use." She had given up on him. I said, "I am going to go and see him anyway. I wanted to see a guy like that." So I went, and I had not said ten words about Jesus until he started to cry, and he said that he wanted to accept Christ into his life. You never know! You do not know whether the very next time you tell someone about Jesus may be the time that the Holy Spirit has prepared their heart! It may be your own father, your own mother, your mate, or your children—do not give up. Paul said, I continue unto this day, I continue witnessing both to the small and to the great. I continue to this day.

Let me read to you a quote about a man who ran for office one time and was a failure in business.

- In 1831, he *failed* in business
- In 1832, he was *defeated* for the Legislature
- In 1833, he *failed* again in business
- In 1834, he was finally elected to the Legislature
- In 1838, he was *defeated* for the Speaker
- In 1840, he was *defeated* for the Electorate
- In 1843, he was *defeated* for Congress
- In 1846, he was finally elected to Congress
- In 1848, he was *defeated* for Congress again
- In 1855, he was *defeated* for the Senate
- In 1856, he was *defeated* for the Vice-Presidency
- In 1858, he was *defeated* again for the Senate
- In 1860, *he was elected President!* Of course his name was Abraham Lincoln!

When he was elected, half of his cabinet opposed him. He was asked, "Why don't you fire them?" His reply? He said, "I'd rather rid myself of my enemies by making them my friends." There is a man who was persistent. How are you going to beat a man like that? He failed and he got up, he failed and he got up, he failed and he got up, he failed again and he got up, he failed and he got up, he failed and he got up, he failed and he got up. You cannot beat a man who will not quit!

Acts 15:35, says, *"Paul also and Barnabas continued in Antioch, teaching and preaching the Word of the Lord, with many others also."* These guys stayed where they were. They stayed at Antioch until God told them to move. That is my challenge: Stay where you are in ministry and service until God tells you to move. There is no one who had more of a burden than Paul did. He looked at Asia, he looked at Macedonia and he wanted to move; he wanted to leave, but he stayed at Antioch. He stayed where he was until God said to move. If God has called you to be a Sunday School teacher, then continue until God tells you to quit. If God has called you to be in the choir, then continue until God calls you to quit. If God calls you to work with the boys and girls in AWANA, then continue until God tells you to quit. Do not quit because your schedule is messed up, do not quit because you get tired; only quit if God tells you to do something else.

Years ago, Pastor Mike Miller told a story that stuck with me all these years. It was a story about a little old bowlegged bulldog. The bulldog was walking down the alley one day. There was a chain-link fence behind a house, and there were two big old German shepherd dogs in the backyard. They were growling, the hair bristled up on their backs as this little old bulldog was walking by. There was a hole under the fence, not big enough for them to get to him, but big enough for him to get to them. That bulldog crawled under that hole, into the yard with those German shepherds. They attacked that bulldog, pulling him around like a rag doll and stretching him out. Finally, after about an hour of vicious fighting, limping and dragging a leg, he went back to the hole and crawled under. He went back home. The next day, without hesitation, he crawled under that fence, into the yard with those big German shepherds, and they gave him another whipping. Day after day, for a couple of weeks, every day, he would walk down that alley and, without hesitation, crawl in their yard. Every day, those German shepherds would give him the whipping of his life. Finally, by the end of the second week, he came limping down the alley again. He dragged that leg they had been chewing on and, without hesitation, he crawled under the fence. Both those German shepherds began to whine, and they began to run from that old bulldog. They tried to get under the house and they tried to climb over the fence. They could whip that bulldog, but they did not want to any more because he kept continuing, continuing, continuing! You cannot beat a dog like that! You cannot beat a man or a woman like that. The devil cannot beat you if you continue. Continuing—that is what life is all about, not giving up. Galatians says, *"And let us not be weary in well doing: for in due season we shall reap, if we faint not."* Sometimes it does not look like your life is accomplishing anything, but do not give up, because in due season you are going to reap. Do not give up in a battle.

A battle took place on March 15, 1915, when the British Navy attacked the Turks at Dardanelles. A tremendous naval battle ensued with a heavy barrage from the guns on shore. Three ships had been sunk. Finally, at noon, the British Navy withdrew, never to take the point during the engagement. What the British Navy did not know was that the Turks had only sixty seconds of ammunition left. At that very moment they were preparing to surrender. Had the British Navy been persistent for sixty seconds more, they would have won the battle! Had they continued to press the battle, they would have taken Dardanelles, split the enemy forces, ended the war years earlier and saved thousands of lives. They lost the battle because they did not continue! Napoleon, the great general, once said that in every battle there is a fifteen-minute period when victory could go either way. The general who knows that period and throws everything into the battle at that time will win.

Much like the battle Napoleon spoke of, you are going to find in your Christian life that there is a fifteen-minute period—sometimes it is much longer than that—when you want to quit. You may want to quit on God, and you may want to quit on the church; or you may want to quit on your mate, you may want to quit on your children, or you may want to quit on what God has called you to do. There is a period of time when you will be tempted to quit. It is at that time that you must press the battle and not give up. It was Edmund Burke who said, "Never despair, but if you do despair, press on and work on in despair." I like that! When I think about the great workers and the great preachers for the Lord Jesus from the past, I always think about men and women who continued, who kept at it.

This week I watched an interview on television between Pat Robertson and W.A. Criswell. Criswell was the Pastor of First Baptist Church in Dallas, Texas, for forty-four years. He has been preaching for over sixty years. I marvel at the longevity of his ministry. Through world wars and skirmishes, through the ups and downs of economic woes of that city, he has been faithful in that pulpit preaching the Word of God. I know there were times when he must have wanted to quit. I know there have been times when he must have wanted to go to another church, and take it easier. But he did not give up, and I admire that in a man. He continued!

I think about the people of this church and the heritage that we have. I think about a man like Hugh Abbott, who is with the Lord today. He was a lay teacher of the Bible. After our church began to mushroom in growth, people packed into his classroom to hear him teach the Word of God. But it was not always like that. For decades before, he had taught when there were not nearly as many people in his class, but he had been just as faithful then as he was when there was a great crowd listening to him teach. I think about Macy Owens, who taught Sunday School for over forty years in different places. Faithful people like Hugh and Macy are the people that I admire because they continued, they continued, they continued!

Sometimes in the press of the ministry, and the greatness of the ministry we have here, I become tired. Sometimes in helping people to bear their burdens, I become tired. People come to me with burdens that no one can solve, let alone me—marriage problems, financial problems, problems with their children, relationship problems, problems that are beyond my ability to fix or make better. I become weary sometimes because of the fickleness of people's commitment who are "up" for God and "down" for God, with no consistency in their life. Our staff becomes weary with the workload that we have, and yet they do not quit. The leaders of our church become weary. You may sit and hear someone teach a Sunday School class, and yet have no idea what's going on in their personal life. Your children go and sit in an AWANA session, and the leaders help them to memorize the Word of God and lead them in the games, but you do not know what is going on in that person's personal life that week. You do not know the heartache sometimes that they have, and yet they're still here. They're still continuing, continuing, continuing! This is the key to ministry, and that is the key to a great church like this one. In the army, if you quit during peacetime, you are a deserter; if you quit during wartime, you are a traitor. Friend I want you to know we are in a battle. If you quit on God, you are a traitor.

My friend, we are in a battle!

- We are in a battle for the souls of this city!
- We are in a battle to reach one more little boy for Jesus!
- We are in a battle to save one more marriage!
- We are in a battle to reach one more teenager and change his or her life for God!

Some day the battle is going to be over. I know that you get tired of the battle, and you become discouraged along the way. But it will not always be a battle! Some day we'll be in the dress parade, and we'll pass before the grandstands, and it will not be a queen that will be standing there. It will be the King of Kings and the Lord of Lords! As we pass before the Lord Jesus, maybe Valley Baptist Church will pass en masse as a great corporate unit before the Lord, and He'll cry, "Where were *you* when the battle was won?" There will be a Sunday School teacher who will step forward and say, "I was in a classroom with a handful of boys and girls, teaching them the gospel message about Jesus, Sunday after Sunday, week after week, year after year." Someone else will say, "I was involved in the bus ministry. I was on the bus when it was hot and the boys and girls were screaming! I was out there visiting them on Saturday and calling week after week." Someone else will say, "When the battle was won, I was in the choir, staying late every Wednesday night, and getting to church early every Sunday morning, using my talent for God." Others will say, "I was in some other ministry," and one by one they'll say where they were when the battle was won. Maybe Jesus will bring some little boy from this church and ask, "Where were *you* when the battle was won?" Maybe that little boy will say, "I was on that bus," or, "I was sitting in that Sunday School class," or, "I was the one who received a dollar every week from my momma, and brought a dime of it and I gave it to Jesus faithfully."

Where were *you* when the battle was won? I tell you, friend, when we march as if in that great parade, when the Lord Jesus asks me, "Where were you when the battle was won?" I do not want to say, "I quit." I do not want to say, "I became discouraged and I gave up." I do not want to say, "I didn't keep the commitment that I made."

When the battle is over I want to hear Jesus say, "*Well done, good and faithful servant.*"

～ 1994 ～

In 1994, for the first time in our history, we baptized over 300 people and added 635 new members.

In the fall of 1994, we began another capital fund campaign entitled "Arise and Build." Valley had a dream to build a new sanctuary in which to worship. In November we rented a tent and filled it with more than 2,000 people in what we called "Miracle Sunday." Our people pledged nearly $4 million to be given over the next three years.

"Winter is Coming" was preached on Sunday evening, September 19, 1994, at a "Men Only" service. The altar was open that evening as I preached, and during the entire message the altar was filled with men doing serious business with God.

Winter Is Coming

2 TIMOTHY 4:21

"Do your utmost to come before winter. Eubulus greets you, as well as Pudens, Linus, Claudia, and all the brethren." (NKJV)

I struggled with what to preach tonight. I thought about preaching a message exclusively targeted toward men. Instead, I want to preach a message tonight that's more generic. It is a message that could be preached to ladies as well as men. If I target my message just for men and preach to the specific needs of being a husband or a father, then I am going to be preaching to the mind, trying to instruct. Most of my preaching is to the mind. I try to be instructive, but tonight I want it to be more inspirational than instructional. I want to preach to you from my heart!

It was eleven years ago that God led me to come to California, although I had previously been here for about three years, during which time I started a church on the south side of town, known as Panama Baptist. I left California to attend seminary in Dallas. The last thing on my mind was ever coming back to California. I wanted to settle in the Midwest, where I'd grown up, raise my family there, minister and preach. In the meantime, I received the call to come back here to a little church in Oildale that had been on the decline, with about eighty or ninety people at that time. Sweet, sweet people, though! When the call came eleven years ago, I did not really want to come, but God laid on my heart to come. I will never forget driving up on Panorama late one night, struggling with whether or not to accept the church. God had clearly shown me in my mind that He wanted me to come back to Bakersfield. I prayed that night, and the prayer that I prayed was this: "Lord, I will come if You will give me men to help me build a *great* church."

As I look out at this congregation tonight, I see my prayer was answered. God has given our church some wonderful, wonderful men! I think it was great what Pastor Phil said tonight about the importance of having men in every Sunday School class that we possibly can. Even if you are not the teacher, it says a lot to boys and girls that someone who has whiskers helps with their class! It is important for our children to have role models, to know that men *can* be spiritual and that it is not only ladies who can talk about Jesus' kindness and love. They need to know that some men are not ashamed to talk about spiritual things. I thank the Lord for the men God has given us in our church.

I want us to be open tonight and free. I want to preach from my heart tonight, and I want us to have an invitation that's open. I want the altars to be open tonight, even as I preach. If God begins to speak to you in the middle of the message, I do not want you to wait to come forward to kneel and pray. You come as God speaks to you. Come, as unobtrusively as possible, to pray. I preach in the prison sometimes in Tehachapi, and we have a continuous invitation. As I am preaching, people are coming forward and praying, others are shouting, while someone else is crying. I believe that's the way church ought to be with men. We should be willing to move as soon as God speaks to us. (You are going to have to listen closely tonight. My voice is worn out from preaching three times this morning. I may lose my voice in the course of the message, so I hope you will stay with me.)

From 2 Timothy chapter 4, I want to bring a message this evening called, "Winter is Coming." The apostle Paul said many, many great things.

- In Romans 1:16, he said, *"For I am not ashamed of the gospel of Christ, for it is the power of God to salvation."*
- In Ephesians 2:8-10, he said, *"For by grace you have been saved through faith, and that not of yourselves; it is the gift of God, not of works, lest anyone should boast."*
- In Galatians 2, he said, *"For I am crucified with Christ; nevertheless I live…"*
- In 1 Corinthians 15, he writes an entire chapter on the resurrection of the dead.
- 1 Corinthians 13:13, in the "chapter on love," Paul said, *"And now abide faith, hope, love, these three; but the greatest of these is love."*

No man has ever lived, except Jesus, who had greater insight into human nature than the apostle Paul. No man has ever lived who had greater revelation and understanding of the nature of God than the apostle Paul.

We tend to remember a person's last words as significant, so tonight I want to read for you the last words of the great apostle Paul. To this day, the dying testimony of someone is admissible in court and carries great weight, because the assumption is that a person's dying words are going to be true. A person's dying words are often very significant. We have all heard dozens of sermons on the last words of Jesus, the words He uttered as He hung on the cross. I have preached about fourteen or fifteen messages myself on the last words of Jesus: "It is finished," "Into Thy Hands I Commit My Spirit," "Today You Shall Be With Me in

Paradise," "Father, Forgive Them, For They Know Not What They Do,"—all of those wonderful words.

I remember the last words of my grandfather when he was dying. I grew up on a farm, and my grandfather (I called him Grandpa!), farmed with my dad. When I was a boy, I could hardly distinguish between the two of them. (Actually, it was like having two dads. I thought every boy had two dads!) Every morning Grandpa came over and was there all day as they farmed together. I rode with them both in the pickup truck. When I was little, I could not see over the dash so I would stand in the seat between them.

I surrendered to preach when I was a teenager still in high school. I remember when I began to serve the Lord. One Saturday my grandfather said, "I want you to come and go with me," and he taught me how to be a soul winner. He took me visiting all day long, "marathon soul winning." We went from house to house throughout that community. He'd knock on the door and say, "This is my grandson. He's going to be a preacher and he's going to tell you about Jesus." That was Grandpa's method of teaching someone how to win souls. He used the same method for teaching someone how to swim. He threw them in the river, and they had to swim. They did not drown! I won people to Jesus, so I guess it works!

I was close to my grandfather. He died of cancer in 1976. I was in college at the time, but I drove a couple of hundred miles to his hospital room. He was incoherent and had not recognized anyone for days. They said there was no use talking to him, but I wanted to talk to him one last time. I never went to sleep that night. I stayed up all night with him. With every little movement, I was there by his bed. Early in the morning, he awoke as rational as he'd ever been. We had a wonderful conversation. He told me some things that have had a profound impact upon my life and my ministry. The last words of my grandfather were significant. Last words are *lasting* words.

In 2 Timothy 4, we find the last words of the apostle Paul as he talks to his "son in the faith," Timothy, the young "preacher boy"—perhaps the closest man to Paul on the earth. Paul said in verse 9-12: *"Be diligent to come to me quickly; for Demas has forsaken me, having loved this present world, and has departed for Thessalonica—Crescens for Galatia, Titus for Dalmatia. Only Luke is with me. Get Mark and bring him with you, for he is useful to me for ministry. And Tychicus I have sent to Ephesus."* Paul was in a cold, dark dungeon under the sentence of death. We know he was cold, because in verse 13, he said, *"Bring the cloak that I left with Carpus at Troas when you come—and the books, especially the parchments."* Maybe Timothy had some of the scrolls of the Old Testament, and Paul, a man who knew more than anyone about God, wanted to spend his last days in the dungeon learning more about Jesus. Before he said farewell, his very final words in verse 21 were, *"Do your utmost to come before winter."*

Winter is coming! Paul wanted to see Timothy one more time. Paul would never live to see the spring. His time was short. It was autumn; the days were getting cold. He knew that once winter set in, travel was going to be impossible. If Timothy were going to come, he would have to do it now. He's saying to young Timothy, "Whatever you do, do it now before it is too late."

I grew up where it was cold in the wintertime. Certain things needed to be winterized. You had to put antifreeze in your car but, of course, we do not know what that is like here in California. Every winter when we drive back to Oklahoma, I have to put antifreeze in my car before I leave California. When I go to the station here and ask them to check my antifreeze, they look at me kind of dumbfounded. When I tell them I need it rated for about twenty degrees below zero, they do not even know what I am talking about! Before winter, we also had to wrap the pipes. Those of you who grew up or lived in other parts of the country probably remember having to drain the water hoses, so they do not freeze in winter. There are certain things you had to do, because when winter comes, it is too late. It is too late to patch the roof during the rain. It would be a lot better to patch it when it is dry. It is too late to wrap the pipes once it is freezing. It is too late to drain the hoses after winter has come. Paul said to Timothy, "Winter is coming! Come quickly! Do what you can now, because it is soon going to be too late." That is good advice for us.

Winter Is Coming for the Lost

We need to listen to the words of the imprisoned apostle Paul, because winter is coming. We need to come before winter. First of all, I believe we need to come before winter to the *lost*. Let me do a little survey tonight with you. I am going to ask you a question, and I want you to respond. How many of you, *after* you became a Christian, have ever had a stranger hand you a tract, or tell you about Jesus? I am speaking of someone who came up to you in a confrontational way, and perhaps asked you a diagnostic question: "If you died today, do you know whether you'd go to heaven?" If you have ever had that experience, would you raise your hand? All right, that's less than half of you. Do you find that interesting?

Sometimes you hear stories about a guy who witnesses to someone, or he tries to lead someone to Christ, and then the next day or two that person has an accident and dies. Such stories make you realize that you must live your life with a sense of urgency. I cannot tell you how many times I have preached the last message someone heard before they died. Maybe I preached to them on a Sunday morning or a Sunday night, and within twenty-four or forty-eight hours, they died suddenly, unexpectedly! The last message they ever heard, the last opportunity they ever had was delivered in a message that I preached. That has happened to me dozens and dozens of times. You might be saying, "Oh, well that's never happened to me." There still needs to be a sense of urgency in witnessing.

Less than half the people here have ever had anyone try to share their faith with them. Do you know what that tells me? That tells me that if you take the time to try to lead someone to Christ personally, you are probably the last one who is ever going to talk to that person about Jesus. The fact is that many people live their entire life without anyone ever telling them, in a personal way, about Jesus. No one ever has asked them whether or not they are going to heaven when they die. No one has ever given them a tract. No one has ever asked them about Jesus. They have lived their whole life without that experience. So if you try to tell someone about Jesus, even though they may live ten more years, twenty more years, or forty more years, the fact is that you are the last one between them and hell. You may, in the span of their life, be the only person who has ever told them about Jesus, or ever will tell them. When you witness to someone and invite him, or her, to come to Jesus, that may be his or her last chance! They may live fifty more years, but it could be the last time they ever have someone confront them with the claims of Jesus. Winter is coming!

Recently I had the opportunity to witness to a man in the hospital, and I put it off. I had promised him that I'd go on a certain day, and I did not go that day but went the next day instead. When I got to the hospital early that morning, his bed was empty. He was dead! Winter had come!

I preached a revival a few years ago in New Jersey with Pastor Larry Wood, a friend of Pastor Phil and myself. Larry talked to me about an incident that happened just a few weeks before I got there. He said one day he was in his office and the phone rang. A lady asked, "Are you a preacher?" He said, "Yes, ma'am." She asked, "Are you a Baptist preacher?" He said, "Yes, I am." She asked if he could come over to her house and talk to her. She said they had a terrible problem. He said, "Okay," and went to her house. She met him at the door, and both she and her husband expressed a concern about their son. They said, "We are worried about our son. We are afraid he's into some kind of a cult or Satanism." They led Larry into the young man's bedroom where there were all kinds of paraphernalia of Satanism. Larry thought that he was probably into some really bad things. They asked Larry if he could come back the next day and talk to their teenage boy about Jesus, and he said, "Sure."

Larry said the next day was a very busy day. Even though he was busy doing other things, all day long it was in the back of his mind that he had promised to talk to this teenage boy. The parents had said they would have the boy at the home that day waiting for the preacher to come. All day long he thought about it, but was busy. In fact, once he got in his car and started driving over to their house but remembered something else he had to do. In the afternoon, he forgot about it entirely. Late that evening he remembered that he had promised to talk to that boy about Jesus. He could hardly sleep that night because he'd broken his word.

The next morning he got in his car and drove over to the boy's house. He walked up to the door, and knocked. The door opened and it was the boy's mother. When she saw him she began to cry and even sob. She grabbed him around the neck and held him and sobbed into his shoulder. He asked, "Oh, what's wrong?" She pointed out in the front yard to a huge tree like they have back east in New Jersey. Hanging from the tree was a rope. She said, "Last night our son hung himself right there." The rope was still hanging from the tree. Brother Larry drove me by that house and said, "Right there is the tree." As we sat in the street, this big man began to sob.

His whole body began to shake as tears spilled down his face and he said, "Right there, right there is where a young man went to hell." There are lost people all round us, and *winter is coming!*

Some day it is going to be too late to reach the lost. I try to make my preaching as relevant as possible on Sunday mornings. Occasionally I preach an entire series of messages about marriage, or about stress, or self-esteem. Such messages are called "felt needs," the needs that people *feel,* such as loneliness. But this spring God led me to preach pure gospel messages. I preached a series on the basic Bible stories of the New Testament. Week after week, I told stories about Jesus, and the people with whom He came in contact. We had more people saved in our services during that period of time than any other time, especially little children as they heard the stories of Jesus. I received a lot of criticism for that series! You probably would not think that we ever get criticized around here, but sometimes we do. People criticized me saying, "You are preaching on salvation all the time. You are not doing anything to help us." In fact, one lady came up to me right in front of the church after hearing the sermon and asked, "When are you going to preach something relevant?" I replied, "Well, I do not know of anything that's more relevant than getting people saved."

Even though we had a lot of people saved that morning, I understood what she meant. She continued, "No, when are you going to preach something to help me in my marriage? When are you going to preach something that will help me with my children?" I sympathize with her, and I am not necessarily criticizing that lady. I know what she was talking about, but I tell you, *winter is coming,* and people are lost!

Do you know how lost people are without Christ? Jesus talked about the ninety-nine sheep in the fold, and yet one was lost. He said to leave the ninety-nine and go after the one that is lost. I cannot stand in front of a thousand people and not think about the one that is lost. On a Sunday morning, there may be some little boy who has brought his daddy, who does not simply need a message on kindness, or self-esteem. He is lost and that may be the only time he is ever going to be here. I have got one shot at him, that's it! He will go to hell after that if someone does not reach him. He may live ten years, twenty years, thirty years, but will probably never hear another message about Jesus. Not one! That is what the statistics show. I cannot help it, but if I preach on kindness or on marriage, at the end of the message I must make an appeal to that one who is lost.

Oh, the one lost! I care about the ninety-nine and I want to feed you. But I am also concerned about the *one* who is out there, the one who is outside of the fold because I know winter is coming. The judgment of God is coming, as sure as autumn gives way to winter. The grace of God is going to give way to the judgment of God. We need to come before winter to the lost!

Winter Is Coming for the Lonely

We also need to come before winter to the lonely. A wise old preacher once said, "If you preach to the lonely, you will never lack for a congregation." We live in a lonely world. The world is full of lonely people. In fact, the number one cause of suicide in our country is loneliness. When David, the great king, was running from Saul, he crawled into the cave of Abdullah and wrote in one of the Psalms, "No man cares for my soul." I wonder if there are people in our city who could say that.

We are having fun tonight! It is fun to get a bunch of men together, to preach and sing and eat watermelon, but there are people in this city who are alone. They do not know the fellowship of the brotherhood of Christ. When I have traveled to big cities like Chicago or New York City, one of the things that impress me as I walk down the street is the *loneliness* of people. Right in the midst of huge crowds, you will see thousands of people with expressions of loneliness.

In New York City, a woman inexplicably threw her three little children off an overpass onto the expressway. They were just toddlers, scurrying alongside her and, one by one, she quickly threw them off the overpass. It was all over the news! On the street below, tires were squealing and screeching as people tried to stop. But by the time all the traffic came to a halt, all three little children were dead. The police grabbed the woman, and they asked her why she would do such a thing. As they were putting her in the police car she kept saying over and over, "Nobody don't care, nobody don't care, nobody, nobody don't care, nobody don't care." She did not see any reason for her children to live because her perception of the world was a world where "nobody don't care." That is how many people view life. We are so privileged to know the Lord Jesus and have the joy of His Spirit. But most of the world does not know about Jesus. "Nobody cares," as far as they are concerned.

We live in a city that's full of lonely people. We live in a city full of rest homes where no Christian goes and preaches. I used to preach in rest homes. When I was in college and did not have an opportunity to preach for one semester, I made a commitment to preach in five different rest homes. We went to a different one every night, five days a week. I prepared one message each week, and I preached it five times during the week at five different rest homes. Many rest homes today do not have church services. People are too busy. My sister works in a rest home, and when I was back home visiting, she told about how it is just a "warehouse," a place where people are waiting to die. They lie there day after day, watching the door all day long, all week long, all month long and all year long, waiting for someone who might come in, who might care. For the most part, nobody ever comes. Our lawns might as well be moats; we are so isolated from people! We are uninvolved, too busy in our own lives to care about people.

Did you know that in the pew where you are tonight, you may be sitting shoulder-to-shoulder with someone in pain right now? Maybe there is a man who is going through a divorce? He is hurting, and you do not even know it. His wife may be about to leave him, or maybe she's already left him. It may be that his business is about to collapse, and he does not know where to turn; he is under a great deal of stress tonight, and he feels alone. There are those who are hurt by grief, financial ruin and divorce. Holiday seasons come and go and people who spend them with their families seem so happy. All people are not happy every holiday! Sometimes they are lonely.

I will never forget that first Thanksgiving after my little girl, Charity, died. She died in the fall, September 13, after being hit by a car. All of the family was together on Thanksgiving Day. Oh, we had the turkey, ham, dressing and all the fixings. But the greatest day of pain in my life, other than the day of the death of my daughter, was that Thanksgiving. In the midst of all of that happiness all around me, my heart was absolutely crushed. Right in the midst of a huge family, I felt like I was all alone. There are people like that who are here tonight, and there are people like that in our city. Winter is coming, and we need to learn what it is to come to people who are lonely.

Winter Is Coming for the Lowly

We need to come not only to the lonely, but also to the lowly. In Proverbs 3:34, it says that God *"giveth grace unto the lowly."* In Luke 4:18, when Jesus declared Himself to be the Messiah, He quoted out of the book of Isaiah and said:

"The Spirit of the LORD is upon Me, Because He has anointed Me to preach the gospel to the poor; He has sent Me

to heal the brokenhearted, to proclaim liberty to the captives and recovery of sight to the blind, to set at liberty those who are oppressed..." Think about the ministry of Jesus! He came to the *lowly* people. Some get to the point where socially they are above others and look down on people. Jesus did not do that. One day, a leper approached Him. The law said that lepers had to notify people of leprosy, and so he must have cried out, "Unclean, unclean." The disciples probably scattered, but Jesus walked right up to the leper, whose flesh was rotting, and whose nose and ears were rotted off, and He touched him. He had not felt a human touch for years, but Jesus touched him and made him new. Jesus came to those kinds of people. He was walking one day and there was a blind beggar man sitting beside the road. He had been blind from birth, and though most people had probably ignored him, some people would throw a little coin into his cup. Jesus walked over to the man and knelt beside him. He proceeded to spit on the dirt and make some clay, which he put in the blind man's eyes so he could see. Jesus had time for the lowly. That is what we need to do—come to the lowly. People like that are all around us.

One of the best friends that I have upon the earth, one of the best friends that Pastor Phil has, is a mutual friend whose name is Dan Maxwell. He's a pastor in Oklahoma City. A friend of his told me this story. Dan would never have told me, but a friend of his was with him when this happened. They were in downtown Oklahoma City, the wind was blowing and it was a cold wintry day. It does not get any colder than when the wind is blowing in Oklahoma City and it is freezing. As Dan and his friend were walking downtown, Dan passed a beggar. The man was homeless, was sitting on the side of the street, and obviously was cold. They walked on by, but Dan suddenly stopped and walked back to the man. The man was wearing a thin shirt and a light windbreaker. He was shivering. It was after Christmas, and Dan was wearing a brand new cashmere jacket someone had given him for Christmas. Dan asked the man, "You are cold, aren't you?" The man said, "Yes, sir." So Dan asked, "Would you like to trade jackets with me?" The man stood up and took off that old windbreaker, and Dan took off his new jacket and handed it to him. As Dan put on the old windbreaker, he looked down and saw that the man had old cotton gloves on and the ends of his fingers were sticking out. Dan had on nice gloves that were fur lined, and he asked the man, "Your hands are cold, aren't they?" The man replied, "Yes, sir," and Dan asked if he would like to trade gloves with him. Dan gave him those fur-lined gloves and Dan put on those old cotton gloves with his fingers sticking out. As the two of them were walking off, his friend said that Dan felt as if God spoke to him and said, "Dan, did you see that man's feet, did you see his feet, Dan?" Dan went back, looked at the man's feet, and saw that he had old tennis shoes on and the ends of them were ripped out. He did not have socks on. Brother Dan sat down beside him on the sidewalk, pulled off his shoes and gave them to him. Then he pulled off his socks and walked back several blocks to the car barefoot, in the ragged old clothes of that man. Now, that's what it means to come to the poor. That's what it means to come to the lowly.

Those are physical needs, but all around us there are people who have spiritual needs. In Chicago, many years ago, there was a little boy who went to Sunday school. An obnoxious little guy, he was unruly and the teachers could not handle him so they passed him from one class to another. Sometimes they would send him to the Sunday School superintendent, and he would have a talk with him. Finally, after several weeks, the Sunday School superintendent said, "That is enough. We cannot handle you. You are disruptive, and we do not want you to ever come back." They sent him away. It was not the last time Chicago heard from that little boy, however. As a young man, one evening outside of a theater in Chicago, his body was riddled with bullets and he lay dead in a pool of blood. Photographers from the newspaper came and photographed his body, but it was so gruesome that they were not allowed to publish the pictures. All they were permitted to publish was a photo of the feet of this man. Under the picture of his feet was a caption that said, "Here lie the feet of John Dillinger." What if there would have been someone to guide him in a different direction? A Sunday School teacher and a Sunday School superintendent failed that little boy. They did not come before winter. Winter was coming in that young boy's life. They had no idea about the forces and the violence that were going to be unleashed in that young man's life. Winter was coming, and they had a chance to make an impact on that boy. But they failed him!

The little boys and girls of our city might as well be growing up in third world countries. They will grow up, live and die, and never know about Jesus. The only hope some of them have is that some men in this church will keep those old raggedy busses rolling. That some men in this church will go to their homes and invite them to Sunday School, that some men in this church will stand in a Sunday School class, stammering and stuttering, but let them know that Jesus loves them. We need to come before winter. Winter is coming! Winter is coming! I see little boys and girls riding their big wheels out in their driveways, riding their skateboards and their bicycles. I cannot help but look at them and realize that winter is coming!

Some day those boys are going to be men, but right now they are so tender and innocent. When you tell them that Jesus loves them, their eyes will get big, and they will hug your leg, and they will love on you. But some day, they will be men who will be going down on 19th Street; they will men who will be looking for prostitutes; they will be men whose minds will be racked with pornography; they will be men who will turn to liquor, and their lives will be wrecked because no one came before winter. Winter is coming!

Winter Is Coming for Our Loved Ones

You will not always have your loved ones. When your children are little, or your grandchildren are small, you think that's the way life will always be. But they will soon be grown. Turn around and they will be gone. You need to tell your children that you love them. I am ashamed to say I was twenty-five years old before I ever told my dad or my mother that I loved them. Even though we had a loving family, I was raised in the kind of environment where you did not necessarily say, "I love you." You need to come before winter. You can go to any cemetery in the country on a Saturday, and it will be full of children who are putting flowers on the graves of parents to whom those children never said, "I love you." They waited until winter, the cold wind of winter, and death came before they gave them flowers, before they ever said to them, "I love you, Dad," or, "I love you, Mom."

Herskel Lewis lived in High Hill, Oklahoma. He had three sons. When the boys were grown, they were in business together with their dad. They raised cattle. A man who lived near that area told me this story about Herskel Lewis and his sons. Apparently the boys sold some cattle, and they felt like their dad cheated them, or did not divide the money fairly. There was a big falling out among the family, and they vowed that they would never speak to their father again. During the last ten years of his life, they never spoke to their father, and they denied him even being able to see his grandchildren. Oh, how it grieved their father. They were members of the same little Baptist Church. If the father sat on one side of the church, then the boys sat on the other side. If the father came in and sat close to them, they literally moved to the other side of the little church. They refused to have anything to do with their father. He tried to make it right and straighten things out. He wrote letters, he sent word to them and tried to apologize to the boys. He tried to give them money, but they absolutely refused to receive their father again. Herskel's wife said that he grieved himself to death. He died of a heart attack. The pastor told me that, during the funeral in that little Baptist Church in High Hill, Oklahoma, you could hear those three grown boys sobbing all over that auditorium, weeping and wailing over the death of their daddy. One of the boys, when he walked past the casket, reached into the casket and literally tried to pull his daddy out and through the sobbing, said, "I am sorry Daddy. I am sorry, Daddy. I am sorry." The other boys tried to hold him, until they literally broke down the casket and the table that it sat on. The body almost rolled out onto the floor as they wept and wailed inconsolably, because they loved their daddy so and they had not told him that they loved him. Those young men waited till winter. Winter is coming!

If you have children in your home, do they know you love them? What about your mate? Do you take her for granted? Does she know that you love her? Sometimes people are so cross and angry at one another. So many times in marriage counseling I see how husbands mistreat their wives, and eventually that wife will finally become fed up with it. She has had enough! She says, "That is it! I am leaving!" All of a sudden, that man will change and he will realize that winter is coming, but it is too late. He will realize that he has mistreated his wife and, although he is now showing her respect, it is too late! Winter has come!

My grandmother and my grandfather loved each other. They both grew up in the hills of Kentucky and at age fourteen, my grandmother became an orphan. None of the family members wanted to take her in since it was during a time of terrible poverty in that part of the world. None of them felt like they could afford to raise young May at fourteen. The family got together, and without her input, they decided the best thing to do would be to arrange a marriage for her. My grandfather lived in the community. At twenty-three years old, he volunteered to marry May. The family arranged the marriage, and as soon as they were married he moved her to Oklahoma. She never again returned to her homeland and was never able to see the rest of her extended family. She vowed when she was fourteen years old, and had to marry my grandfather, that she would be a good wife but she said, "I will never tell him that I love him, I will never tell him that."

They grew to love each other. As a little boy, I knew they had a deep love for one another, but I did not know the whole story. I never knew it until my grandfather was dying in the hospital. I learned the story as I was visiting with my grandfather. As he was dying with cancer, I listened to him say to his wife, "May, I do not understand why you will not tell me that you love me? I know that you love me. Why will you not just tell me that you love me?" My grandmother would shake her head. "Please, will you just tell me? Why will you not just say, 'I love you?' We have had a good life together, will you not just tell me that you love me?" Again, she'd shake her head. She never told him! My grandfather died, and in the little Nazarene Church where I grew up in the country, we had the funeral service. I was the only preacher grandson and she had one preacher son, my Uncle Lee. It was our duty to sit on each side of my grandmother, to be with her and to comfort her. When the service was over, everyone left the building except my Uncle Lee, my grandmother and me. We walked her to the casket. I will never forget seeing my grandmother cry, leaning over the casket of my grandfather. Spilling tears upon his cheeks, she cried, "Oh why, why did I not tell him that I loved him? I loved him so much. Why? Why? Why did I not tell him that I loved him?" My grandfather knew that winter was coming, and my grandmother let winter come before she ever told him, "I love you."

I know that you have loved ones and people that you need to come to before it is winter. There are people who you need to tell that you love them and that you care about them.

In 1914, there was a train station in London that was filled with young men who were getting on the train to go and fight the Kaiser. There was a spirit of jubilation and a cheer went up as these young men were going to battle. As a train would come in, hundreds of young men would load onto it. As another train would come, the crowd would chant, "Give them hell!" On the same train platform there was another young man who was going, not to fight the Kaiser, but he was going to the coast to catch a ship to go to Africa as a missionary. Those were the days before missionaries had furloughs like they do today. When a young man went to be a missionary, you knew that he was probably never going to come back home. In the midst of that huge crowd as they were chanting, "Give them hell, give them hell," and a band was playing, a father stood right in front of his son, knowing that his son was going to be a missionary and knowing that he would never see him again. With steam rising out of the train, as it was getting ready to start, and embracing his son with the din of the crowd in the background, this father whispered in his son's ear, "Give them Christ. Give them Christ." He kept cadence with the crowd, as they chanted, "Give them hell." He said, "Give them Christ. Give them Christ. Give them Christ, because they have enough hell in their lives." Winter is coming! We need to come to the lost, we need to come to the lowly, we need to come to the lonely, and we need to come to our loved ones.

I heard about a man who had two sons. The first son, the oldest, was born retarded. He never developed beyond the ability of about a three-year-old. The second son was a straight "A" student and a member of the track team. He made the family so proud. Finally, one day when he was a senior in high school, this son came home, burst through the door and said, "Dad, you won't believe what happened today. I got a four-year scholarship to a college." As they were rejoicing, the retarded son was pulling on his dad's shirt saying, "Daddy, Daddy." The dad pushed him away. Finally, the dad turned to the retarded son and he said, "What do you want, Son?" As he was pulling on his daddy's shirt, he said, "Today, today, today, Daddy, I tied my shoes. Daddy, I tied my shoes today, Daddy." The father looked at that retarded son, who had never tied his shoes in his life, and he looked at that college-bound young man. He hugged the retarded son and he said, "Oh, I love you, I am so proud that you can tie your shoes!"

Wherever your children are, you need to just love them! From the time my children were little, I would hold them in my hands. When they were just babies, one of the things I said ten thousand times to my children, before they could ever understand a word, was "Daddy loves you. It does not matter what you do. Daddy is going to love you. You may break my heart some day, but Daddy is going to love you. You may go out into sin some day, but Daddy is going to love you." I told them when they were babies, "There is nothing on God's earth that you can ever do that will make Daddy not love you!" We need to come before winter! Let's forget about this performance-based love, and let's love our children unconditionally. Come before winter! Spend time with your little children. Spend time with your family.

I started Panama Baptist Church in 1977. On our first Sunday, my wife and I and four other people attended. It is hard starting a church from scratch. It was a lot of work. I did door-to-door visitation. I did not know what else to do! They did not have a lot of books written then about starting churches. I just went door-to-door, trying to tell people about Jesus and inviting them to come to church. I worked day and night. When we started that church, my wife, Ginger, was already expecting a child. Our first child was born in July of that next year. We named her *Charity,* which means, "love." She had blonde hair and beautiful blue eyes. I always thought babies were about as pretty as newborn mice; but to me, she looked like a fragile little doll when I held her. I did not have a lot of time those first two years of her life. The last year I was at Panama Baptist Church, I preached twelve revival meetings, as well as pastoring the church. Then in 1980, when Charity was nearly three years old, we decided to move to Dallas, Texas, because I wanted to attend seminary in order to learn Greek. I was so busy then! I would get up early in the morning; Pastor Phil and I would meet and we'd go to class, sometimes at six. Some semesters we would not have to leave the house until seven in the morning. I would leave before my little girl was up, and by then I had a little son, who was born premature. When we moved to Dallas, he only weighed five pounds, and was about three months old. I would get up early in the morning, I would go to class, and come home for lunch, when I'd have a few minutes with the kids. Then I would go to a job. In the evening, I went to a sales job, came home late at night, usually about ten o'clock, and by then little Charity was already asleep. I would study way into the night, and I would do the same thing the next day, working seven days a week. Sometimes I would work six days a week and preach somewhere on the seventh day. I did not have a lot of time to watch her grow up. Those three years I did not spend much time with her. I was busy trying to learn about Jesus and prepare for life's ministry.

Then when she was five-years old, I became the pastor of this church. Life became very busy with a brand new ministry. I tried to spend time with my family here and there whenever possible. Then in September of 1984 when Charity was six years old, she had her open house at school. Again, I was not there! I was out preaching a revival meeting across town when a speeding car took her life. In an instant, she was gone! *I did not know that winter was coming.* I did not know that the season would be so short. Her death changed the priorities of my life! That was when I began to think about co-pastors and serving with Pastor Phil so that I could have time with my family.

Tuesday of this last week was Charity's birthday. She would have been sixteen years old. This week I would have been helping her get her driver's license. Instead, I went up to the cemetery and lay on her grave, and I thought about this message. I thought to myself, *"I did not come before winter to my little girl."* When she was just a baby, I was starting a church. When she was a toddler, I was in school and was gone. When she was in the first grade, I was visiting day and night. I was feeling guilty about it, and then as I was kneeling there on her grave I thought to myself, "I wonder what she would say to me on her sixteenth birthday. I have a feeling that if she could come back from Heaven she would say, 'Daddy, I am glad you were out visiting. Daddy, I am glad you were telling people about Jesus. I am glad you were across town giving the invitation when I was killed. I am glad, Daddy, that you preached twelve revival meetings the year I was born. I am glad, Daddy, that you did that!' "

You need to spend time with your family, but don't you dare use your family as an excuse not to serve God. Don't you dare use that little child as an excuse not to serve God. Your child deserves someone who will love Jesus. Part of loving Jesus is coming before winter to the lost and to the lonely and to the lowly. Part of serving Jesus is being gone, reaching someone else's little child. I knelt on that grave with my wife and I said, "Dear God, I rededicate myself to preaching your Word. Help me reach someone else's little girl before winter comes. My little girl is gone but there are thousands, tens of thousands, of little children in this city who need some man to reach down and to love them and tell them about Jesus." I said, "Dear God, as you give me breath, help me to be faithful in preaching your Word."

If you become a Sunday School teacher, you may not change America. You are not going to change the world, but we ought to do what we can! We ought to do what we can and reach someone's little boy or some little girl because I will tell you for a fact—winter is coming!

❧ 1995 ❧

Valley Baptist Church continued to grow in 1995. Again, we baptized over 300 people and added nearly 600 new members. For the first time, we averaged over 1,500 people in Sunday School attendance.

In the fall of 1995, we added a fourth Sunday morning worship service. At the time, we did not realize it would be four more years before we occupied a new worship center.

Our choir made their first video recording in 1995 called "Fire of Hope." It would prove to be only the first of many quality recordings of both our choir and orchestra.

"Valley's Vision" was preached Sunday morning, December 3, 1995, on the occasion of our tenth anniversary as a church.

Valley's Vision—1995

PROVERBS 29:18

*"Where there is no revelation, the people cast off
restraint; But happy is he who keeps the law."* (NKJV)

Valley Baptist Church is ten years old! As your pastor, I
believe it is appropriate for us on our tenth anniversary,
to refocus the vision of our church. Proverbs 29:18 says,
*"Where there is no vision the people perish: but he that keepeth
the law, happy is he."* Your translation may not render it **vision**
at all; it may render it, "Where there is no revelation."
Literally, it is where there is no unveiling of God, the people
perish, or as some translate it, the people "wither."

I am constantly asked as a pastor what my vision is for
the future of Valley Baptist Church. Most people want me to
be specific in my response to that question. I know what they
are really asking is, "When are we going to build a new building?" or they are asking, "How big is the building going to
be?" or they are asking, "What kind of target ministries are
we going to have?" Perhaps they are asking when we are
going to be on television, or what I envision the size of the
congregation ultimately will be. Ten years ago this Sunday,
when Valley Baptist was started, we declared that we wanted
to have 2,000 people in Sunday School by the year 2000. We

are ahead of that by about five years. Many people said, "That is the vision of the church, to have 2,000; or that is the vision of the pastors, that we have 2,000 in Sunday School. No, that is not the *vision* of the church. That is a goal, and we are going to meet that goal today. We have a goal for a new building, but that is not the vision.

I have never thought in terms of numbers in relationship to the vision of the church, or in terms of buildings, programs or staff. The vision that I have for this church has not changed, not even a little bit, in the last ten years. I want to share with you some of the ingredients of what my vision is—and yours too, I trust—for Valley Baptist Church.

An Atmosphere of Worship

I hope that we always strive to create an atmosphere of worship. I do not want us ever to become focused upon buildings, budgets or programs. These are simply a means to an end; they are not the end itself. Many times a church gets hung up on such things. They define their existence as to what kind of buildings they will build, who their staff is, or who their pastor is. The primary connection of their church becomes merely social. It becomes merely a place of family and of friendship. I do not want our primary emphasis to be social, I want it to be spiritual. I do not want us to ever get used to what God is doing. I want us to always come with a wide-eyed sense of wonder of God. I do not want this to be a place where we just come and meet friends and family, but a place where we meet God.

A few years ago I had the opportunity to talk to a pastor of a church much larger than ours. In our conversation, I asked him what he believed to be the key to building a great church. He did not hesitate for a moment in his response as he said, "Three things!" I thought to myself, "Now, I'm going to receive some great insight from a man who has been very successful in leading a giant congregation of people." I prepared myself for his answer and hoped I would be able to remember these three things, since what he was about to tell me would be very important. He said, "The number one key to building a great church is parking. Number two is parking, and number three is parking!" I guess they must have had parking problems where he was, because that is what he said to me!

I do understand some of the frustration of administration, providing parking and getting people in and out of a small auditorium. I understand the frustration of not having enough classrooms and using T- buildings. But these are not the things that are important in building a great church. All the buildings that we could build, all the great cathedrals in Europe and all the palatial church buildings in the United States, together, cannot change one life. Not one. That is not what makes a church great! What about the conviction of God, and what about the atmosphere of the presence of God where you sense God during the invitation? These are things that make a church great.

A Japanese businessman once said, "When I meet a Buddhist leader, I meet a holy man. When I meet a Christian leader, I meet a manager." There is something about that statement that *stings*, because there is some truth to it. The modern church today has emphasized programs, staff and buildings so much that sometimes you feel, as a leader in the church, that you are simply managing. I do not want Valley Baptist Church to ever become predictable. I do not want it to ever become manageable. I want us to always be out on the edge where no one knows everything that is going on, where something is happening beyond our understanding. When people ask us, "What is the key to Valley Baptist Church?" I want us to have to scratch our heads for a while and not be able to explain it. I want us to honestly say that we do not know, that it is simply God! I want us to do all that we can, have all the programs and the finest staff we can, build the nicest buildings we can build, but in the end I want us to have a breathless dependence upon God. Unless God does it, it will not be done!

A fancy restaurant has what is known as *ambience*. Ambience consists of several things: the lights are down low, there is soft music playing, (at this time of year Christmas music!) a maitre d' seats you, and you receive a small portion of food when they bring it to you. Usually there are "things" on your plate that are not even edible, like "little green stuff" and "little orange stuff"—it's just there for color! If you are real cultured, you know you are not supposed to eat those things! Something else that is part of ambience is that the bill is high! However, when we are really hungry, do you know what most of us do? We go to a little hole-in-the-wall barbeque place where they have good food, or we go to a great burger place, or we go to a little Mexican restaurant that has good food. When you are really hungry, you are not concerned about the ambience, you go for the food; you do not care about bright lights or what kind of music they are playing or whether someone seats you. You can find your own seat. You are concerned about the food!

One of the problems in Christianity today is that the modern church is hung up on ambience. It is all about being user friendly! It is all about packaging! It is all about market-ing! It is all about making the church look attractive, having the right staff, the right programs, the right buildings, the right ambience! Somewhere in all that ambience, we forget about the spiritual food! The vision I have for this church is that it will always, always be about the food. It will always be about the spiritual food. What is spiritual food? It is Jesus! That is it, and that is why we preach about Jesus:

• His birth in Bethlehem
• His boyhood in Nazareth

- His baptism in the Jordan
- His temptation out in the desert
- His transfiguration upon the mountain
- His trial in Jerusalem
- From the womb to the tomb
- From the cradle to the cross
- From His agony to the ascension
- It is about Jesus!

A Place of Grace

I want this to be a place where people meet God in an atmosphere of worship, but I also have a vision for this church that it will be a place of grace. In the Old Testament, there were cities of refuge. If someone was trying to take vengeance on you, hunting you down to kill you, you could go to a certain city that was a place of refuge. When you were a little kid playing tag, once you touched base, you were safe. They could not get you! When people went to a city of refuge, they were safe. I want this church to be a place of safety for people, a place of refuge. Our city is full of people who have been "beat up" by religion, and hurt by churches. The average church in America averages less than a hundred people in attendance on Sunday mornings, and yet our cities are passing us by. Churches are fighting, fussing and fuming over the color of the carpet, or budgets and personalities, perhaps this faction against that faction, yet they are introverted and barren. I want Valley to be a place of grace. I want the emphasis of this church not to be on rules but on relationships. That is what it is about! So many people's view of God is distorted, and they think that all God is about is a list of things you are not supposed to do and a list of things you are supposed to do. They think it is all about rules. No, my friend, it is about a relationship. It is about a personal relationship with God, where you can enter into a sense of intimacy with God, where God will be your Father and even your friend. The vast majority of people in our culture have the wrong view of God. When they think of God, they think of a giant referee who is about to blow the whistle on their behavior. Some people think of God as a judge, waiting to zap them. Others think of a cosmic cop who is about to pull them over on the road of life. When people come here, I want them to have a right view of God.

You may be asking, "What is the right view of God?" The most consistent image of God in the New Testament is that of a Father. That is God! God is a Father! At times He is a cop, and at times He is a referee, much like every father is sometimes a cop or a referee. But He is a Father. He accepts us, He loves us and He wants to have a relationship with us. I want this to be a place of refuge for people who feel beat up by all the rules, by legalism and by religion. I want this to be a place where people can come after they have been rejected, where they can sit and soak up God's grace, a place where they can heal.

A Family of Fellowship

I want Valley not only to be a place of grace but I want it to be a family of fellowship. You see, the church is to be family, a spiritual family. Families are in trouble in America, so many having become dysfunctional. I want Valley to be a true family. Do you know what a true family is? A true family is made up of people who care about one another. That is why when you miss a day in your Sunday School class at Valley, I want someone to call you that week. I want someone to write you a card, perhaps your Sunday School teacher or a care group leader, not to make you feel guilty because you were not in church, but to let you know someone cares about you. It is not about keeping our numbers up—it is about caring about people. We come week after week and sit shoulder to shoulder with people who have great burdens.

- There are those in this room this morning that are contemplating divorce. You do not know the agony of their home. They have come today, in the midst of a festive atmosphere of celebration, and yet their hearts are broken.
- There are those with us today who are going through the backwash or the wake of a divorce. Their lives are devastated.
- There are those among us today who are in the throes of grief, and their hearts are broken.
- There are those who worship with us today who are terminally ill, and they do not know how they are going to face their own death.

A church is about learning to bear one another's burdens. It is about family, caring for one another. That is the vision I have for this church! My vision is not about numbers, but about being family.

A little girl's best friend's mama died. The little girl went over to see her friend, and she was gone for a long time. When she came back, her daddy asked her why she was gone so long. She said, "Well, I was with my friend whose mama died." Her daddy asked, "What did you tell your friend?" She replied, "I did not say anything to her, I just sat on the curb with her and helped her cry." That is what caring is, that is how a church should be. I hear about problems every week that are beyond my capacity to solve. It would take a miracle from God, and His intervention within people's lives to heal hearts that are so broken. That is God's business, but it is our business to cry with them; it is our business to care about them and to be family.

A Passion to Proclaim

I want Valley Baptist to have an atmosphere of worship, a place of grace and a family of fellowship, but I also want us to have a passion for proclaiming Christ. Do you know that the heart of this church for the last ten years has been leading people to Jesus? That is what our church is about. If you wanted to distill our vision to one thing, it is about a passion to proclaim, to get people to Jesus. I do not know how many people were saved last week, but two weeks ago, besides the seven or eight people who were saved in the service, there were forty-two people led to Christ in their homes by members of Valley Baptist Church. Forty-two people! A couple of Sundays ago, we had a sixth-grade-boys Sunday School class that went to the park for an entire Sunday afternoon and led people to Jesus. Sixth grade boys leading people to Christ! We have youth who go out soul winning. In many churches, the youth do not even want to come to church. We actually have youth that not only want to come to church, but they want to go out and knock on doors and tell people about Jesus.

I wish you could see what I see. Week after week, I stand right here and extend an invitation four times on Sunday morning, and without exception people are saved—every week, every week, every week, every week! I am amazed by it! Some mornings, I think that this might be the week that no one will come. Yet before the day is over, someone walks down this aisle, and usually there are many, many people who are saved. I wish you could see it! No one sees all of it but me. I wish you could see it! I wish you could see as I do, standing right here when someone comes forward. They're facing my direction, as a pastor is praying with them. I see their lips moving, and I see tears flowing from their eyes, dripping off their chin—and I know that right then God is changing that person's life. Their life will never be the same! Sometimes on Sunday evenings, they come and I am privileged to pray with them. I wish you could hear their prayers as they open their hearts to Jesus. In many churches when the invitation is given, people use it as a time to gather up their belongings and get ready to go home. But when we give the invitation, it is a holy moment. People's lives are changed.

I was twenty-eight years old when I became the pastor of this church. I have grown up with this church in the last ten years, and one thing that I have never, ever gotten over is seeing people come forward! Sometimes there's a little child who will walk down the aisle, sometimes with a mom or dad; sometimes they are by themselves. They walk forward and a pastor will kneel with them, and they will pray. As I observe that holy moment, I know that that child's destiny has been changed forever. Years from now when they are forty, fifty, sixty, seventy years old and they look back over the landscape of their life, they will not remember who was preaching or what the message was, and they will not remember who was singing. But they will remember that experience of opening their heart to Jesus. It was *their* day, not my day, not your day, but it was their day when their life was forever changed.

It is a privilege to see people baptized! In the last two weeks, twenty-six people were baptized. Oh, to see them baptized—it is a one-time event in their life. As we observe baptism, for us it is just a part of the service, but for that person who's being baptized, it happens one time in their entire life. It is their day, and I do not want us to ever get over the privilege of seeing people baptized. I do not want us to get over the wonder of God's blessing. Some people ask why we keep pushing, why we installed more T buildings, why we push to build a new building. They say that the church is big enough, we have reached enough, it is manageable and it is a good fellowship. Why don't we just stand still? That is a delusion, a mirage! If we begin to stand still, Valley would no longer be the church that you love. What you love about Valley Baptist Church is that it is a church that does not stand still.

The greatest enemy we have, as a church, is complacency. I fear it more than anything else—that we will become complacent, that we will get to the point where we will say, "It is enough! Let us just stay right where we are." That is selfishness! It is like a house that is on fire. You run out of the house, and you are thankful that you survived the fire. Yet there are others still in the fire. How selfish it would be not to go back into the house and rescue them if you could. My friend, you are saved this morning. You have been saved out of the fire, but our city is still in the spiritual flames. There are still people who need to be saved. We need to do all that we can.

Evangelism is the heart of our church. If you come back five years from now, ten years from now or twenty years from now, I hope that the pastor, whoever it might be, whether it is me or someone else, is talking about getting boys and girls, men and women saved. That is what the church is about, a passion to proclaim. It is not about numbers. It's not about programs. It's about a passion to get people to Jesus!

A Dedication to Disciple

I also have a vision of people who are dedicated to disciple. Once people are saved, we need to help them to grow. What kind of family would it be, if, after a baby was born, the family left the baby to fend for himself? Birth is the beginning, not the end! That is why we have Sunday School! In most churches in America today, Sunday School is kind of blasé; it is relegated to the children; adults do not even go to Sunday School. We have Sunday School because we want people to be discipled, to grow. In an atmosphere of a small group, there is interaction, and Bible study where you can ask questions and learn about Jesus. There are people who will worship with us today who, a few years ago, did not know the book of Job from job. Yet today they are teaching Sunday School because they have been discipled and they have matured spiritually. That is what church is about! It's about growing Christians, not buildings, but believers.

Newsweek Magazine carried an article that said the least demanding churches in America are now the greatest in demand. Isn't that sad? Those churches that demand the least are the ones that people want to attend.

- The lights have gone out in most churches on visitation night.
- The lights have gone out on Wednesday night because there are no services on Wednesday night in most churches.
- The lights are going out on Sunday night in churches all over America because they do not have Sunday night church.

Some people tell us that we expect too much of our people to come to worship on Sunday morning and Sunday night, be involved in Sunday School, attend Wednesday night church, plus come to all kinds of other meetings, work for the Lord in some ministry or sing in the choir. No, my friend, it is not that we expect too much; if anything, we expect too little. When you are saved, God invades your life and He should become the biggest thing in your life! He cleans out little pockets of your heart and your life, and eventually He takes over every area of your entire life.

A People of Conviction

I want us to have a dedication to disciple but I want us to also be a people of conviction. Have you noticed how the line between the world and the church is becoming blurred? Sometimes as pastors, we preach against sin, asking people to give up certain sins. The Christian life is not about rules or legalism. Our motivation is that we love God and want to obey Him.

- I want a church where people will take a stand.
- I want a church where we stand against the atrocity of abortion.
- I want a church where we stand against the social evils of alcohol and drugs.
- I want a church where we live clean lives.
- I want a church where we are committed to holiness.
- I want a church where we do not watch the same movies that the world watches.
- I want a church where we do not use the same filthy speech that the world uses.
- I want a church that, when the world looks at a member of Valley Baptist, they see someone who lives a clean, holy life.
- I want us to be a people of conviction!

That is my vision for the church!

A Spirit of Sacrifice

I also have a vision that we have a spirit of sacrifice. Today on our tenth anniversary, we walk a tightrope between gratitude and satisfaction. It would be so easy for us to spend so much time talking about what God has done, that we miss out on what God wants to do.

Ten years ago today, not many people took notice in Bakersfield as 365 people came together to form Valley Baptist Church. Those 365 people represented decades of struggle of two congregations. Yet, amidst horror stories of church mergers, people came together and bonded. We owe a great debt to the past. In a relay race, the person who runs the second leg of the race owes his best to the one who ran the first leg. If the first guy runs as hard as he can and hands off the baton to the next man, that man who takes the baton owes a debt to the first man—to do his best. The third and the fourth men owe a debt to those who have gone before them, to do their best. That is what I mean when I say that we owe a debt to the past. We have been handed the baton, which gives us great privilege, more privilege than most churches in America today. We also have more responsibility. *"To whom much is given, much is required,"* the Lord Jesus said. As we have been given the baton, we stand in a long line of a great heritage that stretches back, not just decades, but actually centuries.

- I see in our heritage the ancient Christians, bodies scarred with the wounds of persecution.
- I see the martyrs' tombs, stained with their own blood, who died to preserve this Bible.
- I see courageous soldiers strewn across the battlefield, stiff in the embrace of death, dying that we might be free to worship Christ this morning.

We have a debt to the past. But now—now is *our* time! It is our time to sacrifice, but our sacrifice is not in blood and death, but in life, and our time and our money and our talents.

I have been amazed in the last few days to see all of the work that has been done—this beautiful set that was built for the Christmas program, as well as the "Memory Lane" tent that is being used today to celebrate our anniversary. This celebration involved hundreds of people, thousands of hours of work. Some of our folks moved onto the church property, brought their motor homes and have lived here for the last week, working day and night! That is the spirit of sacrifice. That is what makes this church great. As we built this building, there were people in our church who went without buying a car that their family needed, people postponed buying a house and others gave up their vacations to work at Valley. That is the spirit of sacrifice.

A Willingness to Serve

Last, but certainly not least, my vision for this church is that there would be a willingness to serve. If there is a "human key to the success of Valley," it is a willingness on the part of our people to serve! That's it!

That is what makes the church great, a willingness to get involved. The Bible says that the church is a body. Some are hands, others are feet, all of us have different functions within the church. It is a willingness to serve, for *everyone* to get involved, that makes a church great.

During World War II, Sir Winston Churchill pulled England through with the strength of his own will, and would not let them give up. He delivered many great speeches over the radio. There was a time in World War II when the coal miners went on strike. The coal miners provided much of the energy that was needed in the war effort. You could not blame the union for striking because the miners worked in deplorable conditions. The tunnels were narrow; there were explosions. On occasion, it was very dangerous work; plus, it was dark and damp all the time, and some of the tunnels were filled with water. So they went on strike, and declared that they would not return to the mines until the conditions improved.

Sir Winston Churchill knew that coal was important to the war, so he called a meeting of all of the miners. Their vast union assembled, and he addressed them, reminding them of how they were in a battle, that England was in a war for its very freedom, for its future. I am not sure as to the historical accuracy of his words, but the story has been told of what Churchill said that day. "We will not always be in a war. Some day, the battle will be won. Some day England, with the Allies, will win the battle! When we win the battle, there will be a great parade through the streets of London. There will be marching bands, little children laughing through the streets, and we will build a great stand. On that great stand will be the queen, and I will be standing next to the queen. The parade will pass by that review stand, the Navy will come by first, and they will all salute their queen. As they pass by, I will ask them, 'Where were *you* when the battle was won?' and someone from the Navy will step forward, salute and say, 'We were on our ships, we were at our battle stations, manning our guns, when the battle was won!' There will be bands playing, and eventually the Army will pass by. As the Army marches in cadence before the review stand, I will stop them and ask them, 'Where were *you* when the battle was won?' Some young soldier will step forward and say, 'We were in the trenches, at our post, when the battle was won.' One by one the different groups will pass by, and then the Merchant Marines will pass by, and I will ask them, 'Where were *you* when the battle was won?' They will talk about the supply lines and how they were faithful in their assignment when the battle was won. Last of all in the parade, at the very end of the parade, will be you men, the coal miners of England! As the band is playing, you will march together in a great throng, and as you pass before your queen, I will step forward and I will ask, 'Coal miners, where were *you* when the battle was won?' An aged miner will step forward from among you, an old man whose face will be covered with soot, whose shoulders will be stooped from years in the tunnels, and he will say, 'We were in the bowels of the earth doing what we could for our country when the battle was won.'" When he finished his speech, all of the miners cheered and turned in unison and went back to work in the mines, without any conditions being changed, because now they understood that what they were doing was part of the great battle!

Today is a great day of celebration! Make no mistake. Behind the entire celebration, we are in a battle!

- We are in a battle for the souls of this city!
- We are in a battle for some marriage that is about to break up!
- We are in a battle for some heart that is broken, one more child that needs Christ!
- We are in a battle!

Maybe someday in Heaven, there will be a giant parade. Maybe we will pass by a review stand with the Lord Jesus sitting upon it, and maybe we will have the privilege of passing by as a church, as a great family of faith that stretches for decades and decades of service. There will be:

- The Sunday School teachers
- The care group leaders
- The choir leaders
- The AWANA workers
- The ushers
- The building and grounds workers
- The men's ministry and the women's ministry
- One by one, all the different groups of our church will pass by.

Perhaps we will all pass by, and as the Lord Jesus asks where were *we* when the battle was won, we will answer, "We were faithful, serving You, when the battle was won!"

Years ago at the capitol, Martin Luther King made his great speech "I Have a Dream." He dreamed of equality, of brotherhood, of peace. As we begin a new decade of service together, let us dream!

- Let us dream of an atmosphere of worship where God is in this place.
- Let us dream of a place of grace.
- Let us dream of a family of fellowship.
- Let us dream of a passion to proclaim.
- Let us dream of a dedication to disciple.
- Let us dream that we'll be people of conviction.
- Let us dream of a spirit of sacrifice.
- Let us dream of having a willingness to serve.

Let us dream of a great multitude that will pass before the Lord Jesus and hear those words, "Well done thou good and faithful servant."

1985—Worship service in the sanctuary at our first location at 800 Airport Drive.

Celebrating Pastor Roger's 30th birthday at Airport Drive. Pictured are Ginger, Pastor Roger, Andrew and Matthew.

Spring, 1986—Early days at our first location, 800 Airport Drive.

During the early years in our original building on Airport Drive.
L-R: Associate Pastor, Bob Hamlin and Senior Pastors Phil Neighbors and
Roger Spradlin.

1987—Original Pastors on newly purchased property on Fruitvale Ave.
L-R: Phil Neighbors, Roger Spradlin, Mike Miller.

1988—Banquet held at The Civic Auditorium for "Building for Tomorrow"
Stewardship Campaign.
L-R: Pastors Roger Spradlin and Mike Miller.

1991—Roger Spradlin and Builder, Curt Carter, review plans as foundation is begun at current location on Fruitvale Avenue.

1991—Groundbreaking for new building at 4800 Fruitvale Avenue.

1992—Pastoral Staff at new location on Fruitvale Avenue.
L-R: Roger Brumley, Sal Sberna, Phil Neighbors, Gary Mathena,
Roger Spradlin.

1994—Tent for "Arise and Build" Stewardship Campaign for new sancturay.

1998—Groundbreaking for new sanctuary on Fruitvale Avenue.
L-R: Gary Mathena, Phil Neighbors, Ed Green, Curt Carter, Stan Brewer, Randy Fidler.

1998—Construction under way for the sanctuary at 4800 Fruitvale Avenue.

Spring, 1999—Steeple with cross being raised into place on sanctuary.

Spring, 1999—Staff and workers watching the raising of the steeple.
L-R: Mickey Miller, Randy Williams, J.R. Ashby, Fred Buss and Brenda Collins.

1995—Anniversary Sunday celebrating 10 years.

1996—Valley Baptist Church, Multi-Purpose Auditorium.

1999—Aerial view of Valley Baptist Church with the addition of our new sanctuary.

1999—Night view of new sanctuary at 4800 Fruitvale Avenue.

December 5, 1999—Senior Co-Pastor, Phil Neighors, opening in prayer for first baptism in new sanctuary.

December 5, 1999—Pictured are the 136 people baptized the first Sunday evening in our new sanctuary.

December 5, 1999—Three of the 136 people baptized, by Pastors Roger Spradlin, Phil Neighbors and Rich Paradis.

Curt Carter, Sr., builder for all buildings at 4800 Fruitvale Avenue, and Ed Green, Chairman of fundraising for all buildings.

May, 2001—Memorial Day Service, recognizing and honoring World War II Veterans.

Missionary, Karen Watson, gave her life on the mission field on March 15, 2004.

Pastor Phil / Next Step—stewardship campaign for the new children's building.

Ground Breaking for the Children's Building

2005—Vacation Bible School, "Ramblin' Road Trip"

At their Vacation Bible School, Valley Baptist hosts nearly 2,000 children annually. Here popular "earth ball" thrills the kids!

Pictured here are Ed Green and Kathy Redfeairn, Children's Ministry Director, on a Christmas shopping spree with Bus Ministry kids!

*These photos depict
the growth of
Valley Baptist Church
for the past
twenty years.*

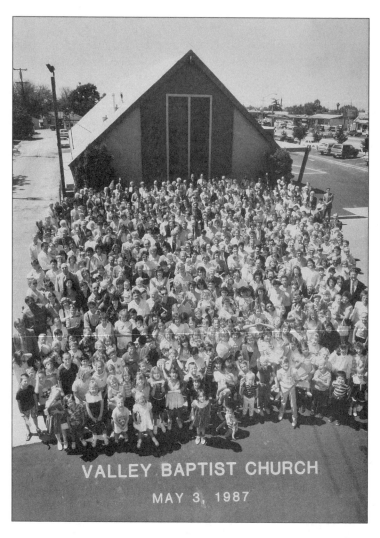

VALLEY BAPTIST CHURCH

MAY 3, 1987

1987

VALLEY BAPTIST CHURCH
MAY 7, 1989

1989

Valley Baptist Church
May 5, 1991

1991

1993

1995

Valley Baptist Church 2002

ᬀ 1 9 9 6 ᬂ

In 1996, we began to feel the pressure of owning only fifteen acres of land. We surged in Sunday School attendance to over 1,700 people. We had a parking problem.

God provided, as always! We bought 11.34 acres from Fruitvale Community Church. This land was across the street to the north of Valley Baptist Church.

Fruitvale Community Church was also blessed by this transaction. They relocated further west and changed their name to Riverlakes Community Church.

"The Ultimate Test" was preached on Sunday morning, June 9, 1996, as part of a series of messages entitled "Faith on Trial."

The Ultimate Test

GENESIS 22

"Now it came to pass after these things that God tested Abraham, and said to him, 'Abraham!' And he said, 'Here I am.' Then He said, 'Take now your son, your only son Isaac, whom you love, and go to the land of Moriah, and offer him there as a burnt offering on one of the mountains of which I shall tell you.' So Abraham rose early in the morning and saddled his donkey, and took two of his young men with him, and Isaac his son; and he split the wood for the burnt offering, and arose and went to the place of which God had told him."

*E*very year, thousands of Southern Baptist pastors leave the ministry, because of discouragement. If you multiply that beyond our own denomination to other denominations, and consider not only those who stand in the pulpit but those who sit in the pews in churches across this country, you will discover that discouragement is perhaps one of the most formidable foes that the church faces. It seems we can deal with open sin and malignant temptation, but we become prey to discouragement as we face trials.

Discouragement comes from failed expectations. We expect life to be one way but when it turns out another way we become discouraged. Somewhere along the way someone has told us that:

- If you are a believer, you will never be sick.
- If you love God, there will never be tragedy in your life.
- If you are serving God, He will exempt you from difficulties.

We know biblically and theologically that these statements are wrong, but deep down we think personally that they are true:

- Other Christians may have tragedy, but not us, because we are serving God.
- Grief will not strike our family because we love God.
- Financial ruin or the loss of a job will not happen to us because we love God.

We fail to see the cycles that God brings us through as believers. Sometimes we are on the mountaintop with God and sometimes we are down in the valley. It is like the old song, "Sometimes I'm Up, and Sometimes I'm Down." The problem is that when we are down in the valley, we have a tendency to give in to discouragement.

In reading the Bible, we have a tendency, as believers, to see *principles* and not *people*. Theory can be sterile and abstract. It is one thing to study the doctrine of suffering; it is another to sit with Job and feel his sores. It is one thing to talk about facing our fears with faith; it is another to spend time with Daniel in the lions' den!

As we look at Bible characters, we need to remember that they were people just like us. Elijah was no superman! The Bible, itself, says that he was a man with a nature like ours. We tend, though, to think that the men and women of the Bible were the varsity squad, and somehow we are second string, or maybe we are even on the bench. The worst thing we can do is to enshrine them, put halos on them and make them plastic saints. Their life message can help us if we look at it as reality. I identify with Abraham, not so much with his faith as with his fears, and not so much his success as his failure. His life is a reminder to me that God is a God of grace. Abraham never parted the Red Sea like Moses, he never called fire out of heaven like Elijah and he never walked on water like the apostle Peter. He was a "garden-variety" man, just like us, yet he was called the "Father of the faith." Abraham and his wife, Sarah, were an ordinary couple. God did not ask them to kill any giants as He did with David, nor did God ask them to build an ark as He did with Noah. But God did challenge them to move across the country, and they obeyed. They believed God in the provision of a child and a family. God did not prepare a fish to swallow them, and yet they demonstrated faith during the ultimate test of life.

Genesis 22:2 was a time when a dark shadow fell across their life, and yet they stood by faith. *"Take now your son, your only son Isaac, whom you love, and go to the land of Moriah and offer him there as a burnt offering."* It is a wonderful story of Abraham going to the mountain and God providing a ram for him to offer as a sacrifice. The story goes on to tell us that Abraham and his son came down from the mountain. We look at this weathered old saint who was willing to give his son, and, from a distance, we applaud his faith. Allow me to help you to enter his world. In essence, God told Abraham, "Kill your son. Kill the son of your old age, the son that I promised you for years, the son whom you waited on, the son whom you named Isaac. Kill your son who filled your empty tent with the laughter of a young child." Can you imagine the shock of that? In whatever way God spoke to Abraham, whether in an audible voice, in his mind, in his heart, or through an angel, those words must have rung in his ear with shock! He was numb, perhaps thinking to himself, "I can not believe that God would want me to do this!"

Shock is always the human reaction to a great trial. People say, "I cannot believe she is dead," or, "I cannot believe that my husband is gone and has forsaken me," or "I cannot believe my son did that," or, "I cannot believe my daughter did that," or, "I cannot believe that my business is collapsing," or, "I cannot believe I have lost my job." Human reasoning follows and we ask, "How could God do this to me? I love God, I am serving God and I am trying to do the best that I can. How could God allow this to happen to me?" The world takes that reaction a step farther, and they begin to question you, "You tell me that God loves you? How could your God allow this to happen? How could a God that you say loves you, allow tragedy and crisis within your life?"

With Abraham there was no such reaction. In verse 3, we are told that he "rose early in the morning, saddled his donkey, gathered the wood, took his son and they left." God spoke to him in the night. It must have been a sleepless night, but as soon as the dawn stretched over the sky, Abraham rose and began the journey of obedience as God had instructed him.

In Hebrews 11, which is kind of a synopsis of this story, there is a verse that says that when he was tested, he offered Isaac. The two verbs tell us that it was simultaneous. In the hour God spoke to him, *immediately* he obeyed God. Procrastination tends to spoil obedience! One of the first phrases a little child will learn is, "Just a minute!" Have you heard that? Go to your room! Just a minute! Turn the television off! Just a minute! Pick that up! Just a minute! Procrastination spoils obedience, but with Abraham there was no procrastination. In the hour that he was tested, he obeyed.

Tests Come from God

Notice some things about this test in Abraham's life. First of all, it was *God* who tested him. It was not fate; it was not an accident. It was God! Verse 1 says, *"It came to pass after these things that God tested Abraham."* Your translation may use the word *tempted*, but do not think of it as a solicitation to do evil. It was a test—a trial, from God.

God will not always build a hedge around us. He does not always insulate us against suffering. There is no such thing as "Disneyland Christianity," where everything runs smoothly and you are totally exempt from life's tragedies and difficulties. In fact, often it is in the storms of life that God proves our faith. This is where we grow! We build faith, not on the mountaintop but in the valley. Sometimes it is not in the valley, but in the *swamp*, in the *bottom* of the valley.

Job was a man whose faith was tested. When his friends tried to console him, they asked a very pertinent question, "Will the rush grow without the mire?" The rush was the most valuable plant of the ancient world. It was a reed type of a plant. The ancient equivalency of paper was made out of the rush. Boats were lined with it so that they would be airtight. Shoes also were made out of the rush. It was a very valuable plant, but the only place that this reed-like plant grew was in the swamp. In order to harvest the rush, you had to wade out into the swamp, out into the muck and mire. During Job's suffering, his friends asked him if the rush would grow without the mire. Is character and faith really built on the mountaintop with God, or is it built in the dark days of trial when we are thrust into a crisis that creates utter dependence upon God? Yet, when we are in the valley, or when we are in the swamp, we ask God to get the mire and the muck out of our lives. We want Him to get the swamp out of our lives, but we never stop to realize that it is in the mire, the muck and the swamp that our faith is built. This is where we mature and grow. Bad things happen in life! Sometimes it is the loss of a job, sometimes it is financial collapse and that is bad. Sometimes a person is sick, and that sickness lasts a lifetime; or a person lives in constant pain. Sometimes a child tears at your heart with his lifestyle, sometimes a mate abandons you, or sometimes you sit across from a doctor and you find out you are terminally ill. It is bad—it is a swamp! But it is in that swamp that the rush grows, it is in the swamp and the muck and the mire of life that God builds character. This test came from God!

God Prepares Us for the Test

God *prepared* Abraham for the test. Verse 1 says, *"Now it came to pass after these things that God tested him."* After what things? After all the other tests that had happened in his life! As a young man, God spoke to Abraham when he and Sarah were living in the Ur of the Chaldees, among a pagan moon-worshipping tribe of people. Again, I do not know how, but God spoke to Abraham. God told him to leave his country and kin and go to a promised land about which he knew nothing. So Abraham took Sarah and all of his belongings, loaded them on the back of camels, and they went to a land, not knowing where they were going. You may be asking, "Well, how was *this* a test?" Have you looked in your garage lately? It would be a great test for me if I had to move everything I have, leave country and kin, and go to a strange land, not knowing where. Abraham did not know when he would receive the land. In fact, they lived in a *tent*. You talk about a test! Maybe that was Sarah's test more than Abraham's, setting up house in a tent all of their lives. Abraham did not own the piece of property that God had promised him until late in life. In fact, the very first piece of the Promised Land that Abraham actually had deed to, was the tomb in which he buried his beloved wife, Sarah. He went, not knowing where; he lived, not knowing when; and he waited, not knowing how. God said that He would make Abraham a great nation through his descendants; they would be innumerable, like the stars above, and like the sands on the seashore. The only problem was, they had no children! They waited, and they waited, and they waited for the child that God had promised them. Abraham was seventy-five, then eighty-five, then ninety-five years old, as he waited for the promise. Finally, when he was one-hundred years old, and Sarah was ninety-five years old, an angel of the Lord declared that they were now going to have the child of promise. Sarah was eavesdropping, listening to the conversation between Abraham and the Angel of the Lord. When she realized that at ninety-five years old, she would have a child, she laughed! Ladies, you would laugh, too! Some of you laughed at forty, but imagine at ninety-five! All of their lives, they waited for this child whom they named Isaac, which means "laughter." He filled their home with fun and laughter—the child of their old age, the child of their faith, the child of promise.

You might look at Abraham and Sarah at this point in their lives and say that God is through with this old couple. He tested them in their youth when they moved across the desert to the Promised Land. He tested them in midlife as they lived in a tent as aliens and sojourners in the land. Surely God is through with them. Actually, there remained one more great test in their lives. In fact, all the other tests were preparatory for this last test. Those earlier tests had built their faith so they could face this great test. God always allows us to climb the lower peaks before we face Mt. Everest. He always allows us to wade in the shallows before we face the rising tide of a great test. The reason David was willing to fight the giant, Goliath, was because he had the *faith*. He remembered that when he was a boy, he fought a lion and he fought a bear. If God could help him defeat the lion and the bear, then God would be with him to face the giant, Goliath. It is in the smaller tests of life that we build faith for the great test that will come. That is why God does not make a Christian's life smooth. You might say, "Well, I am a believer in God, I have placed faith in Christ and I come to church." But then you wonder, "Why is my life filled with daily irritations and frustration? Why doesn't God remove that problem with my boss, why doesn't God remove that physical problem, why can't God remove that irritation and problem in my family?" It is in the routine of life that God is building spiritual muscle for when the "big one" comes. In Southern California, we speak about the "big one"—in reference to a big earthquake! I do not know if the "big one" will ever come as an earthquake, but I guarantee you, as a believer, some day the "big one" will come. Some day, your faith will be placed in the crucible and it will be crushed. Some day your life will be placed in the fire and it will be tested. There will be an "Isaac" in your life. There will be something that God will touch.

- It may be grief.
- It may be a broken heart.
- It may be the fabric of your marriage starting to rip apart.
- It may be the loss of a job.
- It may be terminal illness.

Some day, your life will be tested in an ultimate way, and the only way you will be able to stand is if you have developed faith in the routine of life. From the daily irritations of life, God builds faith in order that you will be able to stand when the test comes.

God Tests Us at the Tenderest Point of Life

Something else about this test I want you to see is that God tested him at the most tender point in his life. There was nothing in the circumference of Abraham's life that meant as much to him as his boy, Isaac. God can order the idols of your heart because God knows all of them. He can order the priorities of your life from one to a hundred. You would be hard pressed to do that, but God could do it instantly. He knows what is of supreme value in your life. He knew with Abraham that it was not the land, it was not the flocks, it was not the material things he had, and it was not even as much Sarah as it was *Isaac*. So God touched the "apple of Abraham's eye."

Corrie ten Boom was a great Christian who spent years in a Nazi death camp, along with her sister. Her sister died at the hands of the Nazis, and years later Corrie ten Boom said, "You'd better learn to hold the things of the world with a loose hand because it hurts when God pries your fingers loose!" This is the message of the story of Abraham. *Nothing* can be ahead of God—not career, not material things, not friends, not even family, can be ahead of God. Jesus said that in order to follow Him, you must hate your father and your mother, and your brother, and your sister. It does not mean literally to "hate" them. It means that the priority of God must be of such magnitude in your life that it dwarfs all the other priorities of life.

> *The dearest idol that I have known,*
> *What e'er that idol be,*
> *Help me to tear it from my throne,*
> *And worship only thee.*

That is hard, but that is the demand of faith!

Sometimes a Test Seems Contradictory

Abraham's test was so difficult because it seemed to be a contradiction. Crises of faith often seem to be contradictory. On one hand, we say that God loves us; we say that God will provide for us, and that He will care for us. On the other hand, there are sickness, grief and trials. How can we reconcile those two things: God loves us and provides for us as a

Father and yet, at the same time, there is pain within life? Abraham's trial was the ultimate contradiction. God told him to take his son, the son of promise who, through his descendants, would be a great nation. Then God told Abraham to *kill* his son. It was not a test as to whom Abraham loved more, Isaac or God. It was a test that involved an apparent conflict between the Word of God and the Word of God. Both were true, "Take your son and kill him," but at the same time, "Your son will be the head of a great nation." How do you reconcile the two? Faith looks beyond what is apparent, and trusts God!

In Genesis 22:2, the Lord said to Abraham, *"Offer him there as a burnt offering."* Abraham knew that command meant the whole carcass. What a difficult thing to even hear when you think of burning your child. In anger, he could have said to God, "Has murder now become piety? Does the God of mercy delight in the blood of children?" He could have thought, "How am I going to face Sarah after taking our son's life? The world will mock the man who slit the throat of his own son." Faith does not argue! Faith obeys! In fact, that is the measure of faith. You can say that you have great faith, but the way to measure your faith is by obedience. You might think, "Oh, I have great faith, I study the Bible, I come to church, I sing and praise the Lord," but the measure of your faith is your obedience. When you scrutinize your life and discover the weakest link is your obedience to God, perhaps in the area of stewardship, or bitterness of heart, or an unforgiving spirit, that is the measure of your faith.

In Hebrews 11, referring to the story of Abraham, the Bible says that God was able to raise up Isaac. Abraham did not understand when God said, "Take your child, who is going to become a great nation and kill him!" How do you reconcile this? Abraham said in Hebrews 11 that he counted that God was able to raise him up. He thought, "I will take his life and then God will bring him back from the dead." He did not understand it all. There are things in life that are difficult to reconcile. We say that God is sovereign, which means God is in charge; nothing happens outside the providence or the power of God. It is a basic affirmation of faith: God is in charge of the world. And yet when you look at our society, you see the righteous suffering and the wicked prospering. Abortion, the murder of unborn children, is legalized and sexual perversion is flaunted. And yet, God is sovereign? How do we reconcile that? How do you reconcile it in your own life? You say that you love God; you have put your faith in God, yet at the same time, you suffer or have trials in your life. Faith believes that God will ultimately triumph! Faith does not look at life in the smallness of one day, or in the smallness of one incident. It trusts that God sees more than we see. That is faith!

Faith Is Contagious

Verse 6 says, *"Abraham took the wood of the burnt offering and laid it on Isaac, his son."* Isaac was no preschooler! You might have in your mind the picture of Isaac being a young boy, but Isaac was a young man, perhaps grown. He may have been a teenager at the very least, but perhaps a man as old as thirty, we do not know. Abraham's faith was contagious. If this young man was strong enough to carry the wood, he certainly could have overpowered his aged father who was well over a hundred years old. Yet, as they arrived at the top of the mountain, Isaac stretched out prone upon the wood, ready to be offered as a sacrifice. Somehow the faith that lived in the heart of Abraham now lived in the heart of Isaac. That is the goal of every parent, to be able to pass the "baton of faith." Abraham did! This is an amazing scene. For three days, Abraham and Isaac journeyed and finally came to the foot of the mountain. Leaving the servants behind, they climbed the mountain by themselves, prepared the wood, and Isaac stretched out on the top of the wood. Abraham lifted the knife high above his son and, with tears spilling down onto his bearded cheek, verse 11 occurred: *"But the Angel of the* LORD *called to him from heaven and said 'Abraham, Abraham!' So he said, 'Here I am.' And He said, 'Do not lay your hand on the lad, or do anything to him; for now I know that you fear God, since you have not withheld your son, your only son from Me.'"*

What a wonderful story! How is it relevant for you and me? Let me give you some application. The first point of application is:

God's Will Always Requires Obedience, But It Doesn't Always Come with an Explanation!

God's will does not always make good sense to us at the time. Trials do not come in thesis form. I wish they did! I wish there was a handbook where we could look at the table of contents, or we could simply read the last chapter. Perhaps we would say, "Oh here is why God did that—it is because He's doing this,' or 'Here is why this happened—it is because He's accomplishing this.'" We see the effect of trials, but we cannot always look back and understand the cause. That is why, when you get knocked down, you shouldn't spend your time looking for explanations. Most likely, you won't find them. So rather than ask why, trust God. That is why it is called faith!

There Is a Cost to Faith

The second point of application is that there is a cost to faith. God touched Abraham at the tenderest point of his life. God has a tendency to do that with us. There is a cost attached to serving God, and there is a cost attached to becoming spiritually mature. Two little children, after Christmas, were playing with a little plastic Noah's ark that one of them had received for Christmas. There were little figurines of Noah and Mrs. Noah, all their boys, their wives and little animals, two by two—plastic elephants, giraffes and hippopotamus. The children played with the animals all day long, walking them up the ramp into the ark. Finally, one of the children who had been to Sunday School said, "We should offer one animal as a sacrifice to God," and both agreed. "Which one should it be?" They looked at all the animals they had been playing with, and finally they decided on a little sheep. They said, "Let's give this one to God." They had no biblical reason for offering a sheep. The fact is that one of the little plastic legs had been broken off, and it could not stand. It kept falling over, so it was not much fun to play with. Because the little sheep was of no value to them anyway, they laid it aside and decided that one would be for God. That is the way we sometimes want to live the Christian life by faith. We want to calculate how we can serve God with the least amount of cost in our life, the least amount of commitment of time, money, energy, talent, and of our soul and heart. Faith has a cost. It cost Abraham!

Trials Bring Maturity

The third point of application is that trials bring maturity. James indicates this is a basic axiom of faith. Abraham is called the "man of faith." How did he become so mature? In the New Testament, when God illustrates faith, He uses Abraham. So how do you get to be the illustration of faith? By facing a lot of storms in life, that is how! God is committed to conforming you to be like His Son, if you are a believer. What does He use in our life? Storms! Much more is learned in the dark than in the light of blessings, and yet we despise the storm when it comes.

One day the rain clouds and a dark storm may come, and people living in the city, perhaps little children, do not want it to rain. They want to go out and play in the park, or maybe they want to have a picnic. They do not like the rain. Far out in the country, however, there is a weathered old farmer standing on the porch with his wife. Together they are watching and scanning the clouds, hoping for rain. He does not mind the wind, and he does not mind the lightning because he knows the rain will bring a harvest. The farmer knows that without the rain, all that wonderful sunshine will turn his crops into a desert. He likes the rain because it brings a harvest. We ask God to remove the storm, wondering why He would allow trials to happen to us. Yet, it is in those storms of life that He is bringing a harvest, a harvest of maturity and a harvest of faith.

Amos, the great prophet in the Old Testament, is called the "gatherer of sycamore fruit." In talking about Amos, one commentator said that as they gathered the sycamore fruit, the migrant workers (of which Amos was a part), would use a piece of metal or a stone to bruise the fruit. It was in the bruising of the fruit that it would ripen and become sweet. If they did not bruise the fruit, it would not be as sweet. The bruises of life come. Sometimes people are embittered by the bruises and become angry, and shake their fist at God. Yet in the bruising of life, God ripens us and makes us sweet. The bruises of life will come. Your choice is how you will react to them. The bruises of life may be:

- An empty place at the table
- A child who breaks your heart
- An illness, maybe a terminal illness.

Don't Waste Your Sorrows

The message is, "Don't waste your sorrows!" Sorrows are going to come. Do not waste them. I know what it is like to be bruised. I know what it is like to hold my firstborn child, limp in death. I know what it is like to open a casket and see the face of a child whom I love. God has used the bruises in my own life in order to bring me to an utter dependence upon Him.

Sometimes a little lamb will run away from the shepherd and he will bring it back, and it will run away and he will bring it back, and it will run away and he will bring it back again. Finally, not wanting that sheep to wander from the flock, with his heart grieved, the shepherd will commit an act of violence against that little lamb. He will take the little lamb that keeps running away, and he will put its leg over his leg, and he'll break its leg. Then the shepherd will put a splint on the lamb's leg, and now the little lamb cannot run away because it is crippled. The little lamb is totally dependent upon the shepherd; it stays by the shepherd's side. For weeks the shepherd feeds and waters the lamb. It is during those weeks when the lamb is wounded that the little lamb develops a relationship with the shepherd. The little lamb becomes totally dependent upon the shepherd. Then one day the pain is gone, the leg is mended, and the shepherd takes the splint off, but the lamb never runs away again. Why? Because that little lamb has bonded with the shepherd! In days of pain, the lamb established such a relationship with the shepherd that it will never again leave the shepherd's side. It will always, always stay close to the shepherd. Sometimes, in the providence of God, there is the bruising of life. In that bruising, we become utterly dependent upon God for our care and our comfort, and utterly dependent on God to sustain our spirits and our life. Even after the pain of a broken heart is healed, the relationship and the lessons that are learned will linger a lifetime.

God Does Not Always Stop the Test

One last point of application is that *God does not always stop the test.* The story of Abraham and Isaac is a wonderful story because of the way it ends. The angel of the Lord stopped Abraham and he pulled Isaac off the altar. They found a ram in a thicket, hung by his horns, and they offered the ram as a sacrifice. It is one of the sweetest scenes in the Old Testament. As the smoke ascended up to God, there was not another human ear on the mountain to hear their songs of praise, as this aged man and his young son knelt in front of the altar offering thanks to God. What a wonderful worship service it must have been! When it was over, they came down off the mountain and journeyed three days back to their camp. When they entered the tent, they must have told Sarah, and she probably shook with fear, realizing how close she had come to losing her son. Certainly Sarah sobbed with joy when she heard the end of the story, the end of the test. Their test lasted three days. Sometimes you come off the mountain alone. God does not stop the test. Sometimes the test does not last three days. It lasts three weeks, sometimes three months, or sometimes three years. Sometimes the test stretches over a lifetime.

When I went through a time of testing in the loss of my precious daughter, Charity, I wrote these words:

Oh, my child, you are dearer than my own life.
I pleaded with God not to let you leave this strife.
I know that you're even happier than before,
You now see Jesus and so much more.
Sometimes in the night though, I think I see you by my bed,
I know it really isn't you, just my mind tricking me instead.
I hear your voice so tender and young,
But I know that you are gone, like a song that's been sung.
It's hard to let you go,
My spirit rebels and says no,
Yet I know that God knows best,
That now you have entered eternal rest.
Will I ever any comfort find,
Those of us who are left behind?
Always when little girls I see,

My heart will break as I think of thee.
I remember Abraham, who offered his son as a lamb,
But God, in His love, provided a ram.
God stayed his hand with a knife,
But of my child he demanded her life.
Abraham went off the mountain with his child by his side,
But mine is gone with a chasm so wide.
I'm left on the mountain all alone,
No child by my side, just a deep moan.
How do I find from the mountain a path,
How can I live my life free from such wrath?
The answer from man I cannot find,
When it comes to such pain, all men stumble and are blind.
Strength does not come from viewing this as fate,
Comfort only comes by leaning on God, who is great.
The answer is, struggle we must,
But in the end, all that can be done is to trust.

~ 1997 ~

Valley Baptist Church had four Sunday morning worship services in 1997, our parking lots were full and the estimated cost of a new sanctuary continued to creep upward!

Early in the year the church adopted the theme, "Whatever it Takes." Late in the year we had yet another capital funds campaign entitled "A Time To Build." This emphasis was for an additional eighteen months beyond the three-year "Arise and Build" pledge period.

Our people responded with generosity and we would soon build a new sanctuary!

"Gray Matters" was preached on Sunday morning, September 24, 1997, as part of a series of messages entitled "Grace Matters."

Gray Matters

Romans 14:1-2

"Receive one who is weak in the faith, but not to disputes over doubtful things. For one believes he may eat all things, but he who is weak eats only vegetables." (NKJV)

Occasionally we are confronted with issues that the Bible does not clearly or explicitly address. Perhaps it is an activity in which we are not sure we should participate, or some belief that we are not sure about. These are the *gray* areas of the Christian life.

The passages preceding Romans 14 deal with issues that are very black and white. Basically, they say that if you are saved, you ought to live a clean life. In Romans 13:13, Paul lists six prohibitions in the believer's life: you are not to walk in revelry, drunkenness, lewdness, lust, strife or envy. He nails down, very clearly, areas in which the Christian should not engage. In other words, if you are a believer, your beliefs should affect your behavior. If you are a believer, your faith should shape the way that you live.

However, in chapter 14, we are looking at the *gray* areas of life. Gray areas concern issues that are not clearly presented in the Word of God, issues that are hard to tell whether they are right or wrong. Sometimes these issues are like moving targets—they change!

When I was a boy growing up in church, at least in the circle of Christians with whom I was associated, it was wrong to go to the pool hall. I remember, as a little boy, walking down the street and wondering what wicked things were being done in the pool hall. I remember when I first heard of churches buying pool tables to put in their basement for the youth. Such churches were considered liberal and corrupt because they had a pool table. It always amazed me that although you could not play pool, you could go bowling. That was okay, unless, of course, the bowling alley had a pool table in it—then you could not go! In our home, we could not play with a regular deck of cards, but Old Maid was okay. I guess it depended on what was on the cards as to whether they were right or wrong.

In certain circles, you could not go to movies of any kind. You could not go swimming on Sunday. In fact, you could not do anything on Sunday! You could not go out to eat on a Sunday, for instance, because that would cause someone to work on a Sunday in preparing the meal. Our family believed that you could not buy gasoline on Sunday. We always had to be sure we had enough gas to get to church, because if we stopped at a station for gas, that would cause someone to work on Sunday.

The only thing you could do on Sunday was go to church and take a nap in the afternoon. As a little boy, I dreaded the long sermons. But what I hated worse than the long sermons was taking a nap in the afternoon, whether I wanted to or not, because there was nothing else to do.

I learned very early in my Christian life that there are many different opinions in the Christian world about what is right and what is wrong. There are even different opinions in our church about what is right and what is wrong.

Some people think, for instance, that it is appropriate to clap during the worship service, and some think that it is not proper to clap. Some people think that, after a baptism, you should only say "Amen," and others think that it is appropriate to clap. So we have the "clappers" and the "Amen-ers" within our church, and other churches as well. People have different opinions about music styles, whether you should sing only choruses and contemporary music, or whether you should sing only hymns.

Opinions have changed culturally about how people should dress when they come to church. When I was growing up, a lady always wore a dress to church. In fact, it was unheard of for a woman to wear pants to church. Gradually that changed during the cold winter months, then on Wednesday evenings, and eventually on Sunday nights. Now, of course, it is not even an issue for most people.

I have been told that many of the Christians in Western Canada feel like it is wrong to wear jewelry. Women who are Christians there do not even wear a wedding ring. Yet as a European Christian, if you were to visit Western Canada, and there was a married lady in the church who was not wearing a wedding ring, you would think *that* was immoral. To Europeans, a woman wears a wedding ring to signal to other people that she is married.

In some circles, even to this day, women are judged if they wear makeup. If a woman is a Christian and she wears makeup, she is judged usually by those who should be wearing makeup!

There are certain parts of the country, certain sects of Christianity, who think it is wrong to drive an automobile—the Amish, for example. They think it is wrong to use electricity, so they sit around kerosene lamps and discuss all the wrongs of the modern world. It is all right to wear buttons, but it is a sin to wear a zipper because that is modernism.

That same group derives their major income from growing tobacco, and yet much of the Christian world would say it is wrong to smoke.

Sometimes there are disputes over doctrinal matters. Churches even split over issues such as predestination and free will. We have both extreme camps within our own fellowship. I heard about a church that split over predestination and free will. One man did not really know which group he belonged to, so he decided he would go with the predestination camp. They asked him, "Why are you here?" He replied, "Well, I came of my own free will." They said, "You do not belong to this group. You need to go and join the other group." He went to the other group and they asked, "What are you doing here?" He said, "I was *sent.*" They said, "Well, you do not belong here if someone sent you. This is for people who freely choose."

The dispute over doubtful things can become complicated. How do you decide about the gray areas of life? Well, that is what Romans 14 is all about.

The church of Rome wrestled with gray areas, although different from our gray areas today. Their gray areas concerned "diets and days." Verse 2 says, *"For one believes he may eat all things, but he who is weak eats only vegetables."* In the church of Rome, there were meat eaters and vegetarians; however, it was not a nutritional dispute. It was a very spiritual issue for those Christians. It is helpful to understand some of the background of this issue. In those days, many of the people in the church of Rome had been saved out of paganism and idolatry. Pagan temples contained idols that the people worshipped. In worshipping idols, they would slaughter an animal, take about half of the animal's carcass, put it on the altar in the temple, and burn it as an offering to the idol. After the sacrifice, they still had half of a carcass left. Since there was no refrigeration in those days, and these idolaters were sort of entrepreneurs, they opened meat markets in the temple itself. So, within the precincts of the temple, there was usually a meat market where you could buy meat, the other half of which had been offered to idols. You could perhaps buy it cheaper at the temple than you could in the regular marketplace.

Suppose you were a Christian walking down the streets of Rome and you saw one of these pagan temples. And suppose they have a special on meat—you know, prime rib for three cents a pound! As you go into the temple to buy meat, another Christian observes you. You are not going in to worship; you are going in to shop! When you go through the gate of the temple, you turn to the right if you want to worship the idol. But if you turn left, then you are in the meat market. The guy on the outside who saw you go into the temple does not know if you are worshipping idols or doing the day's shopping, and he is offended. Finally, after a while when you come out of the meat market, this other Christian asks, "How could you go into a pagan temple? How could you *do* that?" You reply by saying, "Hey, I am free in Jesus! They have a sale on steaks in there!" But that person is deeply offended because they associate the temple with idolatry. So the first issue had to do with *diet*.

The second problem had to do with *days*. Look in verse 5: "*One person esteems one day above another; another esteems every day alike. Let each be fully convinced in his own mind.*" Of course, many of these converts were Jews, and they had been raised to keep the Sabbath. All of their life, they had kept the Sabbath holy which, of course, was Saturday. They did not work on the Sabbath, they did not travel on the Sabbath, and they hardly would even light a fire on the Sabbath. They did not do anything out of the ordinary on the Sabbath. After they were saved, it was very hard for them to stop keeping the Sabbath. Others that were saved were saying, "We do not have to keep the Sabbath. *Sunday* is the Lord's Day, not Saturday. We worship on Sunday, and you ought not to work or do certain things on Sunday because it is the Lord's Day." Others said, "No, we are under grace—every day is the Lord's Day. It is not Saturday and it is not Sunday. *Every* day is the Lord's Day!" Some esteemed one day above another day, and others esteemed every day alike. Eventually it became a matter of dispute. Those were the gray matters of their lives.

I am going to give you some principles on how to deal with the gray areas of life, but I want you to understand that there are some things that are *not* gray in the Bible. For example, the Bible is against drunkenness. The Bible is against lying, stealing, cheating and sexual immorality; these things are *not* gray. Do not think that they are gray areas! Do not read this message and try to apply these principles to areas that are clearly, explicitly addressed in the Word of God.

This passage is about gray areas. It teaches that there are two kinds of believers. Romans 14:1 says, *"Receive one who is* weak..." So the first kind of believer is weak in the faith. But in Romans 15:1, there is the one who is strong in the faith. In this instance, the person who is weak in the faith is the one who thought it was wrong to eat meat. That person is weak. But the one who said it was all right to eat the meat is strong. The one who said that you must keep one day above another is the weak, but the strong is the one who said he had liberty, and every day is alike. The Scripture is talking about individual situations. You may be strong in one area, and in another situation, you may be considered weak. The Scripture is not speaking about how spiritually mature you are in every area of your life, but rather it is about being strong or weak in a particular area of life.

There are not only two kinds of believers, but there are two dangers as well. The danger of the strong is the danger of license. They are tempted to say, "I am free in Christ—anything goes," and to use the liberty of grace as a ticket for sin. On the other hand, the danger of the weak is the danger of legalism, to think that what you *do not* do is what makes you spiritual. This person becomes the "Boy Scout Christian," with a manual that says, "This is right and this is wrong," judging themselves and everyone else by rules instead of relationship.

There are three principles that will help you to decide what is right and what is wrong:

The Consideration Principle—Romans 14:1-3

Learn to be considerate of others. The Bible says, *"Receive one who is weak."* Receive has the idea of *openness*—of opening your arms to them. You are to receive people who are not like you, who do not believe exactly like you, who do not dot every "i" and cross every "t" exactly like you do. You are to receive them, even though you may disagree with them concerning certain issues. There is a big difference between uniformity and unity. We are to be in unity with our brother, but we do not have to be uniform. We do not have to be "cookie-cutter Christians" who believe the same about every single issue in life in order to have fellowship.

Verse 1 says to receive those who are weak. Why do you receive them? Well, the end of verse 3 says, *"For God has received him."* Romans 15:7 says, *"...receive one another, just as Christ also received us."* You are to receive other Christians because God receives them.

You and I did not come to Jesus on the basis of what we do not do. The world thinks that in order to be saved, you must give up certain things and quit your sinning. Then you become good enough to be labeled as a Christian. We know that is not true. We know that you never become good enough to become a Christian. To become a Christian, you come to the point in your life that you know that you have sinned, and you recognize your sin. You confess your sin to God, you accept Christ as your Savior, and you call upon the name of the Lord. That makes you a Christian, and God receives you. It does not matter about all the baggage of your past, or all the things that you have done wrong. God receives you just as you are, as you come to Him in faith. The Bible says that anyone whom God has received, we are to receive, even though they are weak. They may not be as strong as they ought to be in the faith. They may not believe exactly like you believe about every little thing, or dress like you or worship like you. But you are to receive them because God receives them!

Look at the end of verse 1. It says, "...but not to disputes over doubtful things." Let me paraphrase this for you: "Do not jump all over those who disagree with you over doubtful things. Do not become nit-picky." Let me illustrate this in a couple of ways.

When I started out in the ministry in the early 1970s, the big issue of a gray area was long hair on boys. Many in the church said that if you had long hair (and, of course, people defined that in many different ways), then you were not mature as a Christian. In fact, there were those who said that having long hair might have meant that you were not even saved. Yet the fact is that many who had buzz haircuts were wicked! Some who had long hair were trying to serve God.

I remember the first church in which I served as youth minister. The man who had been pastor when I was called there left the church, so they called another pastor who I considered to be a very legalistic Christian. There was an

272

occasion when I wanted to take some young people to hear an evangelist speak. We loaded up two busses with young people, most of whom were lost. I was hoping they would be saved at this revival. The pastor came aboard the bus to have prayer with us before we left, and as he got off the bus he motioned for me to get off the bus as well. He said, "You cannot take most of these youngsters." I asked why and he said, "Well you may not take any of the boys who have long hair." I said, "Pastor, these young men are not saved. They are *lost!* Not only do they have long hair, some of them are even drug addicts. They have all kinds of problems in their lives—they are not even saved!" He said, "I understand that, but they may not go on our church bus and represent our church to hear this evangelist." I said, "Well, Pastor, they are going anyway! You will have my resignation when I get back." I took those young men to hear the evangelist, and watched during the invitation as many of them walked down the aisle and gave their lives to the Lord Jesus, and God changed their lives. I was happy to be able to resign from that particular church when I got back. You may be saying, "Well, if they are saved, they ought to cut their hair." Maybe there is a point when they should cut their hair if it represents rebellion in their life, but the older I get—and the more I notice that my hairline is receding—I kind of admire men who can grow hair wherever they can!

There was another incident in the 1970s, early in my ministry, when I preached a series of revival meetings out in the country, in a little rural church averaging about seventy people in attendance at the time. The Spirit of God moved in, and we had a wonderful revival. After a few days, the building was so full that we opened up the basement and set a speaker down there. Soon the basement was filled, so we opened the windows and people stood around on the outside of the building to hear. We extended the revival for about three weeks, although it was supposed to last only a weekend. Finally, we ended up in a gymnasium that seated more than a thousand people, all from this little church that ran about seventy each week. One night there were sixty-six people saved, which was about what they had in attendance the week before. It was an amazing revival!

I went back to visit that little country church several months later because I wanted to see what had happened in the months that followed that great revival. I happened to be there on a Wednesday night when they were conducting a business meeting. It was a lulu of a business meeting—a real knock-down-drag-out meeting! Do you know what the meeting was all about? Many in the church were upset that some of these new converts were wearing blue jeans to church. This was 1974 in the Midwest, and yet they could not believe that people would wear blue jeans to church. I sat and listened as they continued fighting back and forth for a while, and finally two teenage girls stood up and said, "We do not even know what this is all about, but we heard that if we came to this church someone would tell us how to be saved. We want to be saved." Looking rather dumbfounded, the pastor pointed to me because I had been the evangelist there a few months back. I motioned for these two teenage girls to follow me downstairs where I led them both to Christ. Then I recommended that they find another church to attend because they were both wearing blue jeans as they were saved!

The Bible says to receive those whom God receives. Through the years, I have seen people who were saved, and yet their hair was way too long for the comfort of many people in the church. Or maybe their skirt was too short, or perhaps they were even wearing shorts. Do you know what I have found? If you leave people alone, God's grace is amazing in their life. If they will sit under the preaching of the Word of God and observe the maturity of Christians around them, God will begin to change things in their life if there are things that need to be changed.

The first principle of consideration is to receive them, and the second one is to respect them. Verse 3 says, *"Let not him who eats despise him who does not eat, and let not him who does not eat judge him who eats, for God has received him."* The danger of the strong, those who say it is all right to eat the meat, is that they start looking down their noses at the weak. You will find all kinds of unusual beliefs about what is right and wrong in certain parts of the country. I have encountered Christian people who thought it was wrong to drink coffee because coffee contains caffeine, which they believe is addictive. Because they believe it is wrong for the believer to be addicted to anything, they become very judgmental of those who drink coffee.

Let me show you a verse that will put you out of the judging business. Verse 4 says, *"Who are you to judge another's servant? To his own master, he stands or falls."* When you start wondering about someone, ask yourself, "Whose children are they, anyway?" You would not jump on someone else's child or try to discipline their child. That duty belongs to the parents. Well, whose children are these new converts? They are *God's* children. Whose servants are they? They are God's servants! So let God take care of them! Do you know what I have found? Most people are against things that they do not do themselves, but the things they do themselves are somehow okay. Sometimes those who are against long hair have the longest tongues in the church, and those who are upset about short pants may have the shortest tempers in the church! I am not saying that we should not dress modestly; there are biblical principles of modesty. But the first principle here of deciding what is right and wrong is the consideration principle.

The Conviction Principle—Romans 14:4

"To his own master he stands or falls. Indeed he will be made to stand, for God is able to make him stand." Standing is straightening up. In effect God is saying, "I am able to straighten out My own children." *God* will straighten them out! In verse 5, though, we find an even better illustration. We are not hung up over eating meat or not eating meat because we do not have temples of idolatry today. This verse hits us a little closer to home: *"One person esteems one day above another; another esteems every day alike."* There are entire denominations founded on esteeming one day above another, and in every Christian circle there are those who have opinions about what a Christian should and should not do on the Lord's Day. Many of our beliefs are shaped by our heritage, by the way we were raised. I know that many of my beliefs came from the way I was raised. Our conscience is shaped, not only by God, but it is also shaped by our families. Some people were saved out of paganism.

While I was attending seminary, there was a man in his thirties who had been a Roman Catholic priest, but had never really been saved. He became a Christian, left the priesthood, and came to seminary. For our chapel service, we met in a church building that had kneeling rails, and we were asked to kneel as we prayed, which is a very appropriate way to pray. But this man would never kneel. He would always stand because he associated kneeling with the rituals of his past, and that was wrong to him. It was okay for me to kneel. In fact, it was very worshipful for me to kneel, but for him to kneel would be sin in his own heart. So he always stood when everyone else was kneeling, and I admired him for his convictions.

The Bible says, *"Let each be fully convinced in his own mind."* What God is saying is that there are no absolutes on some issues. To be convinced in your own mind—how do you do that? Let me give you two key principles: Turn to 1 Corinthians 10, where the same issue of eating and not eating meat was taking place at Corinth. Paul sums it up in 1 Corinthians 10:23, *"All things are lawful for me, but not all things are helpful; all things are lawful for me, but not all things edify."* In essence, Paul is saying, "Look, as a Christian, I can do whatever I want. I can eat meat or not eat meat. I can eat all vegetables if I want to. All things are lawful for me, but not all things are going to be helpful. And not all things are going to edify or build up."

Regarding the gray areas of life, the first principle has to do with the question: *"Is this helpful in my Christian life?"* You might be saying, "I am not sure if I should go to this party or not," or, "I am not sure if I should watch a certain movie." Ask yourself, "Is it helpful? Does it build me up in the Christian life or tear me down?" If your response is, "Well, it probably tears me down," there is your answer! You ought not to do it!

The second principle is in verse 24: *"Let no one seek his own, but each one the other's well being."* It is the principle of consideration for others. In other words, if someone sees me at a certain place, will they be offended as a Christian? In the first century, if someone saw you walk through the gates of the temple, they would think you were there for idolatry even if you were there for shopping. Paul said, "Well, then I will eat no meat." The first principle relates to you. Is this activity helpful in your Christian life, or is it hurtful? The second principle relates to other people. Is this activity hurtful to other people, or is it damaging my witness?

The Consecration Principle—Romans 14:6

"He who observes the day, observes it to the Lord; and he who does not observe the day, to the Lord he does not observe it. He who eats, eats to the Lord, for he gives God thanks; and

he who does not eat, to the Lord he does not eat, and gives God thanks." In other words, Paul is saying, "Understand, whatever you are doing, you should do unto the Lord. If you are a meat eater, thank God for steak and eat it! If you are a vegetarian, thank God for broccoli. Go ahead and eat it."

Here is the principle:

Does it *please* Jesus? Do it unto the Lord.
Does it *praise* Jesus? Can you give thanks?

When you are not sure if something is right or wrong, ask yourself those two questions. *Does it please Jesus, and does it praise Jesus?* If your answer is yes, then go ahead and help yourself. But if you say, "I do not think it pleases Jesus, and I do not think I can praise Jesus," then do not do it!

If you wonder whether you should go to a certain party, ask yourself if you can praise God for the opportunity to go to the party. If you say, "No, I do not think I can," then you ought not to go!

If you say, "I do not know if I should dress a certain way," ask yourself if you would be glad to meet Jesus while dressed like that. If you answer, "I do not know," then you ought not to dress that way.

Should I act this way, or should I not act *this* way? Does it please Jesus to act that way? If it does not, then you ought not to do it.

In closing, let me give you three principles for developing convictions:

Interrelation—Romans 14:7

"For none of us lives to himself, and no one dies to himself." Paul is saying that it matters how you behave, not only between you and God, but also between you and your brothers. That is why, in our church, we have some very strict guidelines for church activities. It matters about the church's witness. That is why we also have some very strict guidelines for leaders in our church. We have a covenant that we expect our leaders to keep, some very stringent things where people might cry, "Legalism! Legalism!" It is not legalism, but rather a witness to other people, because we are interrelated one to another.

Lordship—Romans 14:8

"For if we live, we live to the Lord; and if we die, we die to the Lord. Therefore, whether we live or die, we are the Lord's. For to this end Christ died and rose and lived again, that He might be Lord of both the dead and the living." The Lord is the one whom you should try to please. Christianity is not about rules—it is about relationship! But sometimes when you have a relationship, you develop rules in your life. I have a relationship with my wife, so I have certain rules of behavior that I follow. So, out of relationship, sometimes, come rules. If the rules are there because someone else told you that you must conform to the rules, that is legalism. But if the rules are there because of your love for God and your relationship with God, that is not legalism. That is *Lordship!*

I learned early in my ministry that you could not please everyone, so you ought to try to please God. I cannot please everyone in the leadership of this church. Sometimes after preaching a message, I receive letters that say, "You went way too far," and regarding the same sermon I receive other letters that say, "You did not go far enough about what is wrong." I hear comments from people who say we clap too much in church, and others who say we do not clap enough. Some people say we sing too many hymns and others say we sing too many choruses, and it is the same service about which we hear the comments. Do you know what I have learned? I have learned that I must please the Lord. It is about Lordship.

Accountability—Romans 14:10

"...Why do you judge your brother? Or why do you show contempt for your brother? For we shall all stand before the judgment seat of Christ. For it is written: 'As I live, says the LORD, every knee shall bow to Me, and every tongue shall confess to God.'" You may say, "I do not know whether this is right or wrong." Ask yourself this: Would you be able to explain to Jesus why it is right? If you were attending a party and Jesus came back, could you explain to Him what you were doing there? If you were dressed in a certain way, or if you were watching a certain movie when the Lord came back, could you explain to Him why it is okay to be watching that movie? If you are saying, "Well, I do not know whether I could explain it," you had better know, because you will have to explain it some day. That is what this verse says—that we will all give an account before the judgment seat of Christ. This is the judgment where every Christian will stand and give an account of everything done in the body, the Bible says. So you had better be able to explain it, because some day you are going to have to! There are some things that do not have an explanation, and if they do not have an explanation, you ought not to do them. That is the principle—of accountability.

Perhaps you have never received Christ. Let me give you one verse in closing. In Luke 15:2, the Pharisees and the Scribes complained saying, "This man [speaking of Jesus] receives sinners..." Jesus receives sinners, and He eats with them. That is the good news—Jesus will receive you! You may be saying, "Well, you do not know what I have done." I know this: Jesus will receive you! Or you might be saying, "You do not know about my past. I have been wicked." I know this: Jesus will receive you! That is the good news. Jesus will receive you! I have some more good news for you. This church will also receive you. Did you know that? The people in this church have proven over and over that those whom God receives, they will receive. The Church is not a trophy case for perfect saints—it is a hospital for sinners!

~ 1998 ~

We began construction on a new 2,200 seat worship center in 1998. The church also approved an $8 million loan in order to finish construction and refinance the existing $3.5 million loan incurred with the construction of our first building.

In order to gain parking in close proximity to the new sanctuary, the sump on the church property was relocated to the property purchased from Fruitvale Community Church, to the north, at a cost of $261,000.

The dream of a new worship center was finally beginning to take shape!

"The Doctrine of Damnation" was preached on a Sunday evening, March 1, 1998.

The Doctrine of Damnation

"Then Death and Hades were cast into the lake of fire. This is the second death. And anyone not found written in the Book of Life was cast into the lake of fire." (NKJV)

"Hell disappeared and no one noticed!" That's how American church historian, Martin Marty, sums up the attitude of Americans regarding the doctrine of Hell. The fact is, you seldom hear a message about Hell. *Newsweek* magazine published an article titled, "Today Hell Is Theology's 'H' Word, A Subject Too Trite for Serious Scholarship." In the article, Gordon Kauffman, of Harvard Divinity School, believes we have gone through a transformation of ideas, and he does not think there is any future for Heaven and Hell. The fact is, non-Christians do not believe in Hell, Christians ignore it, and even evangelical conservatives are silent, out of embarrassment on the subject. More than any other doctrine in the Bible, Hell seems to be out of step with our time. Yet, Revelation 20:14 says, *"Then death and Hades were cast into the lake of fire. This is the second death; and anyone not found written in the Book of Life was cast into the lake of fire."*

People often say, "I don't think that a loving God would send anyone to Hell." Based on what? Based on our own perception of what we think that God should be like or might be like! We are not to base our beliefs about God upon our opinion, or upon our own conception of what we think He may or may not be like. The Bible is an objective revelation of the nature of God.

Difficulties with the Doctrine of Hell

It is difficult to reconcile the concept of Hell and the love of God. Millions being in torment is absolutely beyond the human mind's ability to grasp. Bishop John A. Robinson, a very liberal theologian who wrote a book a number of years ago, called *Honest to God*, says this: "Christ remains on the cross as long as one sinner remains in Hell. In a universe of love, there can be no heaven that tolerates a chamber of horror. No Hell for any, which does not at the same time, make it a Hell for God. He cannot endure that for that would be a final mockery of his nature." Among theologians, Robinson's view is the popular opinion today regarding the doctrine of Hell. Such opinions are certainly not extracted from the Word of God. They come from a prevalent philosophy of life, not from the Word of God. We live in an age where many want to make the church or the gospel "user friendly," desiring to be as least offensive as possible with the gospel. It's certainly appropriate not to go out of our way to offend people with the message of God.

Years ago when someone would visit our church for the first time, we would have them stand up, introduce themselves, and say something about themselves. Often they would be terrified by the experience. Surveys have shown that the number one fear in America is that of public speaking, and the number two fear is death. So face it—some would rather die than say something in front of everyone at church. Yet we were asking first-time visitors to stand up and tell us about themselves! That was not very user friendly, perhaps even offensive to some people. Consequently, we began to ask guests to raise their hands so we could give them a visitor card. Later we started having everyone else stand so the visitors could remain seated and we gave the visitors a card to fill out. Now most churches do what we're doing. We ask everyone to fill out a registration card so that visitors don't feel singled out, or put on the spot. We should not go out of our way to be offensive with how we do things or say things, but such thinking has led to compromise in Christianity today. In an effort not to be offensive, some have lessened the message of the gospel. Many believe that the doctrine of Hell is going to drive people away.

James Mills, expressing what many have felt, said, "I will call no being good who is not what I mean by good when I use the word of my fellow creatures and if there be a Being who can send me to Hell for not so calling him, to Hell I will go." Another man said that he would not want to be in Heaven with a God who sends people to Hell. His preference was to be in Hell so that he could live in defiance of such a God. If such a God exists, he complains, He is the devil. That is not what the Bible says, but that is what our culture believes. Here is the problem. To us, the punishment does not fit the crime.

Last week someone broke into a part of our church. They stole a couple of computers, a printer and some other things. Whenever a robbery takes place, you feel violated. You want the people to be caught and punished. Our sense of justice is that if you steal, then you ought to go to jail. If you kill someone, then you ought to be locked up and they should throw away the key. In a particularly heinous crime, where someone molests a little child, tortures them and takes their life, we as a society say that person should forfeit his life. In extreme cases, most believe in the death penalty because the punishment should fit the crime. The punishment should not be more than the crime, neither should it be *less* than the crime. When we think of God sending someone to Hell forever who has rejected the gospel, that strains our sense of credulity and our sense of justice.

Most Americans believe in life after death, or at least varying degrees of bliss. Most people in our culture believe that everyone is going to live after death, but some are going to have it better than others, but that no one is going to be sent to a place called Hell.

Alternatives to the Doctrine of Damnation

There are two alternatives to Hell that have been accepted in our culture, even in some Christian circles. One takes the *Hell* out of forever and the other takes the *forever* out of Hell. The first is universalism. Universalism says that everyone will eventually make it to Heaven, or at least some form of Heaven. This theory says that God will overcome all evil, and all rational creatures will be redeemed some day, even the devil. They love to quote verses like Ephesians 1:10 that says, "*...in the dispensation of the fullness of the times He,*" [speaking of Jesus] "*might gather together in one all things in Christ, both which are in heaven and which are on earth, in Him.*" They quote Colossians 1:20 that says, "*And by Him to reconcile all things to Himself, by Him, whether things on earth or things in heaven, having made peace through the blood of His cross.*" They say, "There you go! At the end, God is going to reconcile all things and all creatures to Himself, even Satan." There is a serious weakness in their belief, because Hebrews chapter 2 teaches that Jesus did not die for Satan, and He has absolutely no grounds upon which to pardon the fallen angel. The Scripture says in Revelation 20:10, "*The devil, who deceived them, was cast into the lake of*

fire and brimstone where the beast and the false prophet are.
And they will be tormented day and night forever and ever."
The Bible clearly states that Satan will not be redeemed.
There will be a day when Jesus restores order to the universe. There will be a day when justice will prevail, but that does not negate Hell. That actually necessitates it.

Universalists often quote Romans 5:18 where it says,
"Therefore, as through one man's offense judgment came to all
men, resulting in condemnation, even so through one Man's
righteous act the free gift came to all men, resulting in justification of life." They reason that everyone died in Adam;
therefore everyone is going to be reconciled in Jesus. That
theory fails for two reasons: Number one, you cannot isolate one verse from the rest of the Bible. The Bible clearly
teaches, particularly in the New Testament, the doctrine of
the judgment of God.

Also, the Bible is explicitly clear that repentance is what
triggers forgiveness. Our culture does not believe that. We
not only do not believe that about God, but we do not
believe that in regard to one another and forgiveness. It disturbs me when we talk about "indiscriminate forgiveness"
in our culture. Several months ago, in Paducah, Kentucky, a
young man walked into a school in the early morning hours
with an automatic weapon and killed several other young
people who were engaged in a Bible study and prayer meeting. The next day students hung a big sign out in front of
their school that said, "We forgive you, Mike, we forgive
you." That disturbs me. The reason it disturbs me is because
the Word of God teaches throughout Scripture that forgiveness is tied to repentance. Jesus said, *"If your brother sins*
against you, rebuke him; and if he repents, forgive him. And if
he sins against you seven times in a day, and seven times in a
day returns to you, saying, 'I repent,' you shall forgive him."
God's forgiveness is always attached to repentance. God
loves everyone, but God does not forgive everyone. That

does not mean that if someone offends you and they never ask for forgiveness, you should not at some point release the hurt. Sometimes we are to release the wound and hurt simply for our own spiritual healing and restoration. The Bible connects the idea of repentance and forgiveness.

The second reason that universalism should not be based on Romans 5:18 is that God uses the word *all* in a restrictive sense throughout the Bible. It is *all* in the sense of a category. In Mark chapter 3, it says that *all* went out to hear John the Baptist. Luke chapter 2 says that Caesar Augustus caused *all* to be taxed. In John 3:26, it says that *all* were following Jesus. Was that literally so? No, it was in a broad sense that *all* was used. In Romans 5:18, *all* die in Adam and *all* in Christ are made alive. Not indiscriminately, not everyone will be saved, but *all* that are in Christ. Matthew 12:32, is the deathblow to universalism. It says that anyone who speaks a word against the Son of Man, it will be forgiven him, but whoever speaks against the Holy Spirit, it will not be forgiven him, either in this age or in the age to come. This verse refers to an unpardonable sin! If there is a sin that is unpardonable, then it logically follows that everyone is **not** going to be saved. In fact, in Mark 3:29, speaking of the unpardonable sin, it says, *"...but he who blasphemes against the Holy Spirit never has forgiveness, but is subject to eternal condemnation."*

Universalism leads to *inclusivism*, which says that it does not matter what you believe as long as you believe. The gospel is very exclusive. It does matter what you believe. We can only come to God through Jesus. Inclusivism teaches that every religion is equally valid. Every "ism," every philosophy, is equally true and acceptable. Some people use the illustration, "If you want to go to the post office, you can go this way, I'll go that way, someone else will cut through the heart of the city, and we'll all end up at the post office." The problem is, we are talking about Heaven, not about the post office. If you go to Heaven, you go one way; that is through the Lord Jesus Christ. I'm not talking about a Baptist way. People will be saved out of virtually every denomination, with every kind of belief about the minutia of Biblical interpretation. But there is only one way to God the Father, and that is through His Son, the Lord Jesus Christ.

If universalism were true, and everyone ultimately is going to be saved, then there is no pressing need of the Great Commission. We can just relax! Why are we telling people about Jesus? Why send people out on visitation to lead people to Christ? Let us just relax! Everyone is going to be okay. That is not true! That is not what the Bible says.

The second great substitute for this doctrine is not only universalism but *annihilationism.* Universalism takes the Hell out of forever and annihilationism takes the forever out of Hell. Annihilationism teaches that not all will be saved, and that is true, but it goes on to teach that neither will any go to Hell. God will judge the wicked at the end of the age and cast them into the lake of fire, and they will be consumed. In other words, they will cease to exist. The reason they come to that conclusion is because they say that it's difficult enough to defend God in the light of the problem of evil, but it's impossible to defend a God who would send people to Hell. Think about that! Why do you have to defend God anyway? What we are really trying to defend is our concept of God. We want to defend what we believe about God. God is not a Being who needs our defense. He simply needs our proclamation. He has given His own self-disclosure of what He is like, whether we like it or not. The favorite verse of annihilationists, though, is Matthew 10:28 where it says, *"And do not fear those who kill the body but cannot kill the soul. But rather fear Him who is able to destroy both soul and body in Hell."* Annihilationists say, "God is going to cast people into Hell, and not only their body, but also their soul is going to be destroyed." The word "destroy" in Greek is the word *"apolesain."* There is not a single instance in the New Testament where it is translated as meaning "to cease to exist." If you look it up in any Greek dictionary, you will find that it means to "deliver up unto eternal misery." That is what the word means. Annihilationism does not wash with Biblical truth. Matthew 25:46, says, *"And these will go away into everlasting punishment, but the righteous into eternal life."*

Jesus said that some are going to Heaven and some are going to Hell. If there is no Hell, then there is no Heaven because they are tied together in the same verse. In the Old Testament age, people did not have as clear a delineation of afterlife as we do in the New Testament. Yet Daniel 12:2, says, *"Many of those who sleep in the dust of the earth shall awake, some to everlasting life, some to shame and everlasting contempt."*

Three groups in American religious life sprang up about a century ago that are considered deviant groups in mainline Christianity, particularly in evangelical Christianity. Cults are the most wrong at this point. The Mormons are universalists. They say everyone is going to make it to Heaven. It may be celestial or it may be terrestrial, but everyone is going to make it to some degree of Heaven. The Adventists and the Jehovah Witness believe in annihilationism.

The Basis of Hell

Hell is based upon the justice of God. At the root of the debate is the question, "Is Hell fair?" It seems that the punishment is inappropriate for the offense. For some, the doctrine of Hell makes God appear cruel, unjust, vindictive and sadistic; because culturally we think deep down that the purpose of punishment is redemptive. When you spank your child, or you send your child to his or her room, that is called chastisement. You are doing that for the child's sake. You are not punishing the child; you are chastising him or her. You are using correction to help your child in the future. People whose punishment of a child is not connected to chastisement or correction are considered abusive. As a parent, if punishment is an end in itself and it is not for correction or for teaching, then it is abusive.

In our culture, we even believe that prison is to be rehabilitating and redemptive. That was an issue a few weeks ago when Carla Tucker was put to death in Texas. She had committed a heinous crime of killing another human being with a pickaxe. In prison, she found the Lord, her life had been radically changed, and it appeared that she had been completely rehabilitated. Yet society said she still had to die. Why? Because society said that capital punishment is not redemptive, it is punitive. If you are sentenced to death, rehabilitation does not matter because the purpose of the punishment is justice! Hell is punitive rather than redemptive. Hell is not about rehabilitation. If it were, we would call it purgatory, and people would be released after a period of time.

Judgment is based upon our actions. Every individual will be judged. Revelation 20:12, says, *"And I saw the dead, small and great, standing before God, and books were opened. And another book was opened, which is the Book of Life. And the dead were judged according to their works, by the things which were written in the books."* We are not saved by our works, but our works become the basis of judgment. You may ask, "What about the people who have never known about Jesus? How could God judge them?" The Bible says in Romans 1:20, *"For since the creation of the world His invisible attributes are clearly seen, being understood by the things that are made, even His eternal power and Godhead, so that they are without excuse."* In Romans 2:14 and 15, it says, *"For when Gentiles, who do not have the law, by nature do the things in the law, these, although not having the law, are a law themselves, who show the work of the law written in their hearts, their conscience also bearing witness, and between themselves their thoughts accusing or else excusing them."* God says that even those who have never heard the name of Jesus can look up at the heavens and realize that there is a Creator and that we are accountable to Him. The law of God is written on their hearts. They have never read the Ten Commandments, but they know that it is wrong to lie, they know it is wrong to steal, they know it is wrong to murder. God holds them accountable for the knowledge that they have. I do not know how all that is going to play out, but that is what the Bible teaches.

The Bible clearly teaches degrees of punishment in Hell. Some people think that if they go to Hell, everyone is together. That is not what the Bible teaches, otherwise why would there be a judgment? The judgment of God is to determine punishment, otherwise God would sort people at the end of time and say, "If you are saved, come over here. If you are lost, go over there." The saved would go to Heaven and the lost would go to Hell. There is such a judgment but there is also a judgment that determines severity of punishment. There is even a judgment for believers. We will be judged according to what we have done, in order to determine the reward level that we will have in Heaven. Matthew 11:20 says, *"Then He began to rebuke the cities in which most of His mighty works had been done, because they did not repent: 'Woe to you, Chorazin! Woe to you, Bethsaida! For if the mighty works which were done in you had been done in Tyre and Sidon, they would have repented long ago in sackcloth and ashes. But I say to you, it will be more tolerable for Tyre and Sidon in the day of judgment than for you. And you, Capernaum, who are exalted to heaven, will be brought down to Hades; for if the mighty works which were done in you had been done in Sodom, it would have remained until this day. But I say to you that it shall be more tolerable for the land of Sodom in the day of judgment than for you.'"* Jesus is speaking of the severity of judgment against certain cities.

In Luke 12, Jesus tells this parable: *"And that servant who knew his master's will, and did not prepare himself or do according to his will, shall be beaten with many stripes. But he who did not know, yet committed things deserving of stripes, shall be beaten with few. For everyone to whom much is given, from him much will be required; and to whom much has been committed, of him they will ask the more."* Clearly, the Bible teaches the degrees of punishment.

Luke 20, beginning in verse 45, says, *"Then in the hearing of all the people He said to His disciples. 'Beware of the scribes, who desire to go around in long robes, love greetings in the marketplaces, the best seats in the synagogues, and the best places at feasts, who devour widows' houses, and for a pretense make long prayers. These will receive greater condemnation.'"*

Revelation, 20:12 says, *"And I saw the dead, small and great, standing before God, and books were opened. And another book was opened...And the dead were judged according to their works."*

John chapter 19 says, *"Then Pilate said to Him, 'Are You not speaking to me? Do You not know that I have the power to crucify You and power to release You?' Jesus answered, 'You could have no power at all against Me unless it had been given to you from above. Therefore the one who delivered Me to you has the greater sin.'"* I do not know where the idea started that sin is sin, that one sin is just as bad as any other sin. If you murder someone, that is sin; if you tell a little lie, that is sin. It is all the same in the sight of God. No! There are degrees of offense against God. There are degrees of offense in our own sense of justice in our society. Is it the same thing to steal a piece of candy as it is to molest and murder a child? No. Is one sin the same as another? In one sense it is.

James 2:10 says, "*For whoever shall keep the whole law, and yet stumble in one point, he is guilty of all.*" What does it take to condemn a person? It takes one sin. Does that mean then that all sins are absolutely equal before God? No, it does not. There are some sins that will receive a much greater condemnation from God. Some sins bear a much greater consequence in this life and in the next life. That is why there is going to be a judgment. Every day of a person's life is going to be analyzed, every hidden thought is going to be examined, every motive is going to be laid bare. So there will be no mistake regarding the innocent or loopholes for the guilty. There are degrees of punishment. That is justice, so all blame will be settled. A child who turns to drugs to escape the abuse of his parents will be judged. The parents who rejected that child will be judged. All blame will be settled. Heaven is a comforting doctrine; Hell is a comforting doctrine also because every court case will be reopened!

- Every rapist will be caught!
- Every murderer will be brought into account!
- There will be no unsolved crimes before God!
- No one will get away with anything!
- At the end, there will be just retribution by God.

That is why we do not have to take matters into our own hands regarding retribution.

The second point in this area is that unbelievers are eternally guilty. Hell exists because no human suffering can pay for sins. If human suffering could pay for sin, then people would go to Hell and suffer for a while—maybe a year, two years, five years—and then they would get out because they would have paid the penalty. The doctrine of Hell exists to show us that no human can pay the price of sin. That is why Jesus had to die. If a human being could pay the price of his own sin, then that nullifies what Jesus did on the cross. It mocks God in sending His Son to die for us. It lessens the effect of redemption for man. Sir Francis Newton, a man who ridiculed Christianity, is quoted on his deathbed as saying these terrifying words: "Oh, that I was to lie a thousand years upon fire that is never quenched, to purchase the favor of God, and be united to Him again, but it is a fruitless wish. Millions and millions of years would bring me no nearer to the end of my torments than one poor hour. Oh, eternity, eternity, forever and ever, oh, the insufferable pains of Hell." He should have cried for mercy but he did not, yet he understood that if he went to Hell he could never pay the penalty.

We Cannot Comprehend the Seriousness of Sin

Hell is offensive to us because we are insensitive to sin. Is there anyone who would blame a parent whose child was abducted, molested, tortured and put to death for crying out on television for the death penalty for the murderer? No, we do not blame such a mother or father because we realize the gravity of the offense committed against them. The greatness of sin is determined by the greatness of the one that is offended. It is God who has created us, it is God who sent His Son and it is His own beloved Son whom the world has rejected. Hebrews 10 says, *"For if we sin willfully after we have received the knowledge of the truth, there no longer remains a sacrifice for sins, but a certain fearful expectation of judgment, and fiery indignation which will devour the adversaries. Anyone who has rejected Moses' law dies without mercy on the testimony of two or three witnesses. Of how much worse punishment, do you suppose, will he be thought worthy who has trampled the Son of God underfoot, counted the blood of the covenant by which he was sanctified a common thing, and insulted the Spirit of grace? For we know Him who said, 'Vengeance is Mine, I will repay,' says the Lord. And again, 'The LORD will judge His people.' It is a fearful thing to fall into the hands of the living God.''*

God declares that when the world rejects Him, they are tracking through the blood of His Son. As a parent cries for the death penalty for someone who has molested and tortured their child, God says that when you reject My Son, it is an infinite crime that cannot be paid for in this life nor in the next, so infinite punishment must be meted out. The reason we are offended by the doctrine of Hell is because we do not correctly perceive the seriousness of our offense against God. When the Bible describes sin, it talks about sin as a dog that returns to its vomit, it talks about sin as a poison serpent, it talks about sin as filthy rags, it talks about sin as a rotten corpse in a sepulcher, it talks about sin as leaven, it talks about sin as leprosy.

God loves us, but God is also a God of justice. Suppose a certain judge was given the responsibility to mete out justice, and a murderer or rapist appeared before him. Imagine the judge saying to the criminal, "I love you so much, I am going to release you, I am not going to hold you accountable. I know that you have committed these heinous crimes, but because I love you I am going to release you." Would you say that he is a good judge? No, of course not! He is not a good judge. A good judge metes out justice. Would God be good if He did not mete out justice? No, He would no longer be a God of justice. We must balance the concept of the love of God with the justice of God. We must accept God as He is revealed in the Word of God. It is foolish for people to say, "If God is like that, I do not want to go to Heaven. I will just go to Hell and defy Him." Well, that will really show Him, will it not? That is making the point the hard way. It would be like a mouse standing in a field in front of the farmer's tractor, saying, "I am going to stand before this tractor and I am going to defy the farmer.

No, that little mouse is going to get plowed under! As the tractor is beyond the mouse, God is infinite beyond us. When we stand in defiance of His justice, all we will receive is His wrath.

God allows suffering today. He has allowed suffering for thousands of years, so what makes you think that He will not allow suffering in eternity for those who have rejected His Son? You may feel that your sense of justice is superior to God's. What are you going to do? Are you going to go to Heaven and straighten God out regarding His sense of justice? That is what Job tried to do, and God said to Job, "Where were *you* when I created the world, where were *you* when I laid down the ABC's of what is right and wrong. Before there was anything, I set the ethics of the universe, and I determined what is right and wrong."

A Description of Hell

In the New Testament, Hell is called *Gehenna*, which was a garbage dump outside of Jerusalem. Incidentally, it received its name from Ahaz, who offered his children as a burnt offering, a human sacrifice in the valley of Henna. The people decided not to farm that spot of land but instead they would use it as a dump because a king sacrificed his children there. Jesus identified *Gehenna*, the garbage dump, as what Hell must be like. You may think that Jesus would not talk about Hell. The word *Gehenna* occurs twelve times in the New Testament, and eleven times it was out of the mouth of Jesus Himself! Jesus talked more about Hell than He ever talked about Heaven. Luke 16 tells us about a rich man being in torment in Hades. He lifted up his eyes and cried out, *"Father Abraham, have mercy on me, and send Lazarus that he may dip the tip of his finger in water and cool my tongue, for I am tormented in this flame."* Hell evidently is a place of memory. He said, *"...I have five brothers, that he may testify to them, lest they also come to this place of torment."*

You may wonder if there is literal fire in Hell. That is the language of the Bible. You may wonder if it is merely symbolic. It may, in fact, be. I do not know, but I do know that the reality is always greater than the symbolism. If there is not literal fire in Hell, then it is a reality beyond what our ability is to even grasp. In Matthew 8:12, it says, *"But the sons of the kingdom will be cast out into outer darkness. There will be weeping and gnashing of teeth."* I have heard people say, "Well, if I go to Hell, then I will have a big party with my friends!" No, there is isolation and darkness in Hell, but no companionship. In Matthew 25:41 Jesus said, *"Then He will also say to those on the left hand, 'Depart from Me, you cursed, into the everlasting fire prepared for the devil and his angels.'"*

Jesus said in Mark chapter 9, *"If your hand causes you to sin, cut it off. It is better for you to enter into life maimed, rather than having two hands, to go to hell, into the fire that shall never be quenched where 'Their worm does not die, And the fire is not quenched.'"* Jesus declared that if your eye causes you to lust and that's going to keep you from being saved, it would be better to gouge out your eye than to go to Hell. He declared that if your hand is going to steal and that is going to keep you from God, it would be better to cut off your hand and be crippled and enter into Heaven. That is the awfulness of Hell!

You might say, "It is not fair. We have such a brief life. We live sixty, seventy or maybe eighty years, and then we are condemned forever because of the decisions that we make during this brief time of life." Let me ask you this. If someone goes into a 7-11 store and points a gun at someone's head, how long does it take to pull the trigger? Half a second? In perhaps a fraction of a second, a criminal pulls the trigger, and for what he did in a second we punish him for a lifetime. Thirty, forty, fifty years in prison. It took only a second, and yet the rest of that criminal's life he is punished. Do not think because life is brief that there will not be punishment. In fact, it is the grace of God that we have so much time in life while He calls us and He pulls us to Himself.

Implications of the Doctrine of Hell

What are the implications of this doctrine? Number one, we should try to win souls. If you were driving home tonight and your neighbor's house was on fire, would you not try to do something about it? You might not be able to put the fire out, but:

- Would you not try to get them out of the house?
- Would you not do whatever you could?
- Would you not even risk being offensive?
- Would you not, if they were unconscious, pull their bodies through the broken glass of a window in order to rescue them because of the seriousness of the situation?

We talk about those who are saved, meaning those who have accepted Jesus, and those who are lost who have rejected Christ. The word "lost" is an awful word, is it not? What a terrifying thing to be lost! We live in an age that has lost its way. We have an obligation, as part of the family of God, to go to those who are lost and tell them about Jesus.

The second point of application and implication of the doctrine of Hell is that we ought to search ourselves. We ought to make sure that we are saved! That is the most important issue of our life! You may be saying, "Oh, well, I do not believe in Hell." Let me ask you this. Do you think there's at least a one in ten chance that this doctrine is true, and that there is a Hell? Most people would say, "Well, yeah, there is probably a one in ten chance." As you board an airplane, the stewardess makes announcements about putting things in the overhead bin, placing carry-on luggage underneath the seats, buckling up your seat belt, and so forth. They go on to say that, if you are traveling with a small child, make sure you secure your oxygen mask first before placing one on your child. After all that, suppose she says, "Oh, by the way, we want to remind you that one out of every ten of our planes crashes and burns and everyone on board is killed!" Boy, I would be getting that seatbelt off, wouldn't you? I would be getting out of that plane if there was a one in ten chance that it was going down! Do you believe there's at least a one in ten chance that there is a literal Hell? I think I would get to Jesus real quick!

The third and last implication of this doctrine is the seriousness of sin. If sin is such an offense to God that those who reject His Son are sent to eternal condemnation; after we are saved, we should consider sin as very serious to God!

Some Christians teach today that once you are saved, you do not ever have to confess sin. There is no condemnation for the believer, so do not ever confess anything to God. I understand what they are saying and, in a sense, they are right because there is no condemnation to those that are in Christ Jesus. There is no sin that will condemn you to Hell once you are saved. What an arrogant position for a believer! That is like saying to God, "Now that I am saved, I know that sin is offensive to You, but hey, You have taken care of it, so I am never going to confess anything!" Should we not instead, when we are caught in failure, have an overwhelming sense of contrition, confession and repentance? Should we not say, "Oh, God, I know that I am in Your grace, and I know that I am going to Heaven when I die, but I have committed an offense against You. I know sin ordinarily would be punished by death, and yet in Your love You have pardoned me. Oh, God, restore this broken fellowship between You and me, and help me to live right!"

This was a tough message! It was a tough message for me to prepare and preach, and I know it is hard to hear. It is not what our culture believes, it is not what we would want to believe, but it is what God has revealed in His Word. Our obligation is to bring our life in line with what God says rather than what we think, or what is politically correct!

1999

The cost of the new sanctuary continued to soar. We had raised money for three years through the "Arise and Build" emphasis and extended the giving period by eighteen months with the "A Time to Build" emphasis. We had voted to borrow $8 million, and still we were short of funds.

We had one final capital funds campaign called "A Place for Changing Lives." These gifts were used to buy the pews for the church. There was an air of excitement as our goal of a new worship center was now in sight!

On the fourteenth anniversary of the founding of Valley Baptist Church, December 5, 1999, we met to worship for the first time in our new sanctuary. On the first Sunday, 136 people were baptized. The 2,200 seat auditorium was overflowing for both Sunday morning services. In the weeks that followed, hundreds of people joined Valley Baptist Church.

"The God of a Second Chance" was preached on a Wednesday evening, March 24, 1999. On Tuesday evening of that week, I met with a teenage girl who had grown up in our church as part of a wonderful Christian family. She had made some terrible decisions in life that had taken her far from the values of her church and home. She was deeply remorseful, but hopeless. With her life before her, she felt that she was unredeemable, that she now could never become the woman that God intended her to be.

Wednesday morning, as I was praying for her in my study, this verse from Jeremiah came to my mind. That evening I preached from my heart that God is the God of a second chance.

Incidentally, that girl is now a young woman, actively serving the Lord. She, along with millions of other believers, is living proof that failure need not be final!

The God of a Second Chance

JEREMIAH 18:1-10

"The word which came to Jeremiah from the LORD, saying: 'Arise and go down to the potter's house, and there I will cause you to hear My words.' Then I went down to the potter's house, and there he was, making something at the wheel. And the vessel that he made of clay was marred in the hand of the potter; so he made it again into another vessel, as it seemed good to the potter to make. Then the word of the LORD came to me, saying: 'O house of Israel, can I not do with you as this potter?' says the LORD. 'Look, as the clay is in the potter's hand, so are you in My hand, O house of Israel! The instant I speak concerning a nation and concerning a kingdom, to pluck up, to pull down, and to destroy it, if that nation against whom I have spoken turns from its evil, I will relent of the disaster that I thought to bring upon it. And the instant I speak concerning a nation and concerning a kingdom, to build and to plant it, if it does evil in My sight so that it does not obey My voice, then I will relent concerning the good with which I said I would benefit it.' " (NKJV)

On occasion, God spoke to Jeremiah and told him to go to the temple, and Jeremiah stood at the gates as the people came in to worship. He preached a powerful message about how their worship was shallow, and how they were engaged in idolatry. This time, however, God did not tell Jeremiah to go to the temple, but to the place of simple craftsmanship, to a potter's house, where God would give him His Word. God taught Jeremiah one of the most important theological lessons of life. The lesson? Failure need not be final! It is a message that, from time to time, all of us need to hear.

I do not know about you; maybe this is more of a "guy" thing, perhaps not applying so much to the ladies, but when I watch television, I watch it with my finger on the remote control, ready to change the channel at a moment's notice. In fact, I cannot remember *when* I have watched a complete show on television. I am always changing the channel, watching five or six programs at one time! Eventually, when I am finished watching television, I wonder what I really watched! I watched a little bit of everything. Once in a while as I am surfing through the channels on cable television, I find a program that my son and I watch together. It is a rather bizarre program called *The Antiques Roadshow.* People bring their antiques to the show, which is usually held in a civic center, and experts examine and assign a value to their treasures. You have got to be really bored to watch this show!

I play a little game where I try to beat the experts in guessing the value of an item. My son, Andrew, and I were watching the show last week, and we were yelling at the experts because we thought they were wrong. Someone brought a very small picture of a little boy and girl from a hundred years ago. I did not particularly like the picture because the little girl was in a dress and so was the little boy! I realized that was a cultural thing but I could not quite get past it, so I did not care for the picture. The lady asked, "How much did you pay for this picture?" The man replied, "$5.00." The lady said, "Well, it may surprise you to know that it is worth somewhere between twenty-five and thirty thousand dollars." I yelled at them because I did not think it was worth that! I certainly would not pay that for it!

On the same show, they had a very unusual item. Evidently, when you apply for a U.S. patent, you must submit several schematics as well as a model of the item. Someone brought several models of things for which people had applied for patents. One of them was a miniature model of a mechanical clothesline for drying clothes, from over a hundred years ago. It was a unique invention but, of course, it was never produced. The model was a pot-belly stove with a pipe coming up which forked into other little pipes. The pipes sort of looked like helicopter blades. You were to hang clothes on these various pipes at the top. As it was heated with wood, the heat would rise and cause the pipes to circulate, causing the heat to fan out on the clothes. I thought it was pretty neat. The experts said that it worth $1,500. I do not know why I am telling you this—it has nothing to do with the message!

What is fascinating about this show is that, from time to time, they will have a piece of pottery on the show. It is amazing to see the value of certain vases or pieces of earthen pottery. I have discovered from watching this show that if Josiah Blake Wedgwood made the pottery, it has incredible value! He lived from 1730 to 1795 and was a master craftsman. Born the son of a British potter, Josiah Wedgwood, when just a child, became an apprentice potter. He had the ability to tone, texture and touch the clay in such a way that has never been equaled before or since.

When he was fourteen years old, he suffered from yellow fever, resulting in one of his legs being amputated. He still found a way to work the pedal on the potter's wheel, and for two hundred years now he has been the definitive artist of pottery. So if you find a piece of pottery that has Josiah Wedgwood's signature on it, it is incredibly valuable. Wedgwood's name is synonymous with the ability to shape clay so that it becomes more than what it was.

The art of pottery is one of the oldest arts in the world. It has remained virtually unchanged from the ancient world. A potter takes a lump of clay and cuts it, crushes it, twists it, kneads it until it is soft and pliable and has no lumps or bubbles in it, and then he "throws" it. That is what artists call it; they throw it, or put it on a wheel. The wheel is worked with a foot pedal. The potter turns the wheel around and around with his fingers, pressing, probing, and molding until a beautiful vessel emerges. This method has not changed over thousands of years. You probably would not have to go very far in our own city, or in any city in America, before you would find a potter's wheel in someone's garage. Or perhaps in someone's workroom you would find a moist piece of glistening clay going round and round on a wheel, while someone is trying to mold it into a beautiful vessel.

When I was in college, I was required to take a number of electives, so I took a class in pottery. I had these grandiose ideas that I was going to make this huge pot. I started out but gave up on the idea pretty quickly. I reshaped the clay until it became smaller and smaller, and finally I made a twisted looking little ashtray. Of course, no one in my family smoked, so it had no value to us. I have no idea where it is today! It was kind of a grotesque looking thing anyway. I found out that it is a much more difficult art than what meets the eye.

THE GOD OF A SECOND CHANCE

As the art of pottery has not changed over thousands of years, the truth about God, which He tells Jeremiah, has not changed. The lesson is this: *When you put your life into the hands of the Divine Potter your failure is not final!* When you fail, the last chapter of your life has not been written, because God is the God of a second chance!

A Created Vessel

God tells Jeremiah in verse 2 to go to the potter's house to hear God's Word. In verse 3 it says, *"Then I went down to the potter's house, and there he was, making something at the wheel."* The potter was creating something almost out of nothing, something that would be beautiful. The process became to Jeremiah a living parable.

Obviously, God is the potter. In verse 6, God identifies Himself, *"O house of Israel, can I not do with you as this potter,' says the Lord? 'Look, as the clay is in the potter's hand, so are you in My hand, O house of Israel.'"* God is the Potter, the Master Workman. God is absolutely sovereign. He can shape our lives, He can probe our lives, and He can pressure our lives any way that He desires. Something else about the potter is that, as He is shaping the pot or the vessel, He has a plan. Someone who is not the Master Craftsman cannot see the potential in the clay that the Master Craftsman sees. When God looks at a lump of clay, He sees the potential and has a plan to make something both beautiful and useful. God has a plan, not just for preachers and missionaries, but for your life as well. You may not be called to "full-time" Christian service or Christian work, but if you are a believer, you are called to be a "full-time" Christian! God has a plan for our lives. He loves us and wants to make something beautiful out of our lives.

The difference between this potter and God is that the human potter is limited to work on one lump of clay at a time. But God is sovereign and infinite. He is working on a million plans at once, a million possible scenarios in an individual's life for thousands of people around the earth. There is no limit to God as the Master Craftsman.

If God is the Potter, who is the clay? Well guess what? You and I are the clay! The Bible says that Adam was shaped out of dust, literally out of the clay of the earth. The clay, apart from the Master, does not really have much value. In the same way, you and I are nothing, apart from the work and the touch of God. The deepest truth we can know about ourselves is that you and I were made to yield to the press of the Divine Potter's hands. You can measure your life in terms of relationships, your job, your performance or whatever, but the clay can do nothing about itself. The clay cannot make itself into a useful or beautiful vessel. There are many people in the world who think they are going to be self-made and mold their own life. Well, you will end up "moldy" all right! But, you will not shape your life into anything of value. It takes the touch of the Master Craftsman. He knows where to push, He knows where to pull and He knows the right amount of pressure. The difference between us and the clay upon the wheel is that the clay upon the wheel never jumps off the wheel! We have a tendency to do that. The clay on the wheel never rises up and nails the hands of the potter, as human beings did to God's Son.

God is the Potter and we are the clay, but what is the wheel? The wheel is the daily turning of life, the circumstances of life. Whether they are good days or bad days, whether adversity or blessings, God uses the turning of life to shape and to mold us. He uses relationships, He uses circumstances, He uses finances, He uses illness and He uses everything that comes into our life. Sometimes the Master Craftsman turns the wheel very slowly as He is shaping us, but sometimes it is turning very quickly. At times, the days drag by; at other times the days spin by so fast that we get nearly a sense of "spiritual vertigo," spinning past births and deaths, victories and failures. Whether the days are moving slowly or whether they are moving quickly, there is no way to get off the wheel! God's destiny, for all of us, is that we are on the wheel of circumstances. Sometimes you feel like your life is going in circles. In a sense, it is! We are the clay and God is shaping us, and we cannot understand every mark that the Craftsman makes, or the need for every pressure, or every probing that comes into our life.

Isaiah, the prophet, said in Isaiah 55, speaking for God, "'For My thoughts are not your thoughts, nor are your ways My ways,' says the Lord, 'for as the heavens are higher than the earth, so are My ways higher than your ways, and My thoughts than your thoughts.'" Sometimes we question God, "Why is this revolution in my life, why are the circumstances of my life turning in a certain way?" God does not always answer. It is not that God is mute or that He cannot speak, or that God cannot explain His actions. The inability does not lie with God—it lies with us. We, as clay, are incapable of understanding the complexity of God's mind. He says, "For as the heavens are higher than the earth, so are My ways higher than your ways, And My thoughts than your thoughts."

Sometimes we think we could do a better job than God. Have you ever heard someone say, "Well, if I was God…?" That is a scary thought! Some people say, "If I was God, I would not do that; if I were God, I would do it this way, or I would do it that way." A boy was sitting under an acorn tree out in the middle of a watermelon patch. He thought to himself, "I would do things differently if I were God. Here is this strong tree holding up these little acorns, and these weak vines with big watermelons on them." About that time, an acorn dropped and hit him on the head. He was thankful it was not a watermelon!

Not only are God's thoughts different than ours, but also His methods are different than ours. When the children of Israel were in the wilderness, serpents began to bite them. The people were dying from snakebites. You might wonder why God did not kill the fiery serpents. That is not what God did! Instead, God told them to raise up a serpent on a pole, look at it in faith, and be healed. Man would have never thought of that, but God did. We might ask why God does not just kill the devil, why God does not eradicate evil. Instead of killing the devil, He put His Son on the cross that He might be killed. God's ways are not our ways! We must remember while we are on the wheel, the foot that presses upon the pedal and turns the circumstances of our life has a nail scar in it. As we are on the wheel and we feel the probing and the pressure of those hands upon us, we must remember that those hands are scarred in love for us. He has a plan for our life. That does not mean that we will be famous or rich, but it does mean that God has a plan. It means that we can live a fulfilling life. Any time we believe that God is probing too deeply, any time we believe that God is pressing too hard, we need to write over that circumstance Romans 8:28, *"All things work together for good to those who love God, to those who are the called according to His purpose."* If we will learn to yield, God has a way of working it together for good. He has a way of turning Calvary into Easter and tears into laughter and dark clouds into the harvest as the song says, "He can make something beautiful of our life."

A Vessel Marred

The vessel that Jeremiah saw was marred. In verse 4, it says, *"And the vessel that he made of clay was marred in the hand of the potter; so he made it again into another vessel, as it seemed good to the potter to make."* The vessel was marred. It is literally the word *"ruined."* Everyone looked at the vessel and said it was ruined. Everyone thought that except the potter. The potter looked at the vessel and said, "I can reshape it; I can remake it." The potter had a piece of clay on the wheel, and as Jeremiah was watching, perhaps a frown came over his face. As it was going around and around, he felt a brittle place, maybe a little rock. Every time it spun around, he felt maybe a vein of iron. What he could have done was take that lump of clay and throw it aside, and no one would have blamed him. He could have put another lump of clay on the wheel and started over, but that is not what the potter did. And that is not what God does!

Often we think that our life is ruined. We think that we have gone so far in sin that we cannot turn back, after we stood at the fork in the road and took the wrong path. The fact is, every day we stand at a new fork in the road, and every day we make a new decision as to whether we will yield or whether we will resist the plan of God for our life. Sometimes as we are reading our Bible, or as someone sings a wonderful song, or as the message is preached, we feel the hand of the Potter probing our heart. He finds that weak place, and He finds that resistant place, and He finds that hard place and that dry place, that unsurrendered place within our life—and gives us a choice as to whether we will yield. That place may be:

- A relationship that is wrong,
- A hidden habit in our life upon which God lays His hand
- An addiction
- An attitude of bitterness
- An unforgiving spirit

The question is this: If you find a place in the clay that is marred, is that the fault of the potter, or is it the fault of the clay? It is the fault of the clay that it is unyielding, but there are more than a few who blame the potter. Some say to God, "You have dealt me a bad hand—if I would have had different parents, if I would have attended a different school, if I would have had more money—but You stacked the deck against me. You have been unfair to me." There are many things that are decided without your choice. I was born in 1955; if you want to do the math on that, I am 44 years old. I had no vote on when to be born, and you had no vote on when to be born. I had no vote on where to be born. I was born in Western Oklahoma. In God's sovereignty, I could have just as easily been born in London, I could have just as easily been born in Moscow and my life would have been radically different.

Who are you, as the pot, to say to the Potter that He is unfair? It is the prerogative of the Potter to create the pot as He desires. But it is our prerogative whether or not we will yield. Some blame God and some blame the wheel. Some say, "Pastor, you do not understand my circumstances," but it is not about circumstances. It is about our willingness to yield to the Divine Potter.

There were two men who met Jesus at about the same time and began to follow Him. Both of these men heard every sermon that He preached, both of these men saw virtually every miracle that He performed. One of them became the great apostle Peter who preached on the Day of Pentecost, when three thousand were saved. Later he penned two of the books of the New Testament. The other one was Judas, the Betrayer, who hung himself in a potter's field. The difference was not about the circumstances of their life. Their circumstances were virtually identical: they heard the same message, they saw the same miracles and they felt the touch of Jesus' love upon their life. But one yielded and one refused to yield!

Shifting the blame, whether it is to God or to circumstances, is as old as Eden when Adam said, "That woman that Thou gave me." The question is, are you willing to yield? Why are we marred? The vessel is marred because there is some hidden impurity in the clay. Maybe we are marred because there is some hidden impurity in our life. The clay is marred because it is not pliable. Have you ever said to God, "I will do whatever you want, I surrender wholeheartedly to you"? We are afraid to do that. I hear people talking about their fear. "I am afraid to yield totally to God because He will make me a missionary, or my children will die or He will strip me of my money." That is the devil's talk. The devil will tell you that you cannot trust God and so do not yield to Him. The Father knows best. If we had sense enough to know it, we would want exactly what God wants in our life no matter how difficult the adversity or the problem might be. We sing the song, "Fill my cup, Lord, I lift it up, Lord." Maybe we should sing, "Fix my cup, Lord; I have messed it up, Lord."

A Vessel Restored

Not only is this vessel created and marred, but it was also restored. That is the message of Jeremiah. In verse 4, it says that it "...*was marred in the hand of the potter; so he made it again into another vessel, as it seemed good to the potter to make.*" He made it again, a second chance. It may be that God called you. I meet people all the time who have said, "When I was a teenager, God called me to be a missionary, or God called me to vocational ministry, or God called me to be a preacher, or a pastor." They go on to say, "I said 'no,' and now my life has slipped away and the circumstances are such that it is impossible to follow my calling." Does that mean that God is through with you? Because you make one mistake in life, or stand at the fork in the road and decide to take the wrong path, does that mean that God washes His hands of you? No, no it does not mean that at all.

At Cape Kennedy, they have a flight plan for every missile they fire off, but it may be "Gee or Yaw or Gimble," a little bit one way or the other because the fuel may burn faster than anticipated, or it may burn slower than anticipated. It never, or at least it would seldom ever, follow the precise flight plan that was laid out. But on board, there is a gyroscope that will correct the course. There are computers that, in an instant, will recalculate the rate the fuel is burning, or wind factors, and set it on a new course. It was not the first plan but it is still in the air, and it is still a plan. If a human being can do that with a computer, imagine what God, in His infinite mind, can do!

If we choose the wrong road and then come back to Him, imagine how He can recalibrate and recalculate what our life should be. Life does not end with failure. Once in a while, a missile decides to head straight back and when that happens, they push the button and destroy it. I hope that God does not have to push the button, the "destruct" button, on any of our lives. You may feel that you missed the call of God upon your life, or that you went to the wrong school or that you married the wrong person. You had better not say that very loud! You can bring your failures to Jesus, and He will rewrite the plan. It is not going to be a bad plan. It will be a good plan that He rewrites for your life.

In verse 6, Jeremiah is talking about Israel. God said, *"Israel is like clay in My hand,"* and in verse 7, *"The instant I speak concerning a nation, and concerning a kingdom, to pluck up, and to pull down, and to destroy it, if that nation against whom I have spoken turns from its evil, I will relent of the disaster that I thought to bring upon it."* God has been saying through Jeremiah for years, "You have sinned, and because of your idolatry, God is going to destroy you. In the instant that you repent, I will relent of the evil and the destruction that I was going to bring into your life." He declares that He will bless a nation and pour out His blessing; yet in the instant they turn from God, He will change that blessing to a curse. It is all about whether we yield. It does not matter whether you are a saint or sinner, saved or lost; God is the God of a second chance! He restores broken lives if we simply bring the pieces and give them to Him. He is the same God who caused Jacob to go back to Bethel, who caused Sampson's hair to grow again, who gave Jonah a second chance, and today if we bring the broken pieces of our life to Him, He gives us a new start.

There is a process implied in this, though it is not explicit. Jeremiah does not state this, but the process of pottery involves fire. An unfired pot is useless. Pottery is dull when it is painted, but when fired it becomes lustrous, with a beautiful sheen. The fact is, God, nearly always, matures us in the fire! We want to take a shortcut to maturity. We want to mature without the trials, without the spinning of the wheel or without the probing of the Potter. There are no exceptions. In our life, at times, there is the fire of family, of finances, of vocation, of physical illness; there are academic fires, ecclesiastical, and most of all, there is the fire of failure. Someone said to Dwight Moody, who was a great preacher a hundred years ago, "I would give the world to be able to preach like you do," and Moody said, "That is exactly what it cost me!" He gave up the world!

A Vessel Destroyed

In chapter 19, the scene changes radically. *"Thus says the LORD: 'Go and get a potter's earthen flask, and take some of the elders of the people and some of the elders of the priests.*

And go out to the Valley of the Son of Hinnom, which is by the entry of the Potsherd Gate; and proclaim there the words that I will tell you.'" Jeremiah, a pictorial prophet, preached with living illustrations. He led a procession outside the city of Jerusalem, which was a mixture of the ministerial alliance of the priests and the city council. He came to the Valley of Hinnom. On the very brow of that valley, after buying an expensive earthen vessel, he took it and threw it down. It shattered in a thousand pieces, and his message in verse 10 was: *"Then you shall break the flask in the sight of the men who go with you, "and say to them, 'Thus says the Lord of hosts: "Even so I will break this people and this city, as one breaks a potter's vessel, which cannot be made whole again."'"* Jeremiah and God are saying, "It is one thing to be marred. God can fix and remake your life, but when a brittle bottle is broken it cannot be put back together."

Remember the nursery story, "Humpty Dumpty sat on a wall, Humpty Dumpty had a great fall. All the king's horses and all the king's men could not put Humpty Dumpty together again." We can resist for only so long. Israel had been on the wheel for years. God had been spinning the wheel of circumstances for decades. They would come to God, He would fix them, and then they would fail. He would fix them again, and they would fail; their heart grew harder and harder. He talked about how their necks grew stiffer and stiffer as they resisted the Spirit of God in their life. Finally, God said, "Your heart is so brittle, it will never be fixed. All that awaits you is to push the 'destruct' button and your life will be utterly destroyed." God is saying that there is a point, a "fail safe" point where we cross a deadline. We ought not ever presume upon the patience of God. I hope that no one is at that point.

There is something that Jeremiah could not see, that you and I *can* see, as New Testament believers. He would have never dreamed that one day the Potter would become the clay and that God would become flesh and throw His own incarnate life upon the wheel of circumstances. He would be crucified upon the cross. The Son of God can now hold up His nail-scarred hands before us. He bears on His body the stigma, the scars. As He molds us upon the wheel, the Potter smears us with the blood of His own hands because He loves us!

You may be resistant. You may blame your parents, a boss, a mate or circumstances. You need to simply surrender, to yield to His probe, to His press, to His touch, to make whatever changes He desires.

~ 2 0 0 0 ~

In the summer of 2000, Valley had a special evangelistic emphasis called "Frontliners." That summer, scores of teenagers came to Christ. In fact, the church baptized 460 people that year.

The budget grew by over $1 million from 1998. The 2,000 barrier was broken when the church averaged 2,110 people in Sunday School attendance for the year. Over 700 new members were added to the church. The year 2000 was the greatest year of growth ever for Valley Baptist Church.

"Hurry Up With the Benediction" was preached on Sunday morning, September 20, 2000. This message was originally preached as part of a series of sermons entitled "Major Messages from Minor Prophets."

Hurry Up with the Benediction

Amos 8:1-4

*"Thus the Lord GOD showed me, Behold, a basket
of summer fruit. And He said, 'Amos, what do you
see?' So I said, 'A basket of summer fruit.' Then the
LORD said to me: 'The end has come upon My
people Israel; I will not pass by them anymore.
And the songs of the temple Shall be wailing in
that day,' Says the Lord GOD, 'Many dead bodies
everywhere, They shall be thrown out in silence.'
Hear this, you who swallow up the needy, make the
poor of the land fail.'"(NKJV)*

I want to look at the prophecy of Amos in three ways. I
want to think about Amos as a man, the method of Amos'
ministry, and the message of Amos.

Who was Amos, the man? What was he like, and where
was he from? We know something of his background from
Amos 1:1, where it says in the words of Amos, *"Who was
among the sheepbreeders of Tekoa, which he saw concerning
Israel in the days of Uzziah King of Judah, and in the days of
Jeroboam, the son of Joash, King of Israel, two years before the
earthquake."* We do not know anything historically about
that earthquake, but we know a great deal about Uzziah, the

King of Judah, and about Jeroboam, King of Israel. Therefore, we know something of when Amos lived.

He was a contemporary with Isaiah and also with Hosea. He was from Tekoa, a little village about twelve miles to the south of Jerusalem. On a clear day, he would have been able to look to the west and see the Mediterranean Sea as he was taking care of his sheep. He could look to the north from the ridge on which Tekoa was built and see the sprawling city of Jerusalem. He could look to the east across the desert terrain with its scrub brush, to the glimmering Dead Sea. There in the solitude of being a shepherd, the Word of the Lord came to him. He was not trained in any theological or rabbinical school; neither was he trained in elocution or speech. He was simply a herdsman, a keeper of sheep.

Later in his prophecy, he tells us the type of sheep he took care of were the "*noqed*," They were a stubby, ill-formed, ugly looking black sheep. They were the "bottom of the barrel" sheep in those days. So not only was he a shepherd, he was a keeper of the "*noqed*," the ugliest sheep of his day. He was also a gatherer of sycamore fruit, which was a poor man's fig. In the spring, he would leave the little village of Tekoa, and take the sheep to graze in the green pastures on the surrounding hillsides. As the fruit ripened, he would leave the sheep, perhaps with someone else, and go to the orchards where he would gather fruit. So he was a migrant worker. He followed the sheep in the spring, and the harvest at different times. His was a hereditary lifestyle. His father before him was probably a keeper of the ugly sheep, the "*noqed*." His grandfather and his great-grandfather before him were probably migrant workers as well.

The profiles of the prophets are interesting. God used a wide range of personalities among His prophets. Isaiah was of an aristocratic heritage. He was a statesman, a poet, a literary genius! Jeremiah was a boy prophet who was timid and uncertain. When God spoke to him the Word of the Lord, he protested that he was a youth and could not speak. Jeremiah had a melancholy personality, and was depressed most of his life. Daniel was of noble birth, a brilliant man and an erudite scholar. Hosea was a man whose heart was broken when he married Gomer, who became a harlot. And, of course, there was Amos, the migrant fruit picker from Tekoa, the keeper of ugly sheep named the *"noqed."*

What was the common denominator? How could God use these men in such a tremendous way when they were so different one from another. I believe the common denominator is found in the words of Isaiah, when the burden of the Word of the Lord came to him, and Isaiah said, *"Here I am, send me."* That was the attitude of the prophets—a willingness to be used. They weren't used because of their personalities. Their personalities ranged from an extrovert like Ezekiel, who used to act out his messages like an actor on a stage, to a timid introvert like Jeremiah. They ranged from the brilliant intelligence of a statesman and a scholar like Isaiah to a backward country preacher named Amos. The common denominator was that they were men willing to be used by God, to say, "Here am I—send me."

Sometimes people say, "I cannot be of use to God. I don't have the proper education," or, "I am not extroverted in my personality," or "I don't have certain gifts or talents." God uses people of different personalities and different backgrounds. All that is necessary is to say, "Here am I, send me."

Hundreds of years before the prophets, there was a man named Gideon, who lived during the time of the judges. An Angel of the Lord appeared to him and said, "Hail, mighty man of valor." Gideon turned around and said, "Who, me? You must be talking to someone else." God desired to use him as a great judge, but Gideon protested, "I am of the smallest tribe of all Israel. I am of the half tribe of Manasseh. Why don't you get someone from the tribe of Judah, or Benjamin, or some of the other tribes?" He thought, "I cannot be used. Of all the families of Manasseh, my family is the most insignificant; and of my family, I am the runt of all my brothers." Yet God chose to use him! Gideon learned a valuable lesson that "one plus God equals a majority!"

Amos, this unlearned, unskilled, uneducated country man from Tekoa, this keeper of the ugly, ill-formed stubby black sheep, "*noqed*," was used mightily of God. You can be used of God, too, in whatever circle your life takes you, if you choose to say, "Here am I, Lord, send me." You may not be used in the same way as the great scholar, Isaiah. You may not be used like a Jeremiah, but everyone can be used like Amos—to stand before others and say, "Thus saith the Lord God."

The Method of Amos

When the Word of the Lord came to Amos, he did not do as the Apostle Paul—who left for three years and went out into the desert, giving himself to study, and trained under the stars by God Himself. As soon as the Word of God came to Amos, he immediately left his sheep and the basket of sycamore fruit, going north to a nation that was not his, leaving his precious nation of Judah. He went to the nation of Israel to the north, and when he came to the first village, he began to preach on the street corner.

Can you imagine this country shepherd, preaching on the street corners to the affluent people of Israel in the north? There was no sanctuary that housed the people to whom he spoke, there was no beautiful wooden pulpit to stand before, so he stood on the corner. He stood in the marketplace and declared a scalding message as he accused the people of sin.

He began by denouncing the sin of all the surrounding nations of Israel. He spoke about the sin of Damascus, Gaza, Tyre, Edom and Moab. One by one, he preached against the nations around Israel. He talked about their sin and called for the judgment of God. You can nearly see the excitement of the crowd of people gathering around him. They probably invited others to hear Amos, saying, "You must hear this country preacher from Tekoa. You have never heard a man speak like him. Come hear the message as he preaches about the judgment of Moab, Edom and Tyre, and the nations that are around us." They must have cheered and said, "Amen, brother, you preach it," as he preached concerning the judgment of the neighbors of Israel.

But then he turned those same spiritual guns upon the nation of Judah, and upon the nation of Israel. He began to preach, not to the neighbors of Israel, but to the nation itself. He brought accusation after accusation of sin against the people of God. Amos called for the destruction of other nations, and then declared that if the people did not repent, God was going to destroy them as well. Sometimes we have a theological problem with such preaching. We wonder why the God of the Old Testament would allow whole nations, because of their sin, to be destroyed by pestilence, or by the armies of invading forces. Why would God allow that?

Suppose that a little child is sick in the middle of the night. Someone drags him off his bed and rushes him to a strange place as he is crying in the middle of the night, and shines bright lights in his face. Then someone renders him unconscious, takes a knife and cuts into his body. We would say that is abuse. That's a terrible thing to do to a child! But, on the other hand, it may be a great act of mercy. If that child needs surgery and is taken under the bright lights of a hospital room, and the loving care of a skilled surgeon renders him unconscious and takes a knife and opens his body to repair some damage, it is not so much a cruel act as it is, in fact, an act of mercy. That is what takes place in the Old Testament! Sin is like a cancer that invades the body, and will ultimately destroy the whole body. God looked at humanity and, on occasion, He saw nations that, because of their sin, were like cancers on the intention of creation. God allowed the surgeon of armies and the surgeon of pestilence to remove or eradicate whole civilizations. Never be quick to judge the great plan of God.

Amos attacked the people's materialism. He did not do it in a very easy or acceptable way. In fact, when you read the words of Amos, he appears to be rude and crude. On one occasion when speaking to the women of Israel, he called them "fat cows of the stalls." Such a statement might not endear you as a pastor. He declared them to be like "fat cows of the stalls" because they lived for materialism in an affluent society, and yet they had forgotten the poverty and the social injustice of the oppressed.

Amos attacked the religion of his day by declaring that the people preferred rituals, festivals, and feasts and so forth, but they never brought forth a sin offering. In arrogance, they thought they had not sinned.

The Message of Amos

In Amos 1:2, he said, *"The LORD roars from Zion, And utters His voice from Jerusalem; The pastures of the shepherds mourn, And the top of Carmel withers."* He compares God to the roar of a lion. Amos, being a keeper of sheep, knew what it was like to be awakened in the middle of the night by the predatory roar of the lion. Amos knew that once the lion roared, it was too late. The lion would stalk the sheep, and right before he was ready to pounce, he would roar, in order to freeze the prey. Amos knew that in the middle of the night, once he heard the roar of the lion, one of those little ugly sheep was gone! His message from God was that God has roared! He did not declare that judgment was coming—that was the message of *Jeremiah* and *Hosea*. The message of Amos, instead, was that *judgment is here!*

He was not standing as an "eleventh hour prophet," saying, "Judgment will come." He was standing as a "twelfth-hour prophet," saying that the judgment of God is, in fact, here! We are going to see how the judgment of God came upon the people of God. What is interesting is the context of this chapter. In chapter 1:1, he said that he prophesied during the days of Uzziah, King of Judah, in the days of Jeroboam, who was the King of Israel in the north. The King's name, *Uzziah*, meant, "The Lord Jehovah is my strength." You might wonder, "Why judgment during King Uzziah's reign?" Uzziah was one of the most godly kings of his day. Why not judgment during the awful reign of Ahab or Manasseh, who were terrible kings? Why during Uzziah's time? He was one of the most successful kings. The Philistines had been defeated in the west, the Arabs in the south had been swept away; they had fortified the walls in Jerusalem. In the north, in the nation of Israel, Jeroboam was king. His name meant, "Let the people multiply." The sanctuaries of God were filled with people worshipping. The borders had been pressed to the extreme, yet Amos said that the judgment of God had come. Three decades later, the Assyrians came in and destroyed them.

Why judgment in the midst of what seemed to be the blessing of God? That is the crux of the message of Amos. He was saying that, in the midst of prosperity, the nation had become materialistic. In the midst of the blessing of God, a narcotic type of numbness had settled upon the nation. There was social injustice in the land and shallow religion in their worship. The judgment of God had come!

The people ignored Amos. In their arrogance, they said that God would not judge them. As evidence, they pointed to the blessings and the prosperity. They said that God certainly would not judge them, much like people in America are saying today.

The arm of God's judgment will never rest upon our nation, they said. They were similar to the people in the days and the generation of Noah. They were eating and drinking and partying, and then the flood came. Life was the same as in the days of Belshazaar, who was left in charge as the king by his grandfather. During the time of a riotous party, he allowed the Medes and the Persians to slip in and destroy his nation. They were like the Japanese nation that, decades ago, during the war had leaflets dropped on them warning of an apocalyptic weapon, the likes of which humanity had never seen, yet with a narcotic numbness they ignored that the judgment of God was upon their nation. They were like Chamberlain at the dawn of World War II who came back from the "Wolf Lair" itself, from meeting with Hitler. The headlines proclaimed by Chamberlain, "Peace in My Time," yet they were on the verge of the greatest war of humanity.

Perhaps that is where our nation is today. Thoroughly materialistic, secular, thinking that somehow the arm of God's judgment will never reach into our nation.

Amos 6 is the key to judgment. Amos 6:1, "*Woe to you who are at ease in Zion, And trust in Mount Samaria.*" They were at ease in Zion. Complacency had become a part of their religion. They were apathetic. They were narcissistic, thinking only of themselves. It was an urban society that was built at the expense of the lower classes. They were trusting in their military might. Amos said, "You trust in Mount Samaria." The capital city was surrounded by mountains. They believed, "We are fortified, no invading army can conquer us." Look at the mountains surrounding Samaria. Look at our military might. They were trusting in their might, instead of in God.

Forty times the Old Testament declares that we are to trust in God alone. But they were trusting in their military might.

They were a humanistic society, trusting in themselves, and saying, "We can overcome. We can solve the problems of our society. We do not really need God."

Verse 2 says to go over to Calnah and see, and then go to Hamath the Great, go to Gath of the Philistines. Are you better than these kingdoms? Is your territory greater than their territory? The nations around them had fallen on hard times. Look at the Philistines. Their empire was collapsing! Look at Hamath and the hard times that they have. Does it not remind you of America? We say today we are the only superpower. Look at the crumbling of the Russian Empire and the communistic world in our day. Look at the Third World and the Fourth World countries today, and how superior we are to them. They forgot the essence of life. The essence of life is that you're ultimately as a nation, ultimately as a church, ultimately as an individual, accountable and responsible to God!

They forgot that! They measured themselves in terms of materialism and prosperity. They measured themselves in terms of other nations, and they forgot that they were responsible and accountable to God.

When we look at a panorama of what their life was like in their society, the parallels to our culture are uncanny. Verse 4 says that they lie on beds of ivory, and they stretch out on their couches and eat the lambs of their flocks, and the calves in the midst of the stall. They were given to a life of ease and affluence in spite of the human need that was in their land. They were lying on ivory beds and eating.

It is interesting that in 1945, as archeologists were digging in the ruins of the ancient city of Samaria, they were amazed at the chips of ivory that they found. Ivory, ivory everywhere! God said that is what happened to the culture. They were lying on beds of ivory, and they were entirely apathetic about their spiritual life and about the injustice in the world. They were eating the young lambs, the calves of the stall, or veal.

That was in a day and time in which anyone in the world was fortunate to be able to eat meat once a week, or once a month. There was nothing wrong with eating meat, but they had forgotten their fellow man's needs. They had forgotten God and their whole society had become materialistic.

In verse 5, it says that they sang, idly, to the sound of stringed instruments, and they invented for themselves musical instruments, like David had. Everyone thought they were a "little David." The word is *extemporaneous.* It meant that they were just making up songs that really had no meaning. They were idle and useless; they were not worshipping. In fact, the word for *sing,* interestingly, is the word for *howl* or the word for *screech.* They were a society whose music had no melody; the emphasis was solely upon the beat. That is what has happened to our society. Their music was symptomatic of a nation that had gone awry, away from God.

In verse 6, it says that they drank from the bowl and anointed themselves with the best ointment, but they were not grieved for the affliction of Joseph. The bowls were those instruments that were used in sacrifice, and they were drinking from them. It was not that any one thing was wrong that they were doing—the singing of songs, the drinking from the bowls, and the eating of meat. Simply put, they were insensitive to God. They had forgotten God! They were living only for the moment. They had forgotten the injustices of their society. They were not grieved, in verse 6, for the afflictions of people who were less fortunate than they were.

It reminds me of the parable that Jesus told in the New Testament of a man who was wealthy and affluent, who said, "I am going to tear down these old barns and I am going to build bigger barns to house my crops." God said, "Thou fool, tonight your soul will be required of you." We read that and ask, "Why is he a fool?" Everyone in society probably bragged on this man. Perhaps he was a great civic leader, a wonderful father to his children, a good husband, a leader, and he was prosperous. Yet Jesus called him a fool! Why? Because he had no thought of God! He was so materialistic and so involved with money that that was all he was living for. He had no thought of God. That is how the people of Amos' day were living. Their inaction brought death. Spiritual atrophy set in. In Zion they became apathetic about spiritual things in life, living only for money.

Amos has four visions in this book. The first vision is that of the locust, much like that of the prophet of Joel. In this vision, he saw the judgment of God coming by locusts, utterly destroying the country. After the vision, he begged God and interceded, saying, "Please, God, do not allow the people to be destroyed by pestilence." And God said, "Okay."

Then he had a vision of fire. He saw a fire sweeping across the nation, burning the cities and laying them in waste. He begged God and interceded, saying, "Please, God, desist from the fire. Do not allow us to be destroyed by fire." And God said, "Okay."

Then he had a vision of a plumb line. A plumb line is a string with a piece of metal tied on the end of it that can be held up against a wall. Today it's used when someone puts up wallpaper. It helps to show whether the wall is square. He saw the vision of the plumb line as though someone was holding a string. It was God holding the string, measuring the nation of Israel, saying, "You are out of plumb! I gave you the commandments, and I told you how a society was to function, and how you were to be governed. Now the plumb line is held against you, and you are out of square. You are not living the way I said you should live." God was grieved.

• I wonder if God were to hold the plumb line against our nation, how we would fare. When we look at other parts of the world, we may fare well.

- I wonder if God were to hold the plumb line against our church, how our church would fare. When we look at other churches, we may fare well.
- I wonder if God were to hold the plumb line against us, how we would fare. When we look at other people around us, we may fare well.

But the plumb line is the Lord Jesus. He is the Ruler. He is the Canon by which we are measured. I wonder if we laid our lives down beside a full-length portrait of Jesus, how we would look!

A kindergarten teacher told every little child in the class to draw a straight line on a piece of paper. She was called out of the classroom for some reason, and when she came back to the room, they had all drawn straight lines and had compared them. It was found that the girls' lines were much straighter than the boys' lines. The straightest line was drawn by little Mary. Everyone thought she had a straight line, but when the teacher came back, she said, "Oh, you misunderstood. I wanted you to take your ruler and draw a straight line." She placed a ruler on Mary's paper, whose was the straightest line, and drew a line with the ruler. This showed that even Mary's line was crooked.

When we compare ourselves to others or to pagan cultures, we may fare well. But when you lay the ruler of Christ upon this nation and society, or lay the plumb line of Jesus upon your life and quit comparing yourself to someone else, to the world or some other religion, or even some other believer, the plumb line of Jesus will show that your life is crooked in places.

The fourth vision is found in chapter 8, a vision of the "basket of summer fruit." This vision gives the reason for judgment. It was the time of the Fall Festival. They gathered in the marketplace, and the people were singing and dancing in the streets. They were enamored with the material blessings of their nation. This country preacher felt out of place among all the singing, the partying and the dancing. Walking through the streets, he saw a basket of summer fruit, which suddenly became a vehicle of revelation to him, and the Word of God came to him. The message was, "There is no exit. This generation is a terminal generation."

The vision was a play on words in Amos' mind. The Hebrew word for "ripened fruit" is "*qeyis,*" and the word for end is "*qes.*" As he saw a basket of plums, he also saw Israel plummeting from their power. It is a play on words.

Everyone else was celebrating, and everyone else saw the prosperity and sensed the blessing of God. They had had decades of prosperity and peace in the land. What Amos saw was not renewal, but ruin. They were blind to the condition of their own society. They were like people on the deck of a luxury liner who were dancing and having a party after striking an iceberg, not knowing that the great ship was leaking.

We are in no mood today to hear the message of Amos, just as they were in no mood to hear it. The parallels of this little book, and the parallels of our society are uncanny. Verse 3 says that there would be a day when the songs of the temple would be turned to wailing. There would be a day when all the songsters of the king would be reversed into a lamentation, into a funeral dirge. Their society had become completely secular and irreversibly materialistic, and God had written the word *terminal* across the culture.

What was the attitude of the people? As Amos was giving this revelation of the basket of fruit, the attitude of the people was, "Amos, hurry up with the benediction! We're in no mood to hear this message. Finish the message so we might go on our way!"

They were guilty on two counts before God. They were guilty of social injustice and shallow religion. Amos began with a general indictment in verse 4 when he said, "*Hear this, you who swallow up the needy, And make the poor of the land fail."*

There is nothing wrong with affluence. Affluence in any society, or in any person's life, is not bad. But it is dangerous! In the midst of affluence, in the midst of prosperity, and in the midst of peace, it is possible for a society to become humanistic, where it worships the things of humanity instead of the things of God. Their religion was shallow. In verse 5, they asked when the new moon would pass that they might sell grain, and the Sabbath that they might trade wheat, making the ephod small and the shekel great, falsifying the scales by deceit. They went on to say they might buy the poor for silver and the needy for a pair of sandals, and even sell the bad wheat. Do you know what they were saying? "Oh, these interminable religious holidays! When are they going to be over? When will the Sabbath end? When will the hour of worship end, so that we may make some more money?"

What were they thinking about during the hour of worship?

- Were they thinking lofty thoughts of God?
- Were they thinking how God might invade the dark crevices of the heart?
- Were they thinking how God might wash away sin that had accumulated during the week?

No, on the Sabbath as the preacher stood up to preach, they were thinking, "How can we make the ephod smaller?" An ephod was a measure of eighteen gallons used to measure the wheat and the barley. The businessman, while the preacher was preaching, was thinking, "How can we put a false bottom in a container so that the people will think they are getting more than they are actually receiving?"

Others in the congregation were thinking:

- How can we make the shekel great?
- How can we give them less and make it weigh more?
- How can we get the poor people going and coming?

And then someone else over in another part of the crowd was thinking:

- How can I falsify the balances?
- How can I tip the scale?
- How can I put my thumb on it while no one is watching so it weighs more when I'm selling?
- How can I make it weigh less when I'm buying?

That is what was on their mind. They were thinking, as the message was being preached, "Hurry up with the benediction! Hurry, so that we might sell and buy and make more money." Verse 6 says, "*How can we sell them bad wheat? How can we take the wheat that is no good and the wheat that has no kernel in it and pawn it off on the poor people? How can we make more money?*" That is what they were thinking on the sabbath!

Very early in the revelation of God, in the Pentateuch, God said to Israel, "*Just balances, just weights...I am the LORD your God that brought you out of Egypt.*" That seems so anti-climatic to me. You would think that God would say:

- I am the Lord your God that brought you out of Egypt; therefore, have great worship services.
- I am the Lord your God that brought you out of Egypt; therefore, keep the commandments.
- I am the Lord your God that delivered you out of Egypt; therefore, build great churches.

But that is not what God said. He said, "*I am the LORD your God that brought you out of Egypt; therefore, have just balances.*"

333

Always, from the very beginning, redemption and ethics were tied together. Redemption by God is tied to how you live, how you treat the people who are under you and how you treat the people who are over you in society and in the workplace.

That is the reason for judgment. Social Injustice! Shallow religion—saying, "Hurry up with the benediction." The reaction of God is in verse 7, *"The Lord has sworn by the pride of Jacob, surely I will never forget any of their works."* In verse 2, He said He would not pass by them any more. It is a word of sarcasm. When God gave Amos a vision of locusts to destroy the nation, Amos said, "Oh, no, do not destroy the nation by locusts," and God said, "okay." God gave him a vision of fire, and he said, "Oh, no, do not destroy the nation by fire." By this time, the patience of God was at an end, and with a word of sarcasm, God said He would swear by the pride of Israel. It's ironic, because you always swear by something that will not change. God said that He would swear by the pride of an affluent nation, because that never changes, the pride of an arrogant people who think they do not need Me.

A few years later in 722 B.C., that oath of God was kept. The Assyrians came in and destroyed the nation. What is the result of judgment? Verses 8 to 10 tell us that the solid ground became like a flood, like the Nile. The light became darkness, and then the people were in sackcloth. They mourned as if mourning for the loss of the Holy Son. The worst judgment was not the locust, nor the fire, nor invading armies. The worst judgment, and the judgment that I fear for our society, is found in verse 11: *"'Behold, the days are coming,' says the Lord GOD, 'That I will send a famine on the land, Not a famine of bread Nor thirst for water, But of hearing the Words of the LORD.'"* That is the judgment! He told them the judgment would not be an invading army; the judgment would not be a drought, the judgment would not be starvation or famine. God said the judgment would be a famine of the hearing of the Word of God, and that became true!

Before the New Testament time, when the Old Testament closed, there were four hundred years of silence from God. Four hundred years between the Old and New Testament revelation when God, as an act of judgment, was silent! The heavens were as if they were brass. There was no word from God. Two times in the book of Amos, they said to get rid of the preacher. They basically said, "Country preacher, go back to Tekoa. We do not want to hear your message." God responded that there would be judgment, a famine from hearing the Word of God. The worst judgment of God upon a nation is not when God does something to a nation. Rather, the worst judgment of God upon a nation is when God does nothing to a nation. They did not feel the awful arm of God's judgment, but rather fell under the awful silence of God.

That is the fear I have for this nation. My fear is not that we would be destroyed by pestilence, or some invading army; but in the economy of God, His patience would come to an end, and we would suffer under the awful silence of God. Maybe we are already in the beginning of that judgment. If we look at a nation like Russia, we can see the moving of God in that nation as hundreds of thousands are coming to Christ. I sat in my living room and tears streamed down my face as I watched Billy Graham preaching in Moscow. At the end he gave an invitation to the Russians, who had not heard the Gospel message for decades. He said to them, "Please walk, do not run. Please walk, do not run." He knew, from the experience of having preached there the previous night, that when the invitation was given, there would be a mass of people rushing to embrace Christ. He said, "Please walk, do not run. Christ will be here. Do not crush others in the press of getting to

Christ." I thought to myself, "When was the last time that a preacher had to say to our nation, 'Please walk, do not run,' at the invitation time?"

I have heard about the revival taking place in Brazil, as missionaries have come and told the story of how they preach there and thousands come to Jesus. People will come forward, and they will be sent back to their seats. They say, "You do not understand." They will reexplain the message, thinking somehow the people do not understand. They make it as clear as they can about repentance and then give an invitation, and once again, thousands will come to give their lives to Christ.

The same thing is happening in pockets of Africa, Korea and other parts of the world. God is doing something in other nations. I believe that in my lifetime, if the Lord tarries, we will see God do something in the great nation of China. The gospel some day will be preached there once again, and multiplied thousands will come to Christ. God is doing something around the world, and yet it seems as if He is silent in our culture. Here and there are pockets of godliness, here and there are churches that are being blessed; but for the most part, church buildings across this nation today are empty. Invitations are given, and no one rushes to the front giving their life to Christ. We are living perhaps not in the eleventh hour, but we are living on the verge of the twelfth hour. Judgment will not be that God does something to the nation, but His judgment will be that He does *nothing* to the nation—that He will leave us in silence! It says that they will look for a word, from sea to sea, from the Mediterranean to the Dead Sea, they will search for a word from God, that they will grope like blind men, they will stumble like ancient men, but they will not hear the Word of God.

There is already a famine for the hearing of the Word of God in America. Oh, there is not a famine from the preaching of the Word of God. Thank God for that! But there is a famine in the hearing of the Word of God. Most of our nation will not listen. We have severed ourselves from our roots. We have become a materialistic culture; the religion of our day has become shallow. We are much like Israel, we are a "cut-flower" society. When you cut flowers and put them in a vase for a few days, they look so beautiful, and their fragrance fills the room. But after a few days, the death that is there manifests itself because they have been severed from the root and are dead. They are gone! That is a picture of our society, a "cut-flower society." On the surface, our culture has fragrance and beauty. It looks like we are enjoying the prosperity and the peace of God, but in reality we have cut ourselves from the roots, and some day the death that is in this culture will manifest itself.

It can be the same in *your* life. Perhaps you are a believer, and yet you are like a cut flower. Everyone looks at your life and thinks there is such beauty, such fragrance. Actually, within your life, you have cut yourself from the root that gives life. You have become humanistic in your lifestyle, narcissistic in the way you live, materialistic and secular in your outlook. Some day the death that is creeping into your life will manifest itself in open sin.

What was Israel's attitude when they heard the message of Amos? *"Hurry up with the benediction, preacher! We are getting tired of this message of judgment. We are getting tired of this message of sin. Hurry up with the benediction!"*

I have been asked on occasion what I think the responsibility of a church is, or the responsibility of an individual Christian to our culture? What is our obligation? There are those who are part of the religious right, conservative evangelical Christians who say that our obligation is to fight and resist the culture politically. They become religious and political activists who fight and resist with their dying breath trying to recover the heritage of America. There is validity in such actions.

My personal philosophy is this: My view of our society in America is like a great house that is on fire. It is burning, and we can spend our time holding a hose, trying to put out the fire, and God bless those who do that! I have committed my life to another path, instead of holding the hose, or trying to put out the fire in a house that I fear is gone, I have committed my life to saying, "Let us go into the burning house, and let us find as many victims as we can, and let us drag them to safety." Instead of spending our time trying to put out the fire, let's spend our time rescuing, one by one, by the gospel of Christ, pulling them to spiritual safety. God bless those who are led to fight abortion! God bless those who are led to fight the degradation of politics and the entertainment of our society! The commitment that I envision for our church is not to be holding a puny hose trying to put out a fire, but to be spiritual firemen who are willing to go into the house and pull out those you love—neighbors, friends, people you work with—and drag them to safety before the house collapses about them.

Amos was an angry man. The Bible does not end, though, with an angry voice of judgment. It does not end with cities in smoking ruins. The Bible ends in the book of Revelation, after God's wrath has been poured out and exhausted. It ends with a wonderful vision of a new Jerusalem. It ends with the vision of a place where there will be no death, no sorrow, no tears. It ends with hope! That's the way I want to end this message.

The Bible ends with a great invitation. The difference between me and Amos is that Amos stood at the twelfth hour and said, "It is too late!" I stand at the eleventh hour and say, "It is *not* too late!" I stand with a message of hope, saying the Bible ends with an invitation. The Bible ends by saying that the bride says come, the Spirit says come, *"whosoever will may come."*

Today we are in a day of grace and a day of hope, and though our culture may be burning and though it may be collapsing around us, and though we may be on the verge of the silence of God, the word of hope is, *"Whosoever will may come!"*

‑◌‑ 2 0 0 1 ◌‑

By the year 2001, Valley was considering another building project. Our children's Sunday School classes were "bulging."

A three-year capital funds campaign called "The Next Step," was begun. The building committee had proposed the construction of a two-story building that would house preschool Sunday School on the bottom floor and grade school children's classes on the second floor.

The church once again was alive with the excitement of sacrifice. This time our sacrifice was for the next generation.

In the fall of 2001, Valley Baptist Church hosted the annual meeting of the California Southern Baptist Convention. Valley was the first church in recent history to do so.

"Predestination and Perseverance" was preached on Sunday morning, August 26, 2001, as part of a doctrinal series of sermons entitled "What We Believe."

This series was based on the various Articles of *The Baptist Faith and Message*, the confession of faith adopted by Valley Baptist Church.

Predestination and Perseverance

EPHESIANS 1:4-9

"Just as He chose us in Him before the foundation of the world, that we should be holy and without blame before Him in love, having predestined us to adoption as sons by Jesus Christ to Himself, according to the good pleasure of His will, to the praise of the glory of His grace, by which He made us accepted in the Beloved. In Him we have redemption through His blood, the forgiveness of sins, according to the riches of His grace which He made to abound towards us in all wisdom and prudence, having made known to us the mystery of His will, according to His good pleasure that He purposed in Himself."

The doctrine of election is perhaps the most difficult doctrine in all of the New Testament. One of the things that makes it difficult is that the word *"election"* only occurs six times in the New Testament. When did He choose us? The text says that He chose us before the foundation of the world. That was before we ever did anything good, or before we individually ever did anything evil. Before we exercised faith, God chose us. Why did He choose us? Did He choose us because we were good? No. It says, He chose us *"...accord-ing to the good pleasure of His will."*

In verse 5 of Ephesians 1, we find the word *predestined.* The doctrine of predestination obviously has some pitfalls associated with it. It brings to mind *fatalism.* It brings to mind *determinism,* that we really do not have any control over our lives. It raises the question: If everything is deter-mined or predestined, why should we pray as believers? Why should we go to church? Why should we tell other people about Christ? I want to clarify from the Word of God what the Bible says about these great teachings.

The Doctrine of Election Is a Paradox

That may be the most profound thing that I can say about this doctrine. The word *paradox* means "an apparent contradiction, that which appears to be contrary, or a con-tradiction." It is not a contradiction in the mind of God. I believe God's mind is absolutely logical. In fact, it would define logic or reason. However, from our perspective, the whole doctrine of election is a contradiction to many other teachings in the Word of God. I do not think the doctrine of election is in the Bible as an intended intellectual riddle. It is not something about which we should spend our time argu-ing or debating.

I think the doctrine of election is in the Bible as an occa-sion of praise. It is in the Bible for us to be able to say that God knows and works in ways that are beyond our under-standing. It allows us to contemplate the imponderableness of God, the mystery of God's nature. It occurs to me that there are two facts concerning this doctrine that are indis-putable, that are self-evident within life. Number one is that man has a choice, that man has a will, that mankind has volition, that we make decisions. I can choose to raise my hands, for instance. No one puts me under constraint, no one forces me to do so; I do so of my will, of my prerogative. I can put my hands down and no one constrains me or determines for me to do so. When this service is over, I can get in my car and drive home, but I could choose to drive to the supermarket; or I could choose of my volition to drive to LAX for some inexplicable reason; or I could choose to take off cross country and end up in New York City. That is my choice. Yet my will and your will, in many ways are limited and determined by our human nature.

It is a self-evident fact to all of us that we have choices that we make in life, but alongside that fact is another fact— the most profound decisions of life are made for us, and even before us. We had no choice where we are born. We have no choice in our heritage or our parentage either. I was born in Elk City, Oklahoma in 1955. If I had been born ten years earlier in Hiroshima or Nagasaki, my life would have been radically different, I am sure. I could have been born a Zulu or an Australian Aborigine, but I was born an Okie and that determined much about my life. I was born in a Christian home. I could have been born in a Hindu home, a Buddhist home or a Muslim home. I did not make that choice. I did not choose my genetic makeup. I did not choose the color of my hair. Some of you ladies have chosen your color, and that is okay; but I did not choose mine. I did not choose the color of my eyes. God determined so much of who I am and who you are before we were born.

On one hand is the sovereignty of God. God is in control of human history. Alongside that is the idea that man is morally responsible. Those two things are paradoxical; they seem to be a contradiction. How can God be in control of everything and be sovereign, and yet man be responsible for the choices that he makes? In the Bible are two sets of nomenclature, two sets of Biblical words. Let's think about salvation, for instance. There is a set of words that are used from God's perspective, as if God is looking at salvation;

then there is another whole set of words that are used as if we are looking at salvation. From God's perspective, there are words like election, predestination, foreknowledge, sovereignty, omnipotence and omniscience. To God, all of history is in the present. God is outside of time. We are so locked into time and space that we cannot even comprehend otherwise. It is like a parade that is passing by and you peer through people and over their shoulders trying to get a glimpse of the parade. God sees all of the parade at once. He is far above the parade of time. Time is linear and we see only a portion of what is happening. In the parade, we see the clowns and perhaps the elephants. God is not locked in to linear time the way we are. He sees all of time. He sees the clowns at the beginning and the elephants at the end.

When we think about the words pertaining to human beings and how we look at salvation, we talk about moral freedom. We talk about possibility, contingency, choice. Think of the verses concerning salvation from God's perspective. Many verses clearly describe salvation from His perspective. In John 6:37 it says, "*'All that the Father gives me,'* Jesus said, *'will come to Me, and the one who comes to Me I will by no means cast out.'*" In John 6:44, Jesus said, "*No one can come to Me unless the Father who sent Me draws him; and I will raise him up at the last day.*" Listen to Acts 13:48: "*Now when the Gentiles heard this, they were glad and glorified the Word of the Lord. And as many as had been appointed to eternal life believed.*" In 2 Thessalonians 2:13 it says, "*But we are bound to give thanks to God always for you, brethren beloved by the Lord, because God from the beginning chose you for salvation through sanctification by the Spirit and belief in the truth.*" These verses look at salvation from God's perspective. He chose us. It does not say we chose Him, but that He chose us. Listen to some verses that look at salvation from our perspective: John 3:16, "*For God so loved the world that He gave His only begotten Son, that whosoever believes in Him should not perish, but have everlasting life."* Revelation 22:17, *"And the Spirit and the bride say, 'Come!' And let him who hears say, 'Come!' And let him who thirsts come. Whoever desires, let him take the water of life freely.'"* Romans 10:13, *"For whoever calls on the name of the LORD shall be saved."* One set of verses talks about God choosing us; the other set of verses talks about us choosing God.

There are some verses that indicate both. John, chapter 1 beginning in verse 12: *"But as many as received Him, to them He gave the right to become children of God, to those who believe in His name; who were born, not of blood, nor of the will of the flesh, nor of the will of man, but of God."* In that verse, it says, *"As many as received Him."* This is the idea of volition or choice. And then it says, *"They're born not of the will of flesh, but of the will of God."* Luke 22:22, *"And truly the Son of Man goes as it has been determined, but woe to the man by whom He is betrayed."* This verse is talking about Judas Iscariot. It was determined by God that Judas would betray the Lord Jesus. That was the plan from the very beginning, but then it says, "Woe to the guy that does it." That seems contradictory. It was predetermined, and yet Judas was fully responsible for his actions. How can you have both? It is a paradox. It was determined that Judas would betray Christ, and yet he was responsible for the choices he made. There you have both doctrines: the sovereignty of God and human responsibility.

Charles Spurgeon said that the system of truth revealed in Scriptures is not simply one straight line, but two, and no man will ever get the right view of the gospel until he knows how to look at two lines at once. These two facts, divine sovereignty and human freedom, are parallel lines. I cannot make them meet; neither can anyone make them cross each other. It is like railroad tracks. Railroad tracks never meet. You can never bring them together. The Bible teaches both divine sovereignty and human responsibility. Some passages teach God's election. Other times you will look at a passage and it teaches that we choose God. You ask which one is true. They are both true. That is the nature of a paradox. John Broudus, the great professor and president of our seminary in Kentucky in the 1800's, illustrated this truth with the fact that you can see only two sides of a building at once. If you go around the building you will see two different sides, but the first two are hidden. This is true if you are on the ground, but if you are up where God is, you can see all four sides. Our finite minds can take in sovereignty and freedom alternatively, but we cannot view them simultaneously. That is a great illustration. Our perspective is limited because we are on the ground, but God sees the entire building at once. When people finally did start flying, they were amazed to be able to see structures from God's perspective and to be able to see mountains in their entirety.

We can grasp human responsibility and divine sovereignty, but it is very difficult for us to grasp them at the same time. That is how it is with a house. A house has to do with a spatial structure, and we are limited in our perception of a spatial structure, but we can get in an airplane and see all four sides of the house at once. God is like that with time. We do not have a perspective where we can see time's beginning and its end at the same time. We can gain that perspective over a spatial structure, but we cannot humanly gain it over time. God has that perspective not only upon spatial structures, but He has that perspective upon time itself. He sees the beginning and the end all at once. It was John Bunyan, the great British preacher, who taught that when you get to Heaven and enter into its gates, written over the entrance of the gate it will say, "Whosoever will may come." Yet when you walk in the gates and look back it is going to say, "Chosen in Him before the foundation of the world." It is the same gate, but it is a matter of different perspectives.

Election and predestination are strong words. Our temptation is to explain them away. You do not have to reconcile election and human responsibility, because they are both taught in the Word of God. They are a paradox. There are many paradoxes in the Bible. The Bible presents Jesus Christ as fully man and fully God! How can you reconcile that in your mind? How can a human being be God and how can God be confined to the body of a human being? That is a paradox. You cannot fully reconcile the doctrine of the incarnation philosophically or logically within your mind, and yet the Bible presents it as a truth. Jesus was fully human and was fully divine at the exact same time. That is a paradoxical truth—an apparent contradiction—just as election and human responsibility are paradoxical truths.

The Doctrine of Election Is Necessary Because of the Nature of Man

Romans 3:10-11: *"As it is written: 'There is none righteous, no, not one; There is none who understands; There is none who seeks after God.'"* In essence, God says, "Left to themselves, no one would seek after God." Adam and Eve had absolute free will, but you and I have inherited a nature inclined towards sin. Adam and Eve were morally neutral. They could choose to obey God or to disobey God, but all of our choices are tainted by our human nature. Romans 3:23 says, *"For all have sinned and fall short of the glory of God."* You say, "Well, there might be some human being born some day who will choose not to sin." If we have free will, then why is there no one who chooses not to sin? It is because we have a nature that is inclined in its predisposition toward sin. Therefore, God must, of necessity, initiate salvation, because none of us on our own, the Bible says, seeks God. Jesus said in John 6:44, *"No one can come to Me unless the Father who sent Me draws him; and I will raise him up at the last day.*" Jesus said, "No one is going to come. No one can come, unless the Father draws him."

The Doctrine of Election Is Also Necessary Because of God's Promise to Jesus

Somewhere in eternity past, we do not know when, nor do we know what exactly was said or communicated, but at some point in eternity past, the Father promised the Son that if He would die for humanity, He would give Him a people. That someone would be saved. That someone would be atoned for. We do not have any passage we can point to that lays that out clearly, but it is inferred by many of the things Jesus said. In John 6:37, Jesus said this: *"All that the Father gives Me will come to Me, and the one who comes to Me I will by no means cast out."* He said, "All of them, every one the Father has given Me, will come." John 17, verse 6 and then verse 9 says: *"I have manifested Your name to the men whom You have given Me out of the world. They were Yours. You gave them to Me, and they have kept Your Word…I pray for them. I do not pray for the world but for those whom You have given Me, for they are Yours."* The doctrine of election is based upon the promise made by the Father to the Son, that He would literally give Him some to be His people.

The Doctrine of Election Is Not Based Upon Man's Belief or Behavior

There are some who say, "Well, here is what happened. God looked down the tunnel of time and saw who was going to be good, and chose and elected them." Or, "God looked down the tunnel of time and said, 'Well, that person is going to choose Me, and so I am going to choose him. I am going to elect him because I know he is going to choose Me.'" That is a wonderful theory, but that is not what the Word of God says. It says in Ephesians 1:5, that He chose, He adopted us "...*according to the good pleasure of His will.*" Election came out of the heart of God, because otherwise salvation would not be by grace. Salvation is by grace! Grace means unmerited favor. We do not deserve it. We do not earn it. It is not that we were so good that God said, "Oh, that person born in Elk City, Oklahoma, is going to be such a fine person, I am going to choose him." That is not what He said. He did not say, "That person is going to be so intelligent that at some point in his life he's going to choose Me, so I am going to choose him ahead of time." No, that is not being honest with the Bible. The Bible says that it was according to the good pleasure of His will. It was not according to our belief or according to our behavior that He chose us. God initiated salvation.

The Doctrine of Election Concerns Salvation, Not Damnation

There are those who will say that God chose some to go to Heaven and He chose some to go to Hell. That is an absolutely horrible view of God. In fact, I nearly shudder when I say it—that God would choose anyone to go to Hell. Election is never presented in the Bible for the seeker. It is never presented in such a way that someone can say, "Oh, I would love to come to Jesus, but I cannot. I cannot come because I am not one of the elect." Never say that you cannot come. You can only say, "I will come," or "I will not come." It is not the case that anyone *cannot* come; it is the case that they *will not* come. The door of mercy is open. Scripture declares, "Whosoever will may come." The doctrine of election in the Bible is always presented positively, never negatively. If a man goes to Hell, he goes to Hell because he chooses to go there by rejecting the Lord Jesus Christ. There is no such thing as election to Hell. In Ezekiel chapter 33, the Bible says, "'*As I live*', *says the Lord* GOD, *'I have no pleasure in the death of the wicked, but that the wicked turn from his way and live. Turn, turn from your evil ways.*'" In 2 Peter 3:9, it says, "*...the Lord is not slack concerning His promise, as some count slackness, but is longsuffering toward us, not willing that any should perish but that all should come to repentance.*" So the doctrine of election concerns salvation, not damnation.

The Doctrine of Election Does Not Contradict Man's Free Agency

We have the power of choice. Therefore, we are responsible. Our choices are controlled somewhat by our nature, but we do have the power of choice. 1 Timothy 2:14 says, "*And Adam was not deceived, but the woman being deceived, fell into transgression.*" Sometimes we get the story of the fall of Adam and Eve wrong. We think that the serpent came and tempted Adam and Eve and they were deceived, and fell into sin. That is not how it happened. "Eve was deceived," the Bible says. She did not really know what she was doing. She was deceived by the smooth words of the serpent, but Adam knew full well what he was doing. Eve had already sinned, and Adam had a choice to make: "Do I choose to be with God, or do I choose to be with my wife and follow Eve into sin?" He chose freely to sin. Man has a choice to make. In Joshua chapter 24, Joshua says, "*If it seems evil to you to serve the* LORD, *choose for yourselves this day whom you will serve, whether the gods which your fathers served that were on the other side of the river, or the gods of the Amorites, in whose land you dwell. But as for me and my house, we will serve the* LORD.*"* If we have no choice, it would be ridiculous for God to say, "Choose." We *do* have a choice. He said, "Choose whom you will serve." On one hand is the doctrine of election, and human responsibility is on the other hand. The

Bible says in Revelation 22:17: *"The Spirit and the bride say, 'Come!' And let him who hears say, 'Come!' And let him who thirsts come. Whoever desires, let him take the water of life freely."* We do have a choice to make. It is a paradox. It is a mystery. It is imponderable.

You say, "Oh, I cannot live with that. I have got to philosophically tie up all the loose ends. I cannot live with a paradox." We live with paradoxes every day. We live with them in nature, for instance. In nature there is a force that is called gravity. It is so powerful that it holds the earth in its orbit. Yet a little butterfly can fly through gravity. That is amazing. Gravity is a powerful force, and yet I can move my hand back and forth and it does not fall down or get pulled to the center of the earth. It is a paradox, in a sense.

Within nature there is centripetal force. Centripetal force is seen when something spins around an axis. It pulls everything to the center. When you stir water around and around in a bucket, everything is pulled to the middle, like a vortex. That is centripetal force! Also in nature is something called centrifugal force. Centrifugal force is when something moves around the axis and it is thrown outward. That is centrifugal force. Which is true? Is centripetal force true, that everything is pulled to the center when something rotates around the axis? Or is centrifugal force true, that everything is pushed out when it rotates around the axis? Both are true, but they are paradoxical. When you stir water in a bucket, you have centripetal force and centrifugal force in the same bucket. They are both true. In the same way, the sovereignty of God and man's choice, or human responsibility, are both true. They are paradoxical.

The apostle Paul wrote extensively in three chapters of the Book of Romans about how God had elected and had chosen Israel as a nation. Finally, he sums it up this way in Romans 11:33: *"Oh, the depth of the riches both of the wisdom and knowledge of God! How unsearchable are His judgments*

and His ways past finding out!" That is how Paul ended his
teaching on the doctrine of election. He is trying to comprehend it. He is trying to explain it, and finally he just says: "Oh,
the depth of His riches and wisdom, oh, how unsearchable
His judgments, it's past finding out; you cannot completely
reconcile it." If the apostle Paul could not quite figure it out,
neither can we!

Perseverance of the Saints

There is another great question that I want to raise with
you today, and that is this: Can someone who is a true
believer in the Lord Jesus Christ ever lose his salvation? This
is an important question. Amazingly and confusingly, the
Christian world is divided into two camps on this issue.
There are those who say that if you are a true believer, you
can never lose your salvation. There are others who say you
can lose your salvation either through an act of your will by
denying Christ or by perpetual sin. Some would even say you
can lose your salvation by the smallest infraction against the
will of God. That is called "falling from grace." Historically, a
man first proposed it, a man by the name of Jacob Armenius,
from Holland, in the sixteenth century. You cannot find it in
historical writings until the sixteenth century. I do not believe
that Jacob Armenius was right. I do not believe that a true
believer, redeemed by the blood of Jesus, saved by the grace
of God, can ever lose his salvation. That doctrine is sometimes called, "eternal security." Sometimes people call it "once
saved, always saved." Others call it "perseverance of the
saints." Some people call it "preservation of the saints." I have
not always believed this doctrine. I grew up in the Church of
the Nazarene and, of course, they are Wesleyan. John Wesley
was the eighteenth century theologian who popularized the
writings of Jacob Armenius from the sixteenth century. No
individual convinced me of the truth of eternal security. I

read no theological book on it. For a year, I gave myself to studying incessantly every night the doctrine of salvation in the Word of God. I came to the conclusion that the genuine believer cannot lose his salvation for several reasons.

Eternal Security Is Based Upon the Nature of Salvation

Some say that you are saved by your lifestyle. Others say no, it is not your lifestyle; it is some ritual such as being baptized. Or it is by taking communion or by being a member of the church. Some people think that when you die and stand before God that God is going to have giant scales. And God is going to weigh everything good that you have ever done on one side, and He is going to put everything bad on the other side. If the good outweighs the bad, then you go to Heaven. But if the bad tips the scale a little bit, then you are going to Hell. That is not what the Bible teaches. The Bible teaches that salvation, being made right with God, is based upon grace. Ephesians 2:8 says, *"For by grace you have been saved through faith, and that not of yourselves; it is the gift of God..."* Grace means unmerited favor; it is not anything you deserve, it is not anything you earn. For by grace you have been saved, and it is through the mechanism of faith, not of yourselves, *"It is the gift of God. It is the gift of God,"* not of works, not of your performance, lest anyone should boast. Salvation is either something you *attain* or it is something you *obtain*. It is either something you attain by your good works or by joining a church or by being baptized, something you do; or it is something you obtain as a gift from God. It has to be one or the other. It is either something you *achieve* or something you *receive*. I do not think you achieve salvation. I do not think anyone does because the Bible says, *"It is not of works."* If it were of works then you could boast, and have reason for pride. It is something that you receive.

Romans 5:17 tells us that we have received reconciliation, and then it says, "...*who receive abundance of grace and of the gift of righteousness...*" There are a few people I have run into, and you probably have too, that say, "Well, Preacher, I am not going to accept Christ or I am not going to come to church because I just don't think I could live it. I don't think I could live the Christian life, and I couldn't go to church regularly. Therefore, I am not going to come and I am not going to give my life to Jesus." On the surface that seems so humble. You think, "Oh that person wants to be honest, and they have so much integrity, since they do not think they could live it they are not going to come to Christ." Actually it is a very arrogant statement. Because it is a statement that says, "Salvation is up to me. I am weak." Well guess what! You do not have to tell me that. I already knew it. I already knew that you are a sinner. I already knew that you could not do enough to be saved or to stay saved. It is an arrogant statement; it is a statement that is saying salvation is something that I do. It is something that I have to achieve rather than receive. If you come to God by grace, then you have to be kept in God by grace.

The nature of faith is that it is *surrender*. It is not Jesus plus a good life. It is not Jesus plus being baptized, Jesus plus joining the church, Jesus plus your puny performance. It is *Jesus!* It is what He has done upon the cross that saves us and brings us into the right relationship with Him. Faith is about surrendering to that principle. It is about acknowledging that you have sinned and are inadequate to save or forgive yourself, so you ask God to do it for you.

While I was on vacation this summer, on the evening news was a story about a family vacationing on a river. Two boys drowned. One was a fifteen-year-old boy who was swimming when he got in trouble. He had a cramp and went under. The seventeen-year-old dived in to rescue him. Neither one of them ever came up. They both drowned. Do you know what happened? The fifteen-year-old boy was struggling for his life, and when the seventeen-year-old boy got to him the younger boy clamped hold of him and pulled them both down. This is what happens many times in a drowning. The drowning person is thrashing around and struggling. They do not surrender to the one who is there to save them, so they pull the other person down. Faith is about surrendering and saying, "I cannot do this on my own. I am drowning and I cannot do enough to earn favor with God, so I am going to relax in the arms of Jesus. I am going to surrender myself to Him to save me."

How strong does your faith have to be? It can be as weak as a woman's touch on a garment. There was a woman in the New Testament who reached out and touched the hem of Jesus' garment. It was acknowledged by Jesus as a great act of faith on her part. I heard about a hunter in the North Carolina wood. He had his rifle and was hunting in the fall or early winter. He came to a stream that was frozen. He did not know if it was thick enough to hold him up or not, so he very tentatively began to put one foot in front of the other and walk across the frozen stream. Finally when he felt that it might break, he put his rifle over his shoulder and spread out on the ice. He was just creeping across the stream when he heard this crashing noise. He turned and saw a lumberjack driving a big team of horses, pulling a wagon with a gigantic log on it. The lumberjack went right across the stream right beside the hunter. The lumberjack was laughing at him as he passed by. The ice was holding both of them up, but the one guy felt pretty insecure. There are a lot of folks who say, "Oh you can lose your salvation." Thinking that does not make it so. You may live with insecurity, but we have the promises from the Word of God. The nature of salvation being by grace gives us security. If salvation is a gift—and that is what the Word of God says—that means you do not earn it, it is *given* to you. How absurd to say, "It was given to me, but now I have to do something in order to keep it." No, it is a gift; it is grace. That is the nature of salvation. Eternal security is based upon the nature of God.

God Finishes What He Starts

Philippians 1:6 says: "*...being confident of this very thing, that He who has begun a good work in you will complete it until the day of Jesus Christ...*" He will complete it. I think that the issue of eternal security hinges upon your view of the Bible. I believe in the verbal inspiration of the Bible. That is, the very words of the Bible are inspired, even the tense of verbs. The Bible says that He will complete salvation. It is not conditional. It does not say, "He will complete it if you are good," or "He will complete it if you do not ever sin again." It says that *He will complete it.* It is based on the integrity of God. Salvation is a gift. Romans 6:23 says, "*For the wages of sin is death, but the gift of God is eternal life in Christ Jesus.*" What is the gift? It is eternal life. Follow me logically. You are going along in life and you come to a point when you accept Christ, and God gives you eternal life. Now what does eternal life mean? It means *forever!* God says in other places that He gives you everlasting life. It means absolutely forever-life without end! That is my definition. If we believe the verbal inspiration of the Word of God, then we have to accept the words of Scripture, not just the concepts. The words of Scripture have meaning. What do the words *eternal life* mean? They mean "eternal." You are saved at a point in time; ten years go by and you mess up and God says, "Hey, buddy I am taking salvation away from you." Was it eternal to begin with? Remember, the words of Scripture have meaning. If it is eternal life, by definition, it has to be eternal. It is a gift. God gives us gifts and the Bible says, at one point in Romans, that His gifts are without repentance, without change or without being altered. God gives us eternal life.

There are those who counter and say, "You do not really get eternal life until you die and go to heaven," and there is an element of truth to that. We are saved at a point in time, we are progressively being sanctified and we will be saved in glorification. Listen to what the Bible says in John 5:24. *"'Most assuredly,' I say to you, 'he who hears My Word and believes in Him who sent Me has* [that is a present tense verb] *everlasting life, and shall* [that is futuristic] *not come into judgment, but has* [that is present tense] *passed from death into life.'"* If the words of Scripture are inspired, then we have everlasting life as a present tense possession. And we shall, (future tense), not ever come into condemnation or judgment. It says what it means.

The Bible says in 2 Timothy 1:12, *"For this reason I also suffer these things; nevertheless I am not ashamed, for I know whom I have believed and am persuaded that He is able to keep that which I have committed to Him until that day."* This is the apostle Paul's confession. He says, "I have committed something to God, and I am confident and I am persuaded that God is able to keep me." He does not say, "You know what? I am confident that I am going to hold out. I am confident that I am never going to mess up, that I am never going to sin, that I am never going to deny Christ." That is not what he said. He said, "My persuasion and my confidence are in God. God is the one who is going to keep me." The word *committed* is the same word as "to deposit" or "to guard a treasure." God is guarding us. Our faith is not merely a system of belief. It is in a Savior. He says, "I know whom I have committed to, and that one is Christ."

Romans 8:38-39 says, *"For I am persuaded that neither death nor life, nor angels nor principalities nor powers, nor things present nor things to come, nor height nor depth, nor any other created thing, shall be able to separate us from the love of God which is in Christ Jesus our Lord."* Paul runs through a whole litany of things. He said, *"height, depth,"* nothing can separate you from the love of God. Then he adds *"nor any other created thing."* You might think you can separate yourself from God. When was it that you were not a created thing? All of us fall into that category. There is nothing, he says, that *"shall be able to separate us from the love of God."*

Think about what Jesus is doing right now according to Hebrews 7:25: *"Therefore He is also able to save to the uttermost, those who come to God through Him, since [or because] He always lives to make intercession for them."* God says that Jesus is able to save to the uttermost because of what He is doing right now. He is sitting at the right hand of the Father and is making intercession for us. He is an advocate and He says to God, "Do not condemn them because they are My children, they are cloaked in My righteousness. I died for them and they placed faith in Me." Salvation then is an absolute gift by God's grace.

Eternal Security Is Based Upon Specific Promises Given by God

In John 10:27, it says, *"My sheep hear My voice, and I know them, and they follow Me. And I give them eternal life, and they shall never perish; neither shall anyone snatch them out of My hand. My Father, who has given them to Me, is greater than all; and no one* [this includes you] *is able to snatch them out of My Father's hand. I and My Father are one."* What a wonderful promise. He says, "they are in God's hand and I have given them eternal life," which means by lexical definition that it is forever. That is futuristic if we believe the words of Scripture: *"They shall never perish...neither shall anyone snatch them out of My hand.*" It is an amazing promise. Listen to what John 3:16 says: *"For God so loved the world that He gave His only begotten Son, that whoever believes in Him should not perish, but have everlasting life."* How can you say you believe the first part of that verse, *"God so loved the world,"* if you don't believe the second part that says, "You are never going to perish"? How can we believe part of it without taking all of it? How can you say, "Oh, I believe that God sent His Son, but I do not believe that everlasting life is everlasting. It may last ten years, it may last fifteen, but it may not last forever." How can we pick and choose what part of the Word of God is true?

The Bible uses birth terminology about our relationship with God. We are adopted into the family of God. We are born again. That would be a sorry illustration if we could lose our salvation. God is the Father; we are His children. With my children, there is absolutely nothing that they could ever do to cease to be my children. There are many things they might do that would break my heart. There are a lot of things that they could do that might break our fellowship one with another. There are some things that they could do that would bring my judgment upon them as their dad, but there is nothing that they could do where they cease to be a blood relative to me. We are *blood relatives* to God. We are born by His blood. That is what the Bible teaches. There are things that we can lose, but we cannot break the fact that we are born into the family of God.

There is another passage we ought to consider. Ephesians chapter 1, beginning in verse 13 says, *"In Him you also trusted, after you heard the Word of truth, the gospel of your salvation; in whom also, having believed, you were sealed with the Holy Spirit of promise, who is the guarantee of our inheritance until the redemption of the purchased possession, to the praise of His glory."* The nomenclature used in the New Testament refers to God as the One who purchases our salvation. God puts up an earnest, a deposit. If you buy a house, you put up earnest money. What happens if you back out on the contract? You lose your deposit. God says, "Here is what the earnest is, the guarantee that I am going to finish this work of salvation in you. I am going to put up the Holy Spirit. He is the earnest money. The Holy Spirit is going to live within you." The illustration obviously is that if God does not perform and save you then He loses His earnest money, which is the Holy Spirit. The Holy Spirit is God and so God says, "The guarantee of the completion of salvation is Myself. I would cease to be God, I would lose Myself if I did not finish the work of salvation." John 6:37 says: *"All that the Father gives Me will come to Me, and the one who comes to Me I will by no means cast out."* Jesus said, "I am never going to cast them out." That is not a conditional sentence. He does not say, "I will by no means cast them out unless they sin," or, "I will by no means cast them out unless they become rascals." That is not what He says. It is unconditional. It is a promise of Jesus: *"I will by no means cast them out."*

You may have some questions. Number one, we all have known people who have professed faith in Christ and yet have fallen away from their commitment. They are no longer living for Jesus; some of them are living like the devil. You wonder, "Are they really saved?" Once saved always saved! You know what I think a better nomenclature is? Instead of "once saved, always saved," it is *"if* saved, always saved." "Your lifestyle," the Bible says in many places, "justifies or validates whether you really have faith." Your lifestyle is evidence of whether you have faith.

Listen to how John said it in 1 John 2:19, an extremely important verse in this argument: *"They went out from us,"* and He is talking about people that appear to be Christians and yet they do not persevere. *"They went out from us, but they were not of us, for if they had been of us, they would have continued with us; but they went out that they might be made manifest, that none of them were of us.*" That is an inescapable verse. John says that these people who say that they were saved when they were twelve years old and then live like the devil the rest of their lives, they are not of us, they are not genuine believers. They went out from us; in fact, going out from us is a demonstration that they were not of us. You ask, "Can a Christian ever drift into sin?" Yes, I think they can, but I think there is also a time when they come back to Christ. I do not think they are going to spend a lifetime away from God. John did not believe that. I do not believe that.

If you could lose your salvation, you could never be saved again. It is either once saved, always saved, or twice lost, always lost. Hebrews chapter 6, is the passage that ultimately convinced me of the doctrine of eternal security in my youth. Hebrews chapter 6, beginning in verse 4: *"For it is impossible for those who were once enlightened, and have tasted the heavenly gift, and have become partakers of the Holy Spirit, and have tasted the good Word of God and the powers of the age to come, if they fall away, to renew them again to repentance, since they crucify again for themselves the Son of God, and put Him to an open shame."* The writer of Hebrews is giving a hypothetical circumstance and says: "Someone that is genuinely saved, if they fall away, if that were possible, they could never be saved again, because the work of Christ is a once-and-for-all sacrifice applied to our lives." Hebrews 9:12, *"Not with the blood of goats and calves, but with His own blood He entered the most holy place once for all."* It is a perfect tense; once and for all He did it, having obtained eternal redemption. So once you come to Christ, Jesus' death and blood are applied to you, fully, completely. You are saved; you are clothed in the righteousness of Jesus because of what Jesus did. If, and it is a hypothetical "if," you could lose that, then Jesus would have to die again. You say that does not make sense. That is exactly what the writer of Hebrews said. That is the argument he is presenting. It is a hypothetical argument. You are either once saved, always saved or twice lost, forever lost.

There are things that you can lose. There are many passages in the Bible warning about making sure you are really saved. You can lose your *reward* if you do not live the way you should. You can lose your *fellowship with God*. Not the fact that He is your Father and you are His child, but you can develop a broken relationship with Him. You can lose your *joy*. When David got away from God by sinning with Bathsheba, he did not say, "God, restore unto me Your salvation." He said, *"Restore unto me the joy of Your salvation."* He had lost his joy. You can lose your *peace*. We are to live a good life. You do not live a good life in a causative way in order to be saved, but because you *are* saved. You do not live a good life in order to earn favor with God, but because you *have* favor with God. Some people say, "If I believed that, I would just live it up. I would get saved and then I would live however I wanted." Then you do not understand the grace of God, or the change that He brings into your life. It is like if you are on a football team and the coach says, "Hey, you guys are unbeatable. Man, you are the greatest team I have ever had." The parents say, "You are the greatest team that we have ever had in this high school," and the media says, "You are number one." Do you think all of that affirmation is going to make that team play worse? It is going to make them play better. That is positive reinforcement. When God says you are eternally saved, that is a powerful motivation in your life. It is unconditional love.

We say, "I will love you if you act a certain way. If you do not, then I am out of here. I will love you since you are beautiful or since this, or since that." But God says, unconditionally, that He loves us. Unconditional love is such a motivation. Remember the story about the prodigal son? He left home and squandered his inheritance. Jesus told the story of how he came back to the father and said, "I am not coming back as a son. I am going to come back as a servant." But the father would have nothing to do with that because the young man was still his son. He had not been acting like a son and he had not been living like a son, but the father's love was not contingent upon the performance of the son.

People sometimes ask, "What if I lose faith?" Listen to 2 Timothy 2:13: *"If we are faithless, He remains faithful; He cannot deny Himself."* When you become a Christian, God lives within you, and for Him to deny you is to deny Himself. He would have to deny all the promises that He has made, and He is not going to do that. It is like when you are crossing the street with a little child in traffic, and the little child is afraid and reaches up and takes Dad's hand. At the same time they reach up and grab hold of your hand, you, as a father, grasp theirs. They may let go, but the father is not going to let go. There are times of weakness in all of our lives when we want to let go. There was a time in salvation when you reached up and said, "I want Christ in my life," and you grabbed hold of His hand. Some day you may lose your grasp on God, but God will never, ever lose His grasp on you.

~☙ 2002 ☙~

In January of 2002, twenty members from Valley Baptist
Church went on a short-term mission trip to El Salvador.
Beginning in 1999, short-term mission trips became a part of
the church's mission strategy. Valley members on such trips
have won thousands of people to Christ in various countries.

In 2002, plans were drawn for the new children's building and
approved by the church. People continued to give to the "Next
Step." For the first time, the church budget exceeded $4 million.

In addition to the children's building, the church approved the
construction of a new office building and storage building.
Together, these three buildings constituted the largest construction project yet for Valley Baptist Church.

"God's High Expectations" was preached on Sunday morning,
November 10, 2002, as part of a series of messages entitled
"Discovering God's Word."

This particular series of messages was taken each week from a
section of Scripture being read by the congregation, based
upon a two-year commitment to read through the Bible.

God's High Expectations

"LORD, who may abide in Your tabernacle? Who may dwell in Your holy hill? He who walks uprightly, And works righteousness, And speaks the truth in his heart; He who does not backbite with his tongue, Nor does evil to his neighbor, Nor does he take up a reproach against his friend; In whose eyes a vile person is despised, But he honors those who fear the LORD; He who swears to his own hurt and does not change; He who does not put out his money at usury, Nor does he take a bribe against the innocent. He who does these things shall never be moved." (NKJV)

In my opinion, one of the most important books written on the subject of church growth is a book written by Dr. Thom Rainer entitled *High Expectations*. It is a book that deals with the issue of membership requirements for a church. The book does not give answers. Instead, it is a survey book of hundreds of churches across America. It chronicles what is happening as far as the trends in churches.

For centuries, particularly in a Baptist Church, if you were saved and baptized, then you automatically became a member of the church. Now there are many churches across America where you cannot be baptized until you go through an extensive training period, including some classes that last as long as six months. Many of these classes consist of intense catechism-type training and tests to determine if you are qualified to be baptized. There are other churches that say you cannot be a member of their church unless you are involved in ministry or a leadership position. There are other churches, and there are hundreds of them in our country now, where you cannot be a member of the church unless you tithe. If you do not make a commitment to support the church financially with 10 percent of your income, then you cannot be a member of that church.

In our church we do not have those kinds of requirements. We believe that if God accepts you into His family, then who are we not to accept you into our family? We believe that if you are saved, you are in God's family, and you are to be baptized as an act of obedience. When you are baptized, you become part of our church family. However, we do have some rather high expectations. Though not a requirement, it is expected that when people become members of our church, they attend a new-member information class, which explains our expectations of members. In talking to dozens of pastors trying to work through this issue, I have wondered, what is it that *God* expects? I am not speaking in regard to what He expects in order to be a member of this church or that church, but what is it that God expects of us now that we are Christians?

Psalm 15, in my opinion, contains God's expectations of how we should live. He has rather high expectations. As best we can determine from Old Testament history, this great psalm was written by David when he brought the Ark of the Covenant back to Jerusalem to be placed in the tabernacle. The Ark of the Covenant represented the presence of God. Inside a little chest made of acacia wood and covered in gold were the tablets of the Ten Commandments. It was placed in the Holy of Holies in the tabernacle, where only once a year a High Priest could enter, and later in the Holy of Holies in the temple. The Ark of the Covenant had been captured by the Philistines, the arch enemies of the Israelites and the people of Judah. The Philistines had possession of the Ark until they began to have difficulties. They tried to take it back. It ended up in storage in a man's house for a number of years. When David became the new king of the United Empire, both Judah in the south and Israel in the north, the first act of business on his agenda was to bring back the Ark of the Covenant, the symbol of God's presence. He desired to reinstitute the worship of God in the tabernacle on the hill, the holy hill in Jerusalem. In parade-like fashion, they brought back the Ark of the Covenant. People lined the streets, rejoicing and cheering. The Bible says that David danced before the Lord. I do not know if it was kind of a ballet or if he did the boogie-woogie! It was a great time of celebration and of worship. David began to reflect on true worship, and out of that reflection he wrote Psalm 15.

As he began to think about what God really expects, perhaps he was reminded of what happened when they first began to bring the Ark of the Covenant back. They placed it on a cart pulled by oxen, which made sense, since they had a long way to travel. The problem, however, was that very early in the Old Testament, God had forbidden that the Ark of the Covenant be carried that way. There were rings on the side of the Ark and there were to be poles put through the rings. It was to be carried on the shoulders of only Levite priests. They disobeyed, not paying attention to what God's Word said, and they carried the Ark of the Covenant on a cart. They hit a "chuck hole," or a rough place, and a young man by the name of Uzzah reached up to steady the Ark so it would not fall off the cart. Instantly God struck him dead! David was upset, as were Uzzah's friends. David thought that Uzzah's death was unfair. However, as they researched the Old Testament, they found that God had said that anyone who touched the Ark of the Covenant would die! God was expressing how serious He was about the details of His Word.

As David reflected during the celebration, he asked the rhetorical question in verse 1, *"Lord who may abide in Your tabernacle and who may dwell in Your holy hill?"* Such a question must have been uppermost on his mind since the death of Uzzah. He asked God what He expected. Psalm 15 is poetry, so it is symbolic language. He is not talking literally about abiding in the tabernacle in the holy hill. It is a poetic way of asking, "What kind of person do You approve of? What kind of person is qualified ultimately to have a relationship with You?"

Imagine that you travel to London and stand outside of Buckingham Palace. One of those guards in the funny hats is standing rigid, at attention, and you say, "Excuse me, I have a U-haul of stuff out here and I would like to move into Buckingham Palace. Would that be okay?" First of all, he is going to think you are a quack, and if you persist you are probably going to be arrested, because the only people who can live in Buckingham Palace are family—royal family! David is asking the rhetorical question, "Who can live with God? Who can have a relationship with God?" The fact is, the only people who have a relationship with God are family— spiritual family. The important question then becomes, "How do you become a part of God's family?" The New Testament answers that very clearly. In a dialogue between Jesus and a religious leader named Nicodemus, Jesus said, "You must be born again, or you cannot get into the Kingdom of God." You must be born again—regenerated, literally! *Generate* comes from *Genesis,* meaning "beginning," and *re* a "new" beginning. You must have a new beginning, a new birth. You may be asking, "How do I do that? Is it by going to church? Is it by giving a certain amount of money?

Is it by doing good? If the good I do outweighs the bad I do, then does that make me a Christian? Then am I born again?" In Ephesians 2:8 and 9, Paul said, "*For by grace you have been saved through faith and that not of yourselves; it is the gift of God not of works, lest anyone should boast.*" The New Testament declares that we are made right with God, not based upon our works or upon our lifestyle, but as a gift of God. God gives us the gift of spiritual birth! There was no human effort on your part in being born physically. When you are born into God's family, it is not because of human effort on your part, it is a gift that God offers you in response to your faith!

That is not really what Psalm 15 is about. It is not about being born again. It strikes me that there are fundamentally two overarching themes in the Bible:

- The first theme is *our way to God*, which is written to the sinner.
  - How am I made right with God?
  - How can I have a right standing before God?
  - How can I, as a sinful human being, get to God?

That is what much of the Bible is written about. The story of redemption, particularly the New Testament, is about our way to God. Concurrent with that great theme is another theme:

- Not so much our way to God, but *our walk with God*, not written to the sinner, but written to the saint, or the believer.
  - Now that I am a Christian, how then should I live?
  - What should be the attitude and the actions of my life?
  - What should be my character and conduct; what should be my belief and my behavior?

In theological parlance, we call the way to God *salvation.* Our walk with God is called *sanctification.*

Sanctification simply means "to be set apart." It means that you and I, if we are Christians, are to be different. We are not to live the same way the world lives. We are to have different values. We are to have a different worldview and a different lifestyle. We are to be distinct from the world if we have been regenerated. The apostle Paul said in 2 Corinthians 5:17, *"Therefore if anyone is in Christ, he is a new creation: old things have passed away; behold, all things have become new."* The Bible teaches that when you become a Christian, you become a new person, you are born again, you are regenerated. What does a new person look like spiritually?

The New Testament is full of descriptions of the Christian life, but Psalm 15, even though it is in the Old Testament, is an old portrait of a new person. A description of what a believer should look like and how he should live. It is a description of what God's expectations are of us. David asks in Psalm 15, *"Who may dwell in Your holy hill?"* We are guests of God, in a sense. David speaks of God's place! When we get to Heaven, we will be guests in His house. I do not know about you, but when I was a little kid and we would go over to someone's house, especially if we went over to the pastor's house, my mom or my dad inevitably would say to me, "Mind your manners." I knew exactly what that meant. It meant, "You are going to be in major trouble, kid, when you get home if you mess up. Mind your manners." That is what Psalm 15 is saying. It is saying, "If you are going to be a guest of God and have a relationship with God, then mind your manners. God has some expectations of how we should live as believers."

Psalm 15 is not the only time this question occurs in the Bible. Psalm 24 says, in verse 3, *"Who may ascend into the hill of the LORD? Or who may stand in His holy place? He who has clean hands and a pure heart, who has not lifted his soul to an idol, nor sworn deceitfully."* That is quite a list! There is another list in Isaiah 33, where it says, *"Who among us shall dwell with the devouring fire? Who among us shall dwell with everlasting burnings? He who walks righteously and speaks uprightly; he who despises the gain of oppression. Who gestures with his hands, refusing bribes, Who stops his ears from hearing of bloodshed, And shuts his eyes from seeing evil: He will dwell on high."* The rhetorical question, "Who may dwell with the Lord?" is asked in three different places: Psalm 15, Psalm 24 and Isaiah 33. All three answers are similar, but they are very different in detail.

Consistency Regarding Our Character

The five expectations I am going to describe for you in Psalm 15 are not exhaustive. They are representative of how a Christian should live. Number one, as Christians, we are to be consistent regarding our character. In verse 2 of this great psalm, we see that God expects that you walk uprightly, that you work righteousness and that you speak the truth in your heart. In the last two years, practically every major secular magazine has done feature articles on what has been called in America the integrity crisis. Many of the nightly news shows in America have featured programs dealing with the integrity crisis. It seems we have grown accustomed to turning on the television in the evening and watching the news of a scandal, or picking up a paper and reading about the latest political scandal. We have grown accustomed to scandals with celebrities, such as shoplifting. There are scandals on the sports page, of famous sports figures caught with drugs, or even shooting people. In the last year, we have seen scandals in the business section of our newspaper and, at times, even in the religious section.

David begins this great psalm by saying the first expectation that God has of a believer is that you would be consistent in your character. He who walks *upright*—the word literally means "to be whole." It is not that you are strong in one area and weak everywhere else, or that you are strong in all areas and yet you have a glaring open weakness that you are not dealing with. It means to be strong in every area, to be consistent in your character. As a believer, you could live your life morally, going to church, and even be involved in leadership in the church, yet absolutely ruin your testimony in five minutes. That is all it would take! You can spend a lifetime building up credibility as a Christian, and in one unguarded moment you can wreck that with your family, or the people you work with, or with everyone, because even our world expects a Christian to have consistent character. God's expectation is that we walk uprightly, to be consistent so that our life is the same on Monday as it is on Sunday.

I do not know on how many occasions people have come to me as their pastor and talked to me about someone who is a member of our church, perhaps someone we were considering for leadership, and they have said, "You know what? He is not the same person at work. He is different from what you see at church." Or maybe someone will talk about how a person is different in his temper, or his attitude from the way he is at church. Sometimes a young person will say, "You do not know my mom or my dad. They seem so Christian at church, but they are different at home." Character fundamentally is about consistency—about being the same on Monday as Sunday, about being the same at work as in Sunday School, about being the same in every circumstance of life.

There are people who will come to church and worship the Lord, and seem so in love with Jesus, and yet they are shady in their business dealings. Somehow they can differentiate between the secular and the sacred, as if those things can be disjoined in a believer's life. Proverbs 20:6: *"Most men will proclaim each his own goodness,* [Isn't that true?] *But who can find a faithful man? The righteous man walks in his integrity; His children are blessed after him.*" Do you see the connection? There is a connection between a happy home life and consistent character. When you are inconsistent as a believer, it sends an awful signal to the children in your home. Often parents take the stance, "Do as I say, not as I do." The problem with that is that more things are caught than are taught. Most of the time, children end up doing as you do, not so much as you say. They see you go to church and worship the Lord. They may see you even pray or read your Bible; but then they also hear you tell a lie, and they know it is a lie. What signal does that send to a child? Or they know their daddy goes to church and seems to be such a fine Christian, but they know there is pornography on Dad's computer. What kind of signal does that send to a child?

I was nineteen years old when I preached my very first revival meeting. I used to preach a lot of revival meetings, but in recent years, with different demands in my schedule, I have not been able to do revival meetings like I once did. A pastor at a church in Alabama asked me to preach a youth revival. It was the first time I ever flew on a commercial airliner, so I was excited. We had a great revival. Dozens and dozens of young people were saved. Nearly every night I would stay until eleven or twelve o'clock, talking to various teenagers, leading them to Christ. About halfway through the revival meeting, after church, I met a fourteen-year-old girl. At that point in my life, I had never met a person like this girl. She spewed out hate and anger. I tried my best to reason with her, to explain the gospel and win her to Christ. She wanted nothing to do with Jesus! Nothing! She said, "I will never be saved, I will never give my life to Christ." I asked her why. She said it was because of her dad. She said, "My dad is at church all the time, but he's not the same at home." She described to me how abusive and overbearing her father was and then I will never forget, she said, "My dad is the pastor of this church!" For the first time, I understood the power of inconsistent character. Proverbs says that if you will be consistent, if you will walk in integrity, your children will be blessed.

The second half of this verse about character addresses not so much what we are but what we do. Verse 2 says, *"And you work righteousness."* The Christian life is not just measured in terms of being; it is also measured in terms of doing. Sometimes we start thinking the Christian life is only about the absence of doing wrong, maybe pastors feed that misconception. Not doing something wrong is morality, but spirituality is a step further.

- Morality has to do with not doing what is wrong.
- Spirituality has to do with doing what is right, the works of righteousness.

It makes me sick sometimes when I watch the news. Sometimes I even talk back to the newscasters! I have this ongoing conversation with Tom Brokaw once in a while. It makes me sick when I see people in our culture, who claim to be Christians but they are not living as Christians. Lost people living like lost people does not bother me so much, but when I turn on the television and I hear about a priest who is a pedophile, that makes me mad. When I see some Protestant minister who is adulterous or greedy, it makes me angry. If that makes me sick with my expectations, imagine how it hurts the great heart of God with His holy expectations!

There has been a drift in our culture for a number of years now. At one time, virtually everyone in America agreed with what God's expectations of right and wrong were. Not everyone did what was right, but they understood what was right and wrong. That is no longer true today. Now an unmarried couple will come to our church and say they want to be members of our church, but they are living with one another in fornication. We tell them that if they are going to get married, they need to separate until they are married; and if they are not going to get married, then they shouldn't be living together at all. Sometimes when we say that, they are shocked! They ask, "What do you mean? Why can't I follow Jesus anyway? Living together has nothing to do with my spiritual life." Now our culture has drifted so badly that in such moments of confrontation, not only are people shocked, often they are offended! They say, "How dare you sit in judgment of me and my lifestyle!" Even those who are homosexuals will say, "I do not understand why I cannot be a member. I should be able to be a part of the church regardless of my lifestyle because following Jesus has nothing to do with my lifestyle." Yes it does! God has some very high expectations of us. That is what Psalm 15 is about. David said that the first expectation is that you have consistent character.

He goes on and says that you speak the truth in your heart. Honesty is essential to character. I think honesty is *fundamental* to character. The words here, *speak the truth in your heart,* carries with it the idea of being trustworthy—that is what character is all about!

Restrained Regarding Our Words

Now we move from verse 2, which deals with honesty, to verse 3, which deals with our words. As Christians, we are not only to be consistent regarding our character, but we are to be restrained regarding our words. Look at what it says: *"He who does not backbite with his tongue, nor does evil to his neighbor, nor does he take up a reproach against his friend."*

Little children, sometimes, playing together will stick out their tongues, and say, "Sticks and stones may break my bones, but words will never hurt me." You know what? Words can hurt! Words are powerful. A child can wither under the weight of a harsh word. Words can create wounds that last a lifetime. Many times I have had the experience of talking to people who are way up in years—in fact near the end of their lives. Their own parents have been dead for decades, and yet with tears in their eyes they will say, "I could never please my dad. I could never live up to what he wanted." Or I will hear something like this: "My mom or my dad, they made me feel stupid," or "They said that I was worthless." For a lifetime they have wilted under those words. The second expectation God has in Psalm 15 has to do with the restraint of our words. He said that you are not to backbite. What a graphic word. What a word picture—*backbite!*

Imagine another human being taking a big chunk out of your shoulder. Biting—what a graphic word! Not to backbite means not to say mean or hateful things. Some translate it "to slander." Webster says "to slander" means to "utter false charges or misrepresentation that damages another." Our words do not even have to be false, if you are misrepresenting with the intent of damaging. The Hebrew word that is translated "backbite" comes from the root word that means the "hoof of a horse." Actually, we still use the saying today when we say that someone is really "hoofing it." It means they are really moving. First, you get a little tidbit of information, and you start hoofing it around, telling everyone about it. That is gossip! You try to hurt and undermine other people by telling things you should not be saying.

We are not only not to backbite with our tongue, but we are not to do evil to our neighbor. Some translate it that we should not even *listen* to slander. It takes two to gossip! It takes the one to slander, but it takes the other one to listen. When someone starts talking mean about other folks, you should walk away. Why is it that they talk slanderous to you, and not to everyone else? Is it that your ears look like "big garbage cans," and they want to dump something in your head? You need to ask yourself, when someone gossips to you, "What do they think of me as a person, that I would want to engage in gossip?" It says something about your character to listen to it, and it says something about theirs to say it. The Bible goes on to say in the same verse, *not to reproach against his friend.* The word *reproach* means "cutting." It is not a neighbor now; it is a friend. We play word games, cutting each other with little innuendos. Sometimes those cuts have meaning behind them. Someone has said that you can bury your friends with a lot of "little digs." We are to live with restraint concerning our words.

I heard about a woman who was bitten by a dog. She took a while to go to the doctor. Finally when she went, the doctor made his diagnosis. He had horrible news. He told her she had rabies and it was past treating. He told her it was terminal, that she was going to die. She was so broken by the news that she sobbed uncontrollably. Finally, she pulled out a notepad and began to write on it. The doctor, thinking perhaps she was making her last will and testament, but wondering what she was doing, asked, "Are you taking notes about treatment, or what we're going to do from here?" She said, "No, I am making a list of all the people I am going to bite!" That is human nature, is it not?

Our tongue can be sharper than our teeth. Our words can bite. God's expectations are that we live with consistent character and that we live with restraint regarding our words.

Careful Regarding Our Friends!

The third expectation for us as Christians is that we are to be careful regarding our friends. Verse 4, *"In whose eyes a vile person is despised, but he honors those who fear the LORD."* David moves from how we treat people to how we actually regard them in our heart. That word *vile* means "worthless." It means "reprobate," a person who is an avowed unbeliever.

This does not refer to your run-of-the-mill *lost* person who does not know Christ. This is a person who is hostile to the things of God, and there are plenty of those people in our culture. I see them everywhere. I saw a guy on television a while back, a political analyst named James Carville, who cursed Billy Graham! They had to bleep it out because he was taking God's name in vain and cursing Billy Graham and his ministry. Why? Because Billy Graham said that a Muslim must accept Christ in order to go to Heaven. Some celebrities in our culture, like Roseanne Barr and others, are so hostile to Christians, they are vile. The Bible says that you are to despise that kind of lifestyle. It is saying that those who dwell with God do not hang out with reprobates. Sometimes, people will say, "I think I should go to this party to witness to my friends." Here it says you are to despise the reprobate, the vile person. It disturbs me that Christian people sometimes make heroes out of certain sports figures who are vile, merely because they can hit a baseball, throw a football, or dunk a basketball. Our children hang posters of heroes in their bedrooms simply because they can do something with a leather sphere when they are, in fact, vile in their lifestyle. David also said: *"But he honors those who fear the Lord."* He is saying, "You be careful of who your heroes are, be careful who your friends are, be careful of the models you have for your life." Here is the problem. We live in a culture where people would rather be envied than admired. If someone wins the lottery, we envy that person, who may be the vilest person on earth. We envy fame and prestige and money. Men envy the way that a guy can play basketball, or the way he can hit a baseball, yet he may be vile in his lifestyle. In America, we would rather be envied than admired, so we make our heroes those we envy instead of those we admire. David is saying we need to be careful who we allow to influence us.

Demonstrate Integrity Regarding
Our Commitments

The next thing he says is that as Christians we are to demonstrate integrity regarding our commitments. The end of verse 4 says, *"He who swears to his own hurt and does not change."* That means that when you make a promise, you are going to keep it, even if it is going to hurt you. Anyone can keep a promise if it is to thier advantage. How hard is that? God expects, if you make a promise, if you swear to something even to your own hurt, that you are going to keep it. We make a lot of promises in this culture. What about the promise that people make when they stand at the front of the church, in front of a preacher and they say, "For better or for worse?" Anyone can keep that promise when everything is going great. Even an atheist can keep that promise. An ungodly vile person can keep that promise when everything is going great. But what about during difficult times when it does become "worse"? People say, "God does not want me to be unhappy." God wants you to keep your word! People borrow money and say, "Oh, I intended to pay it back, but times are tough." What does God expect? He expects us to keep our word. He wants us to be people whose word is our bond.

There was a time in America when not only did God expect that, but the entire culture expected your word to be your bond. That culture is gone! There was a time when big business deals could be made on a handshake, but now if you buy a house you have to sign in about fifty different places and initial in 810 more places. Do you know why? Because there is the idea in our culture, "If I can take advantage of you, then shame on you for allowing the loophole in the contract." It is not about honesty and integrity—it is about loopholes. In essence, God is saying, what I expect is that when you swear it is to your own hurt, even if it is tough.

Jim Voss was a man who was a notorious criminal in America a number of years ago. He was converted to Christ. Not only did he get wonderfully and gloriously saved, but he was called to preach. He began to preach as an evangelist and was invited to preach a weeklong meeting at a little church down south in Gardena, California. He accepted the invitation and said he would be there on a certain date. After he accepted the invitation, though, there was a huge church in Boston that asked him to come and preach on that very same day. He had a crisis of conscience. He thought about canceling the meeting in the little church in Gardena, and going to Boston. Obviously, it was going to pay more for his ministry—but it was not just about money. His reasoning was, "I will be preaching to thousands of people in Boston, and only a handful of people in Gardena." He was thinking of the impact of the gospel. Then he realized that his word was his bond, and he had sworn to his own hurt. He kept the commitment and preached in the little church in Gardena.

A few days after the meeting, the FBI came calling on him. They knocked on his door and identified themselves as the FBI. They asked, "Are you Jim Voss?" When he said, "Yes," they said, "You are under arrest." He was shocked! "Arrest?" He had been living for the Lord for some time so he asked, "Why? Why am I being arrested?" They replied, "Armed robbery." He said, "Armed robbery? Where and when? What are you talking about?" They were there to arrest him for one of the most famous robberies in American history—the Brinks robbery. Maybe you saw the movie or read a book about that famous heist. In the headquarters in Washington, D.C., as the FBI began to profile, they said that Jim Voss was one of the few men in America who could have planned such a job, not recognizing that his life had been changed. As they questioned him, they asked, "Were you in Boston on January 17?" He said, "No, I was going to be in Boston on January 17, but actually I was preaching in a little church in Gardena, California, all that week, and there are dozens of witnesses." I love that story! Here is a man who swore to his own hurt. Yet God rewarded him and kept him out of hot water because he kept his commitment.

Let me ask you this. Do you keep your word? Even when it is going to cost you money? Or do you try to find some loophole so that you can squirm out of it?

Charitable Regarding Our Money

The last thing David says is that as Christians we are to be charitable regarding our money. Look in verse 5: *"He who does not put out his money at usury, nor does he take a bribe against the innocent."* Usury means interest. Does that mean that you cannot collect interest for your savings account? No, that is not what it means. It is talking about an obscure Old Testament law that prohibited a Hebrew from charging interest to another Hebrew, to his brother. It was not a banking law. It is saying that you do not take advantage of people just because you *can* take advantage. We are to meet the needs of people not based solely upon profit. There are Christians who would never dream of giving to other people, or they would never dream of giving to the Lord's work. There is a "disconnect" in their mind between business and Christianity, and yet Jesus taught a great deal about our possessions. He goes on to say, *"Nor does he take a bribe against the innocent."* He is talking about our priorities. Are you more interested in money than you are in justice? That is His question. Would you take a little money under the table? Or would you take a bribe as a juror against an innocent person because money is that important to you? He says, "God expects something different." The principle is that we are to be giving people and not greedy people.

Most all of us followed the news in recent weeks of the sniper who was killing people in Maryland, Virginia and the Washington D.C. area. He also killed in Alabama and perhaps Washington State, but we did not know that initially. Before the two men were caught, there were fifty truck drivers who were part of a fellowship of Christian truck drivers who drove in that area constantly, who got together for a prayer meeting. They prayed that the guilty person, or persons, would be caught. One of those truck drivers, Ron Lance, was a man who was just days away from retirement. After the prayer meeting, he told a number of people that he thought God was going to use him to help catch this guy. That was a very audacious statement, but he made it.

It was not long until the police received a tip concerning the car and the license plate. The information was broadcast on the radio. Ron Lance pulled into a rest stop, and there was the car with the license plate! The people were asleep in the car, so he took his eighteen-wheeler, blocked their exit, and called 911. He said it was the longest fifteen minutes of his life until the police arrived. The criminals were captured and are now facing indictment. There was a half million dollar reward leading to the capture and ultimate conviction of these men. Ron Lance was a guy facing retirement after working all his life as a truck driver. I would think he could use half a million bucks. Interestingly, though, they asked this Christian man, "What are you going to do with the $500,000 reward?" He said, "I am going to give it to the families of the victims." I don't know if he will ultimately do that, but *that* is a hero! Here is a man who saw the hand of God in his own life. He did not exploit a situation, but was charitable with his money. Let me ask you this: How did you do with this list?

- Are you consistent regarding your character?
- Do you show restraint regarding your words?

- Are you careful in the selection of your heroes, and even of your friends?
- Do you demonstrate integrity regarding the commitments that you make?
- Are you charitable regarding your money?

I do not know about you, but this passage was pretty tough on me. As I looked at the nitty-gritty of this chapter, I saw it like a tough multiple-choice exam. But the end result, he said, in verse 5, is that the person who does these things shall never be moved. That's what we want! We want to be stable; we want to be solid.

What does God expect? Who may dwell on the hill of the Lord? It is the person who meets these five expectations of God.

2 0 0 3

In the summer of 2003, Valley Baptist Church's choir and orchestra were asked to perform at the Southern Baptist Convention in Phoenix, Arizona. Everyone in our church was honored by such a request. We could not have been more proud of Valley's music ministry.

The church voted to borrow $11.3 million in order to build a children's building, office building and storage building, plus refinance our existing loan. The office building and storage building were completed, and construction on the children's building was begun in 2003.

"A Vision of Christian Maturity" was preached on Sunday morning, February 2, 2003, as part of the two-year series of messages entitled "Discovering God's Word."

A Vision of Christian Maturity

ISAIAH 6:1-8

"In the year that King Uzziah died, I saw the Lord sitting on a throne, high and lifted up, and the train of His robe filled the temple. Above it stood seraphim; each one had six wings: with two he covered his face, with two he covered his feet, and with two he flew. And one cried to another and said: 'Holy, holy, holy is the LORD of hosts; The whole earth is full of His glory!' And the posts of the door were shaken by the voice of him who cried out, and the house was filled with smoke. So I said: 'Woe is me, for I am undone! Because I am a man of unclean lips, And I dwell in the midst of a people of unclean lips; For my eyes have seen the King, The LORD of hosts.' Then one of the seraphim flew to me, having in his hand a live coal which he had taken with the tongs from the altar. And he touched my mouth with it, and said: 'Behold, this has touched your lips; Your iniquity is taken away, And your sin purged.' Also I heard the voice of the Lord, saying: 'Whom shall I send, And who will go for Us?' Then I said, 'Here am I! Send me.'"

A t the time of Isaiah 6, Isaiah was a young man, but he was already arguably the greatest prophet of the Old Testament era. King Uzziah, Isaiah's friend, died after serving as king for fifty-two years. The people had grown accustomed to his rule, many having known no other king except Uzziah. Under Uzziah, commerce flourished and the military expanded. In many ways, it was the high-water mark for the nation of Judah. Perhaps Isaiah had a premonition that things would never quite be the same with the death of Uzziah, and he was right. They were never the same.

The death of King Uzziah began the long, slow spiritual decline of the nation of Judah. The king died suddenly, and his death created a crisis for the young prophet, Isaiah. Sometimes when something or someone who is dear to us is taken, it causes us to look up to God, and that is exactly what happened with Isaiah. When Uzziah died, Isaiah was propelled to go to the house of the Lord for a time of worship, where he had a tremendous vision of the Lord, high and lifted up.

In 1974 Gail Sheehy wrote a book called *Passages*, which became a runaway bestseller. The book deals with different epics, or periods of life, that we all face. The first passage she named "Pulling Up Roots," which, according to Sheehy, occurs in about your eighteenth year when you leave the nuclear family and launch out on your own. The next passage she called "The Trying Twenties," when you are getting started in life, figuring out what your life is going to be like. The next passage is what she calls, "The Catch Thirties," where you are tearing up what you found out in the twenties. Following is the next passage that she calls, "The Deadline Decade." Beginning somewhere in your mid- or late-thirties, it stretches through your forties. It is a time where there is either the renewal of the vision and the goals of life, or there is a resignation to what life has brought. In her famous book about passages, there is no mention of God, there is no mention of a relationship with God, yet when I read Isaiah chapter 6, I cannot help but think with the death of Uzziah, it was a passage in the life of Isaiah. He knew that when Uzziah died, life would never be the same, and so he ran to the temple, and it was there that he had a vision of the Lord. There are some who say that he literally saw the Lord! Others say the vision is not objective; it is subjective. I do not know whether it was a vision by day or a dream by night, but either way, he saw the Lord high and lifted up. Isaiah 6 is an amazing description of God and the worship experience that Isaiah had.

Contrast Isaiah's experience with the Roman general Pompey who, with legions of Roman soldiers, invaded Judah in 63 B.C. and annexed Judah as part of the Roman Empire. He captured the city of Jerusalem and the temple itself. He entered the outer courts of the temple, the court of the Gentiles, and walked on through the court of Israel, the court of the women and the court of the priests. Then he stood before the door of the sanctuary itself. The Jewish people fell on their faces by the thousand, begging the Roman general Pompey not to desecrate their temple, but he threw open the door of the sanctuary and walked into the holy place. He walked past the seven-branch lampstand and the table of showbread and the golden incense altar, the very place where King Uzziah was struck with leprosy because he dared enter the temple and act not as a king but as a priest. Then, in one of the most despicable acts of religious contempt of the ancient world, he pulled back the veil that separated the Holy Place from the Holy of Holies and stalked into the Holy of Holies. After a moment, Pompey came out and announced that it was empty, that there was nothing in there but darkness.

Contrast that with Isaiah, who saw the Lord high and lifted up in the Holy of Holies. The pagan Pompey said it was dark and empty. Isaiah said it was filled with the glory of God, that the seraphim cry out, "Holy, holy, holy is the Lord of hosts," and the smoke of the incense ascends forever to the throne of God. Isaiah 6 is the only place in the entire Bible that seraphim are mentioned. They are described as having six wings ready for service to God. The Bible also says they covered their face in an act of humility as they stood before the throne.

It strikes me as I read the vision of Isaiah that it is not unlike our own experience with God. We can see, as Isaiah describes his encounter with God, that his experience was progressive. In our Christian life, our encounter with God follows a similar vein of progression.

An Awareness of Who God Is

First of all, a relationship with God begins with an awareness of who God is. He said, *"I saw the Lord sitting on a throne, high and lifted up, and the train of His robe filled the temple."*

There are not many atheists left in our culture. Very few people today will tell you that there is no God. On the contrary, most people today believe that there *is* a God! However, what that God is like varies among people according to their own philosophical understanding. In the ancient world, people made their god into what they wanted god to be. Their gods were very much like them! They were capricious, vengeful, lustful and greedy in Greek mythology, and even in Roman mythology. They were not unlike the god or the gods that people concoct in their minds today. You can turn on a talk show and hear some theologian trying to describe what the God of the Bible is like, and the host or some other guest will say, "Well, I do not think that is what God is like, I think God is like this, or I think God is like that; or I think God would do this, or I do not think God would do that." They make up God as they go along. People create a god borrowed from Buddhism, or Hinduism, or the force from a Star Wars movie. They roll it all together in their mind, and that is their image of God.

The idolatry of our culture is not someone carving an image out of wood and bowing down before it. It is not that we make a statue out of marble and stone and call that statue God. Instead, the idolatry of our day is metaphysical. With our own minds, we create a god that does not exist. Out of our own egos, we make up what we want God to be like or what we want God *not* to be like, instead of following what the Bible says about God. In Isaiah 6, God reveals Himself to Isaiah. Isaiah does not make it up. He has an experience with the *Living God.*

A.W. Tozer wrote a little booklet called *The Knowledge of the Holy,* in which he says, "The most portentous fact about any man is not what he at a given time may say or do, but what he in his deep heart conceives God to be like." What do you think God is like? Where do you get your image of God? From popular culture or what others say on the talk shows, or from the Bible? Isaiah 6 is a description of who God is, what He is like. No one has seen God. It says in John 1:18, *"No one has seen God at any time. The only begotten Son, who is in the bosom of the Father, He has declared Him."* Speaking of God, 1 Timothy 6:16 says, *"Who alone has immortality, dwelling in unapproachable light, whom no man has seen or can see, to whom be honor and everlasting power. Amen."* No one has ever seen God. Looking upon God would be like looking in the full noonday sun; you would have to avert your eyes, yet Isaiah said that he saw the Lord high and lifted up. His description is really not of God, rather his description is of what is around God.

Isaiah said, first of all, *"I saw a throne,"* speaking of the sovereignty and the power of God. The oldest throne upon the earth today is on the island of Crete in the famous palace of Knossos, but the throne that Isaiah saw was from eternity past. He saw seraphim, literally "blazing ones." They had six wings, wings representing their ceaseless availability to serve. With two they covered their face in humility. With two they covered their feet, reminiscent of Moses when he stood before

God, and God said, "Take off your shoes, for you are standing on holy ground." Their confession as they echoed back and forth in an antiphonal chorus was, "Holy, holy, holy is the Lord of Hosts." The very first step in coming to God, to Christian maturity, is to understand who God is. The image Isaiah had of God was that He was holy. Verse 4, *"And the posts of the door were shaken by the voice of him who cried out, and the house was filled with smoke as they sang, 'Holy, holy, holy is the LORD of hosts."* They sang with such seismic intensity that their voices thundered. Isaiah had to hold on to the doorpost because the whole temple was shaking, and it was filled with the smoke of the incense of worship. That is the image of the God of the Bible! God is powerful, God is holy and without sin!

On October 17, 1990, at 5:04 P.M., an earthquake rattled San Francisco. Some six million people felt it for fifteen seconds as the whole city was shaken, freeways collapsed and people were trapped. Many died. Lisa Charone was renting a car at the time, and she had just sat in the seat of the car with the salesman. All of a sudden the earth began to shake, and she thought something was wrong with the car. About that time, the earth was literally rolling, and a wave came along and flipped the car upside down. Such is the power of an earthquake. In the same way, Isaiah said that when he saw the LORD high and lifted up, the voice—not of God, but of the seraphim—was so powerful that the earth shook and smoke filled the temple. It is a vision of a powerful, holy God. That is not the world's view of God today. The world's view of God is much different from the image Isaiah presents to us.

The big debate in theological circles today is over what is called "open theism." Theism derives from *theos,* meaning "God." Open theism means that God is open, in that He does not know the future. The debate says that man is a free-willed creature and that, if God knows our future decisions, they would already be determined; therefore, we would have no choice. They conclude that God really does not know the future—that God simply reacts to the future. He is not sovereign in His knowledge; He is not infinite in His knowledge. Instead, God is simply reacting to the decisions that we make! It is a naïve way to answer the problem of evil. There is evil in the world, and how can there be evil in the world if God is in control? So the answer is that God is not in control? The evil comes as we make our choices, yet God is impotent to do anything about the world. He is simply watching in frustration. That is *not* the image of God that Isaiah presents.

The image of God that Isaiah presents is that God is high and lifted up. Isaiah looks at the throne, and it is as if the throne of God extends into the heavens. He declared that God is high and lifted up, and these great creatures called seraphim, cry back and forth to one another for eternity, as they cover their faces, "Holy, holy, holy is the Lord of hosts."

There are some who view God as simply one step above man on the evolutionary ladder. Still others have a view of God that He is a "gooey glob of love and tolerance." But Isaiah said that He is holy. Because He is holy, we should not speak tritely of God. It makes my flesh crawl when I hear people speaking of God as "the man upstairs," or "their buddy." Isaiah said He is holy, meaning He is without sin! Not only is He without sin, He is without even the thought of sin. He is righteous! His justice is absolute so that God says the soul that sinneth, it shall die. The wages of sin is death. You may be saying, "Wait a minute, isn't God a Father?" Jesus taught us to pray like this: "Our Father, which art in Heaven, hallowed be Thy name." We can pray to God as a Father, but at the same time He said, "Our Father, which art in Heaven." God is distinct from us, God is separate from us, God is, in fact, transcendent.

Jesus said, *"When ye pray, say: 'Our Father, which art in Heaven, hallowed* [literally holy] *be Your name.'"* Always within the believer's life we hold in tension the fact that God is a Father, with the fact that God is holy. There is a danger for you and me, living in the age in which we live, that the things of God would become mundane, familiar and routine to us. Today there are movies made about the life of Christ. You can turn on the television and see the worship of God, and hear the preaching of the Word of God. You can turn on the radio and as you scan through the stations, you hear constantly the name of Jesus and the preaching of His Word. It is possible, in all of the bombardment of the Word of God that we lose the sense of the transcendence of God. There are those who want to treat God like the legend of the genie in a bottle, where they rub a lamp and a genie pops out, does a few magic tricks, then goes back into the bottle and they cork it again! Many people want to relate to God in that way. "Oh, God, I have this problem in my life. Come out of the bottle and fix it. Oh, God, I have sickness in my life; come out and heal me. Oh, God, I have financial trouble; fix it and then go back in the bottle." Then they cork it, and God has nothing to do with the routine of their life.

In the Old Testament era, on one day of the year, the high priest went into what was called the Holy of Holies and poured out the blood sacrifice. Josephus, not a biblical writer, but a historian, tells how eventually they put bells on the hem of the robe of the High Priest so they could listen for him inside the Holy of Holies. If the High Priest had any sin in his life, as he entered into the presence of God in the Holy of Holies, his life was taken! Josephus said they tied a rope around his waist and listened for the bells, and if they could not hear the bells, they realized that God had struck him dead because of his sin; and they pulled his limp body out of the Holy of Holies. No one wanted to go in and rescue him. What do you think would have happened on that one day out of the year if a priest glibly went in to the Holy of Holies while he was having an illicit affair? I can tell you what would happen. They would have tugged on the rope! What do you think would happen if he had entered the Holy of Holies with alcohol on his breath? They would have tugged on the rope! What do you think would have happened if he had had a *Playboy* or ancient equivalent of pornography tucked within his robe? They would have pulled on the rope! What if he would have had impure thoughts in his mind and in his heart? They would have pulled on the rope!

Isaiah is awed by who God is! If we are not awed by who God is, if we do not have the correct image of God within our mind, then our praying will be empty words, our praising will be mere performance, our preaching will be the professional parroting of memorized phrases.

Understanding and Admitting Our Own Sinfulness

Our relationship with God begins with an awareness of who God is, but it also involves understanding and admitting our own sinfulness. As a result of seeing God high and lifted up, Isaiah said in verse 5, *"Woe is me, for I am undone! Because I am a man of unclean lips."* Isaiah was already arguably the greatest prophet of the Old Testament. If Isaiah said this about himself, then what about you and me? He understood not only the greatness of God, but the character of God—that God is holy. He heard the seraphim echoing back and forth one to another as one cries, *Qadosh,* another one, *Qadosh, Qadosh, Qadosh*—"Holy, holy, holy"—and he wanted to join his lips with their great song. But then he realized that his life did not match his lips. Becoming aware of his sin, he said, *"Woe is me, for I am undone, because I am a man of unclean lips."*

The fact is, the nearer you or I get to God spiritually, the more aware we are of our sin. The opposite is also true. The further you are away from God, the less you are aware of your sin. We live in a culture where people will line up and tell you they have not sinned. Oh, they view someone like Osama bin Laden as a sinner, but they do not view themselves as sinners. It is possible to be so far from God that you are not even aware that you have violated the will and the Word of God. Yet the closer you get to God, the more you are aware of your own sin nature.

You can see that progression in the life of the apostle Paul in his early writings as he identified himself as "Paul, an apostle of God." Later he identified himself as "Paul, the least of the apostles," and then as "Paul, a sinner," and at the end of his life he identified himself as "Paul, the chief of sinners." The closer the apostle Paul got to God, the more he realized his own sin.

Isaiah said that when he saw the Lord, He was high and lifted up and he heard that antiphonal chorus singing, "Holy, holy is the Lord of hosts." His reaction was, *"Woe is me, for I am undone."* Isaiah was suddenly in the presence of the One who was aware of every word he had ever spoken. Isaiah was aware that God had seen every deed that he had ever committed. He was aware that God knew every thought he had ever thought and that before he was formed in the womb, God had known him, and he said, "I am a sinner."

Later he wrote in Isaiah 64:6, *"But we are all like an unclean thing, and all our righteousnesses are like filthy rags."* That is always the reaction when you have a right view of God.

- Adam, when he felt the guilt of his sin, hid himself from God.
- Moses, when he stood before the burning bush, hid his face.
- Manoah, when an angel of the Lord came to him and said that Samson would be born in Judges 13:22, said to his wife, *"We shall surely die, because we have seen God."* He had not seen God at all! All he had seen was an Angel of the Lord, but he was amazed with the power of that Angel and said, *"We shall surely die."*
- Job said in Job 42:5 and 6, *"I have heard of You by the hearing of the ear, but now my eye sees You. Therefore, I abhor myself, And repent in dust and ashes."* Job was, in many ways, the best that humanity had to offer. In fact, God Himself said that Job was an upright and righteous man, yet when Job had a correct image of God in his

mind he said, "I abhor myself and I repent in dust and ashes."
- The apostle Peter, in Luke 5, after seeing the miracle of the Lord, fell down at Jesus' knees saying, *"Depart from me, for I am a sinful man…"*
- The apostle Paul, when he met the Lord on the road to Damascus, fell before Him.
- John, the beloved disciple, wrote in the book of Revelation that when he saw the image of Jesus upon the throne, he fell, as it were, dead at His feet.

That is always the reaction when you have a correct image of God—you understand your own sinfulness. If you do not understand your own sinfulness, it is because you do not have a proper understanding of who God is.

Peter tells us in 1 Peter 1:16, *"…because it is written, 'Be holy; for I am holy.'"* Isaiah wondered after seeing the Lord high and lifted up, how he could measure up.

In verse 6, it says, *"Then one of the seraphim flew to me, having in his hand a live coal which he had taken with the tongs from the altar. And he touched my mouth with it, and said: 'Behold, this has touched your lips; your iniquity is taken away, And your sin purged.'"* We are not forgiven because God says to us, "Do more." God did not tell Isaiah he needed a self-improvement plan. He simply said, "You are forgiven because of the altar, the place of sacrifice." Anywhere you go in the world, whether to a museum in the most sophisticated urban city in the world, or in a mud hut, or in a backward Third World country, you can line people up and ask them, "How do you get to God?" They will all tell you basically the same thing. They will tell you about some ritual to keep, or some diet to eat or not to eat, or someplace to go or not to go, or some ceremonies to be observed or some taboos to be avoided. The only place where God takes the initiative and grace is given, is at the altar. At the cross of Christ, God took the initiative. The

Angel of the Lord touched Isaiah's mouth and said, "Isaiah, you are clean because of the sacrifice of God."

Brokenness for the Lostness of Others

Our relationship with God begins not only with an awareness of who God is, and an understanding that we are sinners, but it leads to a brokenness for the lostness of others. In verse 5, it says, *"Woe is me, for I am undone! Because I am a man of unclean lips, And I dwell in the midst of a people of unclean lips; For my eyes have seen the King, the Lord of hosts."* In many ways, Christianity has become consumer oriented. We tend in Western culture to think that Christianity exists in order to make us happy. The fact is, Christianity and a relationship with God is about our becoming holy, and out of that holiness we become happy. Out of holiness comes a great mission to others. Sometimes we hear of a missionary who speaks of the teeming masses, of the lostness of our world; or they speak perhaps of persecution in other pockets of the world. Sometimes we are moved, and we will weep over a nation, but what about our neighbor across the street? What about the person who lives next door to us, or the person who works in the cubicle next to us or down the hall? They are every bit as lost as someone in a Third World country.

In the Old Testament, on one occasion at a low point in his life, David cried out to God and said, "No man cares for my soul." I wonder how many people in our city would say that. I wonder how many people living under the very shadow of a great church, might say with David, "No man cares for my soul." I wish we could see the lostness of the world as Isaiah saw it. He saw the Lord high and lifted up, on a throne that stretched from earth to heaven, and the earth shook with seismic intensity as the angels cried, *"Holy, holy, holy,"* to God. Isaiah said, *"Woe is me, for I am undone, and I dwell in the midst of a people that are unclean."* I wish we could see people as lost without God. I wish we could see them as blind men.

If there was a person who was blind and we saw him wandering aimlessly toward a cliff, toward a precipice where he was about to fall, we would grab him and rescue him. Yet, all around us there are people who are spiritually blind, family members whom we say that we love, our neighbors, the people with whom we work. They are moving ever so close, one step each day, closer to the cliff that will take them into eternity without God. I wish we could grab them and snatch them back. I wish we could look past the affluence, and past the physical countenance, and see the lostness of our world like Isaiah saw it. He said, *"I saw the Lord, and He was high and lifted up and I cried, 'Woe is me for I am undone,'"* and then he said, *"ah, ah, I dwell in the midst of a people of unclean lips."*

Service to God and Others

A relationship with God culminates in our service to God and to others. In verse 8, Isaiah said, *"I heard the voice of the Lord saying, 'Whom shall I send, and who will go for Us?'"* Then he said, *"Here am I! send me."* Somehow, as Isaiah was in the throne room of God, he heard the triune counsel of God. In the very beginning, God had said, *"Let us make man in Our image,"* and now he hears the triune counsel of God and God muses, *"Whom shall We send?"* Who will go for Us to the lostness of this world? And Isaiah said, *"Here am I! Send me."*

Most of the world thinks that we come to God by doing. No! The Christian life is not about doing, It is about being, it is about God changing you by His grace, but eventually out of that being comes doing. Christian maturity starts with:

- A vision of who God is.
- It progresses to recognition of our sin.
- Then it moves to the expiation of our sin, the cleansing of our sin.
- Then we see the lostness of the world.
- Then we say, *"Here am I, Lord, Send me."*

They did not sing a hundred stanzas of "Just As I Am." He said, *"Here am I, Send me."* He was not drafted. He volunteered and said, "Oh, God, let me be the one who goes, let me be the one who goes." Our call to service for God comes out of our understanding of who God is, our understanding of the depth of our sin that has been forgiven, and our understanding of the lostness of the world.

In the Old Testament, there is a Scripture that says, *"Be sure your sin will find you out."* It is sometimes quoted when someone is having an illicit affair, or when someone gets drunk, or when someone is lying, cheating or stealing. We will say, "You are going to get caught; be sure your sin will find you out." But that is not the context of the verse. It is about the tribes of Reuben and Gad, and the time that the Israelites were about to cross over the Jordan River to possess the Promised Land. The tribes of Reuben and Gad had many cattle, and on the east side of the Jordan, it was said there was wonderful grassland. They told Moses, "We're not going to go into the Promised Land. We're going to stay on the east side and enjoy our cattle and our families." Moses rebuked them and said, "You must go and fight the battle and help conquer the land for your brethren. If you do not serve, be sure your sin will find you out." We are not saved to be sponges to soak up the blessing of God. We are saved to be a river of life to others. Isaiah got it! He said, *"Lord, here am I, Send me."* What does that mean for us today?

- It may mean, for someone, becoming a Sunday School teacher.
- For someone else, it may mean joining the choir.
- For others, it may mean working in the nursery.
- For some, it may mean telling your neighbor about Christ.
- For others, it may mean starting a Bible study in your home.

Some in our church have said, "Here am I. Send me to the jungles of Peru." Others in our church have gone to the urban areas of Eastern Europe, some to the deserts of the Middle East, some to the plains of Africa, to the crowded streets of India, to the masses of Eastern Asia—one by one, people in our church have been called to other places and other pockets in the world. We are here on this Lord's Day in the comfort of this beautiful building because someone else said, "Here am I, Send me."

The torch of the gospel began at Jerusalem, then it moved to Judea, to Samaria, to the islands in the Mediterranean, and then to Asia, Corinth and Athens, and then on to Rome, and to Spain.

Then someone from Spain said, "Here am I, Send me," and the gospel went to Britain. Then someone else said, "Here am I, Send me," and it crossed the Atlantic to Colonial America.

It spread across the Eastern seaboard in the Great Awakening. Then someone said, "Here am I Lord, Send me," and in the Second Great Awakening it made its way across the Appalachian Mountains. Then someone said, "Here am I, Send me," and pioneers in covered wagons crossed the Indian territory. Eventually, the message of the gospel came to our own great state of California. Every step of the way, every time the torch was passed from one generation to the next, from one person to the next, someone said, "Here am I, Send me."

⤙ 2004 ⤚

Karen Watson was murdered in Iraq by terrorists on March 15, 2004 while serving as a missionary. Karen had been a faithful member of Valley Baptist since 1995. The church was shocked and grieved by her death.

Weeks later our builder, Curt Carter, died suddenly. Curt's love for Valley Baptist and his commitment as a servant of the Lord was greatly missed as the children's building was finished without him.

The children's building was occupied in the fall of 2004. Finally, after nineteen years of sacrificial giving and hard work, the church had ample worship space and plenty of classroom space as well.

"God's Amazing Grace" was preached on Sunday morning, January 25, 2004, as part of a verse-by-verse series of messages through the book of Ephesians.

God's Amazing Grace

EPHESIANS 2:8-9

*"For by grace you have been saved through faith,
and that not of yourselves; it is the gift of God, not
of works, lest anyone should boast." (NKJV)*

Perhaps the most famous verse in the entire Bible is in the third chapter of John, where a conversation took place between Jesus and Nicodemus. Nicodemus was a ruler of the Jews, and in all likelihood a member of the Sanhedrin, the Jewish high court. Nicodemus came to Jesus by night inquiring about the nature of Jesus' ministry. He was curious whether Jesus was actually the Messiah. Jesus told Nicodemus that he must be born again. In the flow of their conversation, Jesus gave this wonderful verse, *"For God so loved the world that He gave His only begotten Son, that whosoever believeth in Him should not perish, but have everlasting life."* John 3:16 is often lifted from its context. In fact, entire books have been written about that single verse. As far as our culture is concerned, it is the most prominent verse in the entire Bible.

Ephesians 2:8 is probably the second most prominent verse in the entire Bible, *"For by grace you have been saved through faith; and that not of yourselves, it is the gift of God."*

God's grace really is amazing. His grace, or His unmerited favor, can transform and change lives!

John Newton was a preacher who lived in the 1600's. Though you probably have never heard one, a number of his sermons were published. Although you have probably never read a book by John Newton, he was an author of some renown during his time. However, we have all sung a song that he wrote, "Amazing Grace!"

> *Amazing Grace, how sweet the sound,*
> *That saved a wretch like me.*
> *I once was lost but now I am found,*
> *Was blind, but now I see!*

There is a wonderful story, not only behind that song, but also behind the life of the preacher, John Newton. He had a godly mother who loved the Lord, yet his father was just the opposite. A sailor, absent from the home most of the time, John Newton's father was a wicked man. His godly mother died when he was only six years old. By the age of eleven, he decided to follow in the footsteps of his dad and became a sailor, spending most of his life at sea. It was said that, even as a boy, John Newton could hardly utter a sentence without using profanity. As a teenager, he gave himself to a life of debauchery, and eventually ascended through the ranks until he was the captain of his own ship. His ship's cargo? Slaves! He became a slave trader, buying and selling human beings, the most despicable trade of that period. Eventually, because of some reversal of fortune, John Newton became a slave himself. He not only became a slave, but also a slave of slaves. By his own testimony, in a two-year period of time, he had nothing to eat except the scraps from the table of his mistress that were thrown to him on the floor. He was regularly beaten.

John Newton escaped his life of slavery and became a seaman once again. There were a number of Christians on board the ship with him who became concerned about his soul. They gave him a book by Thomas á Kempis, called *The Imitation of Christ,* which he read in jest, for the most part. He ridiculed other men who were believers in Christ, he ridiculed the book, and he ridiculed anything that had to do with Christ. He was a profane man!

In the course of their voyage, they encountered a violent storm. John Newton was on the deck of the ship, holding on to the railing with all his might, but the storm was so violent that a huge wave swept him into the sea. Disjoined from his ship, with no lifeline, John Newton knew that death was impending and that, within the next few moments, he would drown. Knowing there was no way to make it back to the ship, he cried out to God and simply said, "Lord, help me," and then he prayed, "Lord, save me." Amazingly, the next wave lifted him up, and when the wave had dissipated he found that he was back on the deck of the ship!

In that moment when he prayed for God to save him, not only was he praying he would be delivered from impending death, but also that he would be spiritually saved. The conviction of the Holy Spirit from the previous months, all of the reading that he had done, the writings of Thomas á Kempis, and all the witness of those godly men on board, came to bear in that moment during the violent storm. At the moment he cried out to be saved, his life was radically and dramatically changed forever.

Spiritually, John Newton could not be saved by his good works. He had lived a horrible lifestyle as a trader in human flesh. From the time he was eleven years old, he lived a life of debauchery and open, malignant sin. There was nothing he could do to earn the favor of God, and certainly nothing he had done. There was nothing he could do while he was in the water to atone for his sin, no penance he could perform. He simply cried out that God might save him, and in that moment he was saved by God's grace! Grace means "unmerited favor." When he wrote the words, "God saved a wretch like me," John Newton really *was* a wretch by all standards. He said that he was lost and now was found. For years, He was spiritually blinded to the truth of the gospel, and to the teaching of his godly mother as a little boy, and yet he was saved.

When you think about it, the message of the Bible is one of *amazing grace*. That is what the entire Bible is about! In the Old Testament, God gave the law, the commandments and the requirements. We read the law and realize, in frustration, that we cannot attain salvation. We can never live up to the absolute standard of God. If we are to have a right relationship with God, it must be based upon God's mercy and upon His grace, not upon our performance. There is no deed we can perform, no human achievement to earn His favor. We cannot learn it, we cannot earn it and we certainly cannot buy it!

Christianity is not about rules, although that is what our culture thinks. In our culture, when Christianity is depicted in a movie on television, it is about someone keeping rules and regulations, the ritual of baptism or the Lord's Supper. They think somehow it is all about crossing "t's" and dotting "i's." But the Christian life is not about rules—it is about a relationship with God. That relationship is based upon God's *amazing grace*! Many people in our culture think that being a Christian is based upon a creed, that you have to believe a certain thing, and that if you believe a certain thing, that makes you a Christian. Others say, "No, no, it is not a creed, it is a code. It is a code of conduct. You have to avoid this taboo, perform this ritual and follow these restrictions." Still others say that it is not so much a creed or a code, but it is a cause! You just have to love everybody! Others say, "No, you must be a member of a church or of a certain sect." A relationship with Christ is based upon His grace and based upon our faith. It is not based on creeds! It is not based on codes! If it were based upon performance, then you could never be quite sure. How would you know when you have done enough to earn Heaven? If it were based upon human achievement and performance, then we could never be sure because we might mess up at the end. What if you lived a good life, had all your spiritual ducks in a row, were kind to people and benevolent, and then one day you flew off the handle in a temper, and the next thing you know, you were hit by a Mack truck. You messed up right at the end of life! All of that good living was for nothing. If it is based upon human performance, you can never be sure you have really done enough.

If God's love is based upon your goodness, what if that goodness changes? Then God's love would change. God's love is an action towards us; it is not a reaction to us. God does not change you so that He might love you; He loves you so that He might change you! That is not just semantics, but the crux of the gospel. So many people in our culture hope that there is something they can do to cause God to love them. Maybe they grew up in a home where they had an austere father or a mother who was not expressive of love. Maybe they have a mate who has betrayed them along the way. Maybe they are thinking, "Oh, if I could just do something; if I could just achieve a certain level of goodness in my life, then God would love me. Here is my question, friend: "If a relationship with God is based on our goodness, on our human deeds, on anything having to do with human performance or achievement, then why the cross? Why did God send His Son? Why did His Son die such an agonizing death upon the cross, declaring that He was paying the penalty for our sin? If we can earn our way to God, then why did God send His Son?"

In the New Testament, the primary view of a Christian is that of the sons and the daughters of God. We are viewed primarily as children of God, not slaves, not servants. Occasionally, we are viewed in the Bible as servants of God, but the primary view of a believer is that we are the children of God.

- A servant is accepted on the basis of what he does. A son is accepted on the basis of who he is.
- A servant is accepted based on workmanship. A son is accepted based on relationship.
- A servant has to do with productivity. A son has to do with the position of being in a family.

In some ways, the most radical thing that Jesus said when He came to the earth was when He constantly talked about His Father and our Father. He said that He was sent by the Father, and that He who had seen Him had seen the Father. That was a radical teaching in His day. The Jews spoke in terms of God being a Father in the sense of creation—He is the Father of us all. They spoke of God being a Father in the sense of nationally, but they would never speak of God as being their personal Father. They did not think in terms of familial relationship with God. Jesus said that we, as believers, are the sons and daughters of the Living God. God loves us unconditionally, but such love is foreign to many of us. Oh, we talk sometimes about unconditional love, but we do not really practice it. We think:

- God loves me, since I am trying hard, or
- God will love me more because this week I really tried hard, or
- God loves me because I am one of the beautiful people in culture, or
- God loves me because I am living such a good life, or
- God loves me because I am going to church or because I am tithing, or
- God will love me if I do a certain thing.

God's love is unconditional, and that is foreign to us, because we love *conditionally* for the most part:

- I will love you if you behave, or
- I will love you after you straighten up that certain area in your life, or
- I will love you since you are a lovable person, or
- I will love you if you reciprocate and love me back.

God's love for us is unconditional. It is a matter of *grace*, unmerited favor!

In talking to people about Christ, sometimes we will ask this diagnostic question to try and discern where they are spiritually: "If you were to die today and stand before God, and God were to ask you this question, 'Why should I let you into Heaven?', what would you say?"

It is a pretty good question. If you were to die, which we will, and you were to stand before God, which we will, and He were to ask why He should let you into Heaven, what would you say? Nearly 95 percent of all the answers we hear to that question show that people do not understand that salvation is a matter of *grace*.

Answers vary, but for the most part, people say:

- I do not know, I guess I would say I have tried to live a good life.
- I would say that I have been sincere in my belief.
- I have been a good neighbor.
- I am a very moral person and I have always done the best I could.
- I have always paid my bills on time—as if God is going to consult PG&E about your eternal destiny!

Most people in our culture believe that they are going to Heaven when they die, yet Jesus said that there would be few who enter in. There was a survey done by *U.S. News and World Report.* In fact, they did a feature article regarding the survey. The cover of their magazine said, "Life After Death." They asked people in our culture who they thought were going to go to Heaven when they die:

- Sixty-six percent of the people in America think that Oprah Winfrey is going to Heaven when she dies.
- Sixty-five percent of the people think that Michael Jordan is going to Heaven when he dies.
- Only twenty-eight percent think that Dennis Rodman is going to make it.
- Seventy-nine percent of Americans believe that when Mother Theresa died she went to Heaven. (I would have thought it would have been a higher percentage than that for Mother Theresa!)
- Eighty-seven percent of people in America surveyed think that when they die, they are going to Heaven.

The same people who said they are not too sure about Mother Theresa were completely sure about themselves. Many people think that at the end they are going to do some great deed. Most people believe that it is based upon them, it is up to them, and it is based upon their goodness and their efforts. They believe that at the end somehow they are going to get it together. They may not have it together now, but before they die, they are going to get it together! They are going to live a good life and God is going to accept them based upon their goodness.

Jesus said, *"I am the way, the truth and the life; no man comes to the Father except through Me."* He did not say, "I am *a* way." People today are offended at the gospel if a preacher or theologian stands up and says that the only way to Heaven is through Jesus. People say, "Oh, wait a minute.

What about through being a Hindu or Buddhist—or some other philosophical systems of thought." Jesus said, *"I am the Way."* He preached an exclusive message that He was the only way to the Father. That is not something that comes out of my mouth. That came out of the mouth of the Lord Jesus Christ, that He is the only way, not a way, but the way. He said, "I am the door." The gospel is as narrow as a doorway; it is as narrow as one Man. The only way to God is through the Lord Jesus Christ. It is not through human effort, it is not through performing some ritual; it is only through the Lord Jesus Christ and faith in Him!

Saved!

There are three great words in this verse that I want you to see. They are theological words we do not normally use in our culture, but they are important for us. The first word I want you to see is in verse 8, *"For by grace you have been saved."* "Saved!" This word is not even used in Christianity much anymore. There was a man at Oxford University writing a dissertation, and four of his student friends helped him in his research project. In studying records of old sermons from more than a hundred years ago, they found that before the turn of the last century, this word *saved* was used universally to refer to salvation. When men preached, they would say that you needed to be saved. Then about the turn of the last century, the nomenclature changed. Billy Sunday was the great evangelist of the early part of the last century, particularly in the 1920s, and he said that people needed to be "converted." That means that you need to change. Then about three or four decades ago, the nomenclature changed again. Now we speak in terms of "needing to make a decision for Christ," or you need to "accept Christ." Do you see the drift? Being saved is something that God does. Making a decision is something I do. The Bible uses the term "saved." It never says "make a decision for Christ." You will not find that in the Bible. It does not talk about "accepting Christ." It talks about being saved, about being rescued from our sin! That is something God does. There is a sense of urgency if you say, "I need to be saved," or, "I need to be rescued," but not when you say, "I need to make a decision." Such terms imply, "I can be analytical, take my time and make up my mind about salvation."

What does the word *saved* mean? In normal usage, it means to be rescued from a perilous situation. If a man falls out of a boat and he cannot swim, eventually someone will grab him and pull him back into the boat; and we say he has been *saved*. Let us say there is a building on fire and a child appears in the second-story window. A fireman leans his ladder up against the house, climbs the ladder, wraps that child in a blanket and as he descends with the little child, everyone claps and says the child has been *saved*. The child was in danger, but the child was saved! That is what it means on a spiritual level—that we are sinners under the wrath of God, without Christ, and now, by His grace, we have been saved. It is like a felon who has been found guilty and sentenced, and the governor pardons him and saves him from his fate. It is not just talking about eternity. Oh, we have been saved from Hell and we are going to Heaven, but this is talking about being saved right now. All of the failures of our past haunt us. And we have a lot of them, don't we! We have all failed; we have all messed up! It is like baggage that we are tied to, or like a big old rope that we are tied to. We are dragging it through life, holding on to all these failures, mistakes, broken relationships, and all the things we have done wrong. To be saved means that God cuts the rope! Then we are free, our conscience is clean, our heart is pure and we are right with God. We are relieved from all the baggage, the bondage and the guilt of the past. We are saved, not just eternally, but also temporarily.

Grace!

There is another great word here. Look at what it says in verse 8: *"For by grace!"* What a wonderful word. It means unmerited favor. In the original language, there is a definite article before grace. We are saved by the grace. Grace allows you to enter into a relationship with God. Salvation is not based on trying harder. The gospel is not a self-help program. Yet if you listen to much of the preaching today, that is what it sounds like. Sermons are preached concerning ways to live stress free, as if the gospel is merely therapy. The gospel, the good news, is that God loves you and will save you by His grace, that He will forgive your sin.

The most famous trial in American history, outside of O.J. Simpson and Michael Jackson's, or perhaps the most famous spy trial ever was that of the Rosenbergs. When they were found guilty and sentenced, one of their lawyers in summing up said, "All my clients want is justice." The judge interrupted him and said, "Excuse me, you are not saying they want justice, are you? What they want is mercy or grace." That is what we need. Justice means we get what we deserve! I do not want what I deserve. Do you? Mercy is God not giving us what we do deserve, and grace is God giving us what we do not deserve, that we get to go to Heaven when we die. Sometimes someone will ask, "Are you certain you are going to Heaven?" and a Christian will answer, "Yes, I know I am going to Heaven." Our culture reads that as arrogant. They wonder, how can you know that you are going to Heaven? Our culture thinks you are expressing confidence in yourself, because our culture thinks Heaven is something we earn by our goodness. They think you are saying, "Look how good I am! I am going to Heaven when I die!" Their stomachs are turned by what they think is an arrogant statement. In reality, when we say, "I know I am going to Heaven as a Christian," we are not expressing confidence in ourselves but rather we are expressing confidence in the grace of God. I have absolutely no confidence in myself when it comes to going to Heaven. You should not either, because you should know the darkness of your own heart. Our confidence is in the grace of God, the unmerited favor of God.

Faith!

There is another great word in verse 8. *"For by grace you have been saved through faith."* How do you get the grace? It is through *faith*. Some people say, "You know, it does not matter what you believe, as long as you are sincere." It does matter what you believe! If you drink a big glass of poison and you sincerely think it is orange juice, you are going to be sincerely dead! It does matter what you believe. Faith is not a "cockeyed optimism," nor is it "positive thinking." Biblical faith has to have the proper object, and the proper object of our faith is the Lord Jesus and His finished work upon the cross. How do we express faith? We express faith through prayer. The Bible says, *"... whoever calls upon the name of the Lord shall be saved."* If you get to the point in life where you recognize that you have sinned, and you believe in the Lord Jesus Christ, then you express that faith simply by asking God to forgive your sin and to be your Savior. That is how our faith is expressed. The Bible goes on to say that we are saved through faith, and that not of ourselves, it is the gift of God. What is the gift of God? It refers to everything. To being saved, the grace, the faith! It is all a gift of God! That shatters the last vestige of human pride. I guarantee there is no one in Heaven singing, "I Did it My Way." The song that is in Heaven is, "To God be the glory, great things He has done!" It is God who saves us and rescues us by His grace, and that grace is activated by our faith. Even that faith is a gift of God.

Not of Yourselves!

- There are two negative clauses that are very, very important. Verse 8 contains the first one, *"And that not of yourselves,"* and then in verse 9, the second negative clause, *"Not of works, lest anyone should boast."*
- Not of yourselves—that is secular humanism, man trying to do it on his own.
- Not of works—that is religious legalism.

There are two great substitutes for salvation: Human effort or secular humanism; and religious legalism, thinking that you will do some benign work that will earn salvation. Many people in our culture think that man is ultimately going to save himself, that it is a matter of just trying harder. Okay, you messed up, so start over. Reform your life, and turn over a new leaf. Clean up your character, and do the best you can. Our culture says, "After all, that is all that God expects." My question then is, "Why do I have such a big Bible? Why do we have a leather-bound Bible that is hundreds of pages long?" The full Law had to be written on two tablets of stone for Moses. God could have carved, "Do your best," in the side of Mt. Sinai, and we could make a holy pilgrimage every year and stand there in awe. Every millennium, God could write it in the sky for a new generation to see. Do the best you can. Is that what God requires? No! The best you can is inadequate; even if you did the best you could, which I seriously doubt if you are doing because of our human nature.

The Bible says that all of our righteousness is as filthy rags in the sight of God. All of it together cannot achieve a standing with God. It is not a matter of doing the best you can; it is a matter of Jesus' perfection and His righteousness being imputed, or transferred into our account. Humanism is based upon a Darwinian theory that somehow man started as nothing, and he is moving toward perfection. Given enough time, he will solve the problems of racial prejudice, poverty, moral issues and inequities within our culture. The Bible teaches the opposite. The Bible does not teach that man started as an amoeba and is moving progressively toward perfection. The Bible teaches that man started in perfection, created in holiness before God, and he fell from that perfection and is in need of a Savior. Man needs to be rescued from his fallen state because of Adam and Eve's awful sin.

Not of Works!

Verse 9 says, *"Not of works, lest anyone should boast."* If it was of works, I guarantee you we would boast, would we not? We would say, "Man, did you hear what *I* did? I was so good that God said I get to go to Heaven." We would tell everybody! There are no spiritual peacocks in Heaven. Some people are so proud of their good works that they can strut sitting down. They think they have favor with God because of what they have done. It is not of works.

There are different kinds of works in our culture. There is the work of self-affliction. I do not get it, but it is prevalent throughout our world. If you go to a Hindu land like India, you can see holy men in a trance raise their arms for hour after hour until, because of a lack of blood, their hands become lifeless and useless. They think that by doing so, they will appease God. Certain sects of Hindus will bring the remains of their decomposing dead relatives to the Ganges River and immerse their bodies. Such practices spread death and disease everywhere, but they think that will make them right with God. Holy men with the sign of the sheba in the middle of their forehead will wall themselves into a room, brick by brick, until there is only a little slit where people can pass food and water to them. They do not do that for just a few days or a few weeks; they do it for the rest of their natural life until some disease or infection claims their life. Then others seal up the remaining bricks, and that room becomes their tomb. They think the work of self-affliction will please God!

We saw on television months ago, in the Middle East, during the liberation of Iraq, the Shiites in the south. They took whips and beat themselves until their chests and their backs were raw, and their faces dripped with blood, lacerating themselves, thinking that would somehow appease God. You may be thinking, "Those are Third World countries." Well, go to Japan. During a break, a sophisticated factory worker who holds a high tech job will go to the company's Zen priest. He will bow before the priest as he asks him senseless questions, and when he cannot answer, the priest will beat his back until it is bloody—the works of self-affliction.

Also there are the works of religious ritual all over the world. In Spain, at a certain time of the year, there is the custom of *romaria*. Critically ill family members or friends are taken out of the hospitals. They lay these living relatives in caskets and carry the caskets through the streets. People come behind the casket on their knees, scrubbing the streets until their knees are a mass of blood and torn cartilage. These are sophisticated, educated Europeans thinking that this will somehow appease God. In America on every Lord's Day, there are young families who will bring little babies and stand in front of a church, and someone will throw water in the face of that baby. These families think the ritual of sprinkling water upon these babies makes them right with an eternal God. Works! The American version of good works is kind of the Boy Scout approach. If we just do enough benign deeds, God must accept us. That is as old as Judaism.

People today say, "I am just living by the Ten Commandments." Are you? Jesus intensified the Commandments. In fact, Jesus said,

- *"You have heard that it was said to those of old, 'You shall not murder, and whoever murders will be in danger of the judgment.' But I say to you that whoever is angry with his brother without a cause shall be in danger of the judgment."* (Matthew 5:21-22).
- *"You have heard that it was said to those of old, 'You shall not commit adultery.' But I say to you that whoever looks at a woman to lust for her has already committed adultery with her in his heart."* (Matthew 5:27-29).

Jesus not only made the Commandments harder; he made them *impossible!* There is no one living up to the Ten Commandments, no one! The Law of God is like a wall between a Holy God and us. People try to scale it and some people climb a little higher than others, but everyone falls back down. No one scales the wall. People try with religious ritual to burst through the wall to God, but the wall of the Law of God stands. No one can break the wall. The *only* way is to be lifted up by the grace of God.

Let me close with a modern parable. Suppose that a man is at a pier and falls into the water and he cannot swim very well. He is thrashing around and seems like he is going to drown. He comes up after a while, sputtering and thrashing, and some guy on the pier says, "Hey, fellow, listen—do the best you can! Man, just try harder. Take a deep breath this time before you go under. Have you ever thought about doing the breaststroke? How about floating on your back? You are not even trying!" The man goes under. He comes up again and another guy yells to him, "Hey, fellow, listen, could I sign you up for our swim club? We have never had a fatality from drowning. Anyone who is a member of our little group will never drown. Can I sign you up?" He goes under again, his lungs burning, his sides aching. Suddenly, he feels the strong grip of someone upon him who pulls him to the surface, to the shore, and saves him. *That is the gospel!* Jesus did not say to try harder. He did not say to join some sectarian religion or some church. Jesus came into the mess of the world with us where we were drowning. God became incarnate or "in carcass." Jesus came to the world and He saved us. He saves us, by *His* grace, and through *our* faith!

⸻ 2 0 0 5 ⸻

In the spring of 2005, the church dedicated a wonderful plaza and water feature to "our beloved builder," Curt Carter, Sr..

The year proved to be a year of transitions as a number of long-time staff members retired, or left for other ministry assignments. God supplied new leaders with fresh vision and energy.

The history of Valley Baptist Church is more than a recounting of building projects, attendance growth, and an expanding budget. The real history of Valley cannot fully be told. It is a story of changed lives! Each of the nearly 5,000 people who have been baptized at Valley Baptist Church could tell a unique story of God's transforming grace.

History is incomplete! The best and most fruitful days of Valley are yet ahead, in my opinion. Valley has a wonderful heritage but an even brighter future. Our hats are off to the past—let us take our coats off for the future, roll up our sleeves and go to work in God's vineyard.

"Faith as a Choice" was preached on Sunday morning, February 6, 2005, as part of a verse-by-verse series of messages through the book of Hebrews preached by Pastor Roger Spradlin and Pastor Phil Neighbors.

Faith As a Choice

"By faith Moses, when he was born, was hidden three months by his parents, because they saw he was a beautiful child; and they were not afraid of the king's command. By faith Moses, when he became of age, refused to be called the son of Pharaoh's daughter, choosing rather to suffer affliction with the people of God than to enjoy the passing pleasures of sin, esteeming the reproach of Christ greater riches than the treasures in Egypt; for he looked to the reward. By faith he forsook Egypt, not fearing the wrath of the king; for he endured as seeing Him who is invisible. By faith he kept the Passover and the sprinkling of blood, lest he who destroyed the firstborn should touch them." (NKJV)

Hebrews 11 is the preeminent chapter in the Bible on the subject of faith. One might expect such a chapter to be a rational or logical presentation of definitions and propositions about faith. Instead, it is chock-full of illustrations. The writer goes back to the Old Testament period and borrows from the lives of various individuals, in order to illustrate living by faith.

Moses was arguably the greatest man of the Old Testament. He stood before Pharaoh as a shepherd, with no army to back him up and no weapon in his hand, and said, "Let my people go." Egypt was the dominant civilization at that time in the world, and the Hebrew people had been slaves of the Egyptians for centuries. After a series of plagues and pressure by God, Pharaoh let the people go. Moses led them out of Egypt toward the Promised Land in what is called the Exodus. He led them in such a way that they became bottlenecked. The Red Sea was before them, mountains were to one side, and the expanse of the desert was on another side. In the meantime, Pharaoh had changed his mind, so the army of Egypt was pursuing them from the rear. Moses prayed a very brief prayer, raised the shepherd's staff, and the Red Sea literally parted—in one of the greatest miracles of human history. The Bible said that the people went across on dry land, walls of water on both sides of them, yet there was not even any mud! Moses led the congregation in the wilderness that some say numbered a million, or possibly as many as two or three million people. Besides all of that, he looked like Charlton Heston!

Moses had some great roots. His parents were people of faith. Verse 23 says, *"By faith Moses, when he was born, was hidden three months by his parents, because they saw he was a beautiful child; and they were not afraid of the king's command."* During the time when Moses was born, Pharaoh was concerned about the population explosion among the Hebrews. So, he ordered all of the baby children to be put to death as soon as they were born. Moses' parents, Amron and Jochabed, were people of faith. The Bible says that they hid Moses for three months because he was a beautiful child. I don't know what would have happened if he had been an ugly baby! Everyone who has a baby thinks of that baby as beautiful. Last fall we had our first grandchild. We were talking the other day to our son, Matthew. He and his wife live in Kentucky, so we do not get to see our little granddaughter, Charity, very often. We asked how much she had changed and what she looked like. Matthew said, "You know, I have never thought about babies being very pretty, and I am not saying this because she's mine, but she is the most beautiful baby I have ever seen." And you know what? I agree with him! That is how Amron and Jochabed felt about Baby Moses when he was born. He was a beautiful child to them, so they hid him from the king. Since he was growing, there came a time when they could not hide him any more. So they took him down to the river, made a little ark, a little basket that would float, lined it with pitch and placed him in it. They launched him out among the crocodiles of the Nile River, asking God for protection, I am certain. Pharaoh's daughter was downstream bathing when she saw the little baby in the basket. She fell in love with him because he was a beautiful child, and she adopted him as her own. So instead of Moses dying at the tip of the sword of an Egyptian when he was a baby, suddenly, in the providence of God, he became the adopted grandson of Pharaoh and was raised in the court of Pharaoh. He was raised in the court of Pharaoh! Pharaoh's daughter recruited his own mother to be his nanny, and to take care of him.

In those days, people lived longer than today. Moses lived to be a hundred and twenty years old. His life could be divided into three forty-year periods.

- The first forty years, Moses lived in the court of Pharaoh as his adopted grandson.
- The next forty years, he lived out in the wilderness as a shepherd and a fugitive.
- The last forty years, he was the leader of the nation of God.

Someone has said the first forty years he learned to be somebody in the courts of Pharaoh, the next forty years he learned to be nobody, and in the last forty years we see what God can do with someone who learned the first two lessons! When the writer of Hebrews illustrates the faith of Moses, he says nothing of his boyhood, nothing of his youth, very little about the faith of his parents, nothing about him being the dominant leader of the Old Testament era, nothing about Moses performing miracles. The writer uses Moses as an illustration in a very specific way.

The verses about Moses each relate to a time of crisis within his life, as the writer examines Moses' decision-making apparatus. How did he make choices in life? What was in his mind when he made choices? Hebrews 11 begins with Abel, Enoch and Noah, or the beginning of human history. Then the writer moves to the patriarchs of Abraham, Isaac, Jacob and Joseph. The common denominator of the faith of the patriarchs is that it endured.

- Abraham went, not knowing where, and he waited, not knowing how the promises of God would be fulfilled.
- Isaac waited all of his life for the Promised Land.
- Jacob died in exile in Egypt.
- Joseph waited for God's promises.

Moses' birth is not about enduring; it is about faith as a choice. He chose to follow God by faith. There are several principles concerning faith that we can learn from Moses.

Faith Enables Us to Make Correct Choices

Look at the key words in these verses about Moses:

- Verse 24, *"By faith…when he became of age, refused"* That is a choice!
- Verse 24, He *"refused to be called the son of Pharaoh's daughter."*
- Verse 25, *"Choosing rather to suffer affliction with the people of God than to enjoy the passing pleasures of sin"*

- Verse 26, *"Esteeming"* (or literally accounting or considering) the reproach of Christ.
- Verse 27, *"By faith he forsook Egypt"* That is a choice!
- Verse 28, *"By faith he kept the Passover"* That was a choice!

Faith involves a choice for every human being. Faith involves an initial choice, but it also involves a continual choice. There is an initial choice when we surrender ourselves to God and ask God to forgive our sin and Christ to be our Savior. Throughout our Christian experience, there are choices that we make every day as to what kind of a Christian we will be and how much of our life will be surrendered to the Lordship of Christ. When you choose wrong in the beginning, the further you go, the further away from God you become.

Years ago there was a plane that took off from a western airbase in the United States. They did not know it, but the navigator's instruments had a slight malfunction. They set their course and flew for hours and hours. Finally, they dropped out of the clouds, expecting to see a runway, but all they saw was the vast expanse of the Pacific Ocean. In the beginning, there was a slight miscalculation, yet the longer they flew, the farther away from their destination they were. Fortunately it was a military plane and they had parachutes on board. They tried to make it back to land but ran out of fuel, so they parachuted. It was two days before they fished Captain Rickenbacker out of the water, along with his crew. When you make a miscalculation in the beginning, at the point of departure, the longer you live, the further away from God you become. Eventually one day you wake up and you realize you are so far in sin you cannot even imagine you are doing the things you are doing. You cannot imagine the value system with which you are now living, or the choices in life that you have made, and the consequences that you have reaped. It is important that we not only choose correctly in the beginning but that we stay on course.

CELEBRATING 20 YEARS OF CHANGED LIVES

Faith Enables Us to Renounce Our Old Life

Look at what it says in verse 24: *"By faith Moses, when he became of age, refused to be called the son of Pharaoh's daughter."* The word *refused* literally means he "denied it to be said." There was a point in life when he denied it to be said any more that he was the grandson of Pharaoh. It was not the rebellious act of a youth. It says, "when he became of age," literally the Greek word *megos,* when he became great. It was when he became a monolithic man, a great man, not only in age, but great in other ways. It was the decision of a mature man whose place in history by now was secure. Moses was a great man in Egypt. Philo Judeas, the first-century biographer of Moses, said that Moses was in line for Pharaoh's crown. He was the adopted grandson of Pharaoh, and the favorite in many ways. Ancient literature alludes to the fact that Moses was perhaps the inventor of the Egyptian alphabet. Some scholars say that much of the Egyptian civilization is owed to the genius of Moses. Some have said that the Greek philosophers Socrates and Aristotle owed their philosophical insight to Moses.

Moses was part of the government that dominated the world for several millenniums. Can you imagine that? Think of how young the United States is, and then think of a civilization that was the dominant civilization for several thousand years. Moses was the grandson of Pharaoh. If he walked down the streets, soldiers would say, "Bow the knee, bow the knee." If he floated down the Nile River, it would be on a golden barge. Stephen tells us in Acts 7 that he was not only mighty in word as a statesman, but he was mighty in deed. Moses was a powerful warrior. According to the secular historian, Josephus, when the Ethiopians invaded Egypt, Pharaoh put Moses in charge as the Commander in Chief of the Army. He became a renowned general when he repelled the attack of the Ethiopians.

According to a legend, Moses was playing one day as a little boy in the lap of Pharaoh. Moses reached up and took the

424

crown off Pharaoh's head and threw it down at his feet. The wise men of Egypt, the counselors to the Pharaohs, were shocked and said, "This child is wise beyond his years; he will curse the downfall of you, Pharaoh." They decided to test Moses to see if he knew what he was doing in taking the crown off. They brought two bowls. One bowl was filled with bright red-hot coals. The other bowl was filled with precious gems, diamonds and rubies. They declared if the child picks the rubies and diamonds then he should be destroyed because he is wise beyond his years. The legend states that Moses stuck his little fingers in the hot coals and burned them so severely that when he put his hands in his mouth because they hurt, it burned his tongue, and the rest of his life he stammered and stuttered. That, of course, is apocryphal. It is not true. It is a legend, but it shows how Moses was a person of legends.

The Pharaoh at that time, the best we can tell historically, was Ramses II, who ruled from 1292 to 1225 B.C. He was one of the greatest monarchs who ever lived. One day when Moses was *megos,* when he was already a great man and a general, he pushed past the guards. Walking into the throne room, he said, "Let it never be said again that I am the grandson of Pharaoh. I choose by faith to identify myself with the people of God." He traded security for certain insecurity. Here is a man who had everything going for him—power, position, pleasure, possessions and prestige. He jettisoned all of that, and the Bible says he did so by faith. He made a choice between the world and God! We are called on to make that choice. Maybe not on as grand a scale perhaps as Moses, but we must also make a choice.

Years ago an oil company was drilling for oil in South America. They struck oil, but the problem was that there was not anyone who could communicate with the indigenous people. There happened to be a young man living there who was a missionary translating the Bible into their language, who had good rapport with the natives. The oil company decided to hire this young missionary. They offered him a huge salary, much more than he was making as a missionary, to come and be their liaison or intermediary with this tribe. He refused, so they offered him a bigger salary. Finally they offered him a fortune, or what seemed to be a fortune, and he turned it down. They were perplexed, so they asked him, "How much money do you want?" He said, "It is not a matter of money. It is not that the salary is not big enough, it is that the job is too small." The missionary thought, "I do not want to work for an oil company. God has called me to be a missionary." That's the way Moses felt! Moses thought the job of being the Pharaoh was too small when he said, "I am going to identify with the people of God." He did so by faith.

Every human being stands at some time at a Y, or a fork in the road. We must choose whether we are going to follow what Jesus called the broad road that leads to destruction or if we are going to follow the narrow road that leads to life. Even though we make an initial choice, life still is a series of choices. No matter which road you choose, there are other crossroads and other Ys. Life is constantly a choice between whether we will follow God or the values of the world. Faith does not argue; it does not rationalize. It obeys! He could have rationalized and said, "Hey, I am in line for the crown, and if I just keep my mouth shut, I will be the Pharaoh. Then look what I can do for my people! I can free them!" But he did not do that. He made a renunciation that changed his life and changed the course of history. Consequently, there is no statue today of Moses in Egypt, there is no Sphinx that bears his name; he is not buried in the bottom of one of those massive pyramids in a palatial tomb as he could have been. Instead he's buried in an unmarked grave on a mountain in a desert.

It is unlike kings to renounce their thrones. It has only happened once in modern history. In 1936 after a reign of only 325 days, Edward VIII renounced his throne. He wanted to marry a woman from America who was divorced, and the

Church of England would not allow him to marry someone who was divorced, let alone a commoner. He had fallen in love with Mrs. Wallis Simpson and he wanted to marry her. The only way he could do that was to give up the monarchy, so he renounced the throne. The world was divided about his decision. Some people said he was the hero of romantic love, giving up a kingdom for the one he loved. Others said that he was a jerk for avoiding the responsibility of the monarchy. Moses far outclassed Edward VIII in his renunciation of giving up the crown of Egypt. You and I are called on to make that kind of renunciation of the world. *Theological repentance*, we call that renunciation. When we come to God, not only are we embracing God, but also at the same time, we are letting go of the world. There are many people in our culture who want to have it both ways; they want to hang onto God with one hand, and hang onto the values of the world with the other hand. You can barely distinguish whether they have faith within their life. That is absolutely foreign to everything the Bible teaches. When you come to God, there is a renunciation of the old life—you jettison the old life, and you turn from your sin. That initial renunciation we call salvation. When you come to Christ for salvation, you repent of your sin and embrace Christ as your Savior. In addition to that initial renunciation, there is to be a perpetual renunciation we call *sanctification*. Sanctification is progressive within your life, choosing *daily* to surrender yourself to God.

Faith Enables Us to Set Proper Priorities

There is another principle here, and that is that faith enables us to not only make correct choices and renounce our old life, but it enables us to set proper priorities. In some ways, that's what this passage is about. Look at verse 25: *"Choosing rather to suffer affliction with the people of God than to enjoy the passing pleasures of sin, esteeming,"* or accounting literally, *"the reproach of Christ greater riches than the treasures in Egypt; for he looked to the reward.*" He chose between the treasures of Egypt or Christ, the passing pleasures of sin or following God. He chose to identify with the people of God. On the surface, the people of Egypt seemed to be blessed. The goddess of the Nile River, they believed, caused it to overflow and irrigate their crops. There was the sun god, Ra, who seemed to be a blazing success. On one hand was the strength and might of the Egyptians; on the other hand was a contemptible race of slaves, a servile people called the Hebrews. Moses chose to identify with the slaves and to give up riches. You may be asking how he made such a choice. The Bible tells us that he did not look at the beginning but he looked at the end. It says that he looked at the reward and he did not look at the passing pleasures of sin. The King James Version says, "*pleasures of sin for a season.*" The pleasure of sin is temporary. Initially, it is more enjoyable. There are many people who say that there is no pleasure in sin, but the devil is pretty smart! He's not going to fish without bait. Of course there is pleasure in sin, but the operative word here is the *passing* pleasure of sin. For a period of time, there is pleasure in sin, and even satisfaction, but it does not fulfill and it does not last.

I heard about a man in olden times who was feeding his pigs in the roadway. He had a basket of beans, and as he would throw some beans down, the pigs would eat them. He would walk a few more steps and throw some beans down, and the pigs would run and gather round him and eat the beans. Someone said, "Mister, that is a strange way to feed your pigs." He responded, "I am not feeding them, I am leading them to *slaughter.*" Well, the devil is the one with the basket and guess who the *pigs* are? That is you and me! It is you and I who choose material things and the values of the world. We are being led to slaughter for the passing pleasure of sin.

Years ago, Dr. Gordon, of Boston, wrote a song that we still sing occasionally,

"My Jesus, I love Thee, I know Thou art mine;
For Thee, all the follies of sin I resign."

That is not exactly how he wrote it. He wrote, "All the pleasures of sin I resign," but it was changed because people said, "Let's view sin as follies, it is folly to sin." Sin is pleasurable for a while. All the pleasures of sin, he said, I resign. Moses understood the passing pleasures. He looked to the end; he looked to the reward. *Choosing* in verse 25 literally means "to take for one's self a position." We must take a position. We have choices to make. Life is full of choices. We choose what radio station we will to listen to, we choose what television program we will watch, we choose what we are going to do in the evening and, more importantly, we choose who we are going to marry or who we are not going to marry. We choose in the matter of children, having children and when, how many children we will have. We choose our work life, we choose what school we will attend, we choose where we are going to live, but more important perhaps than that, we make choices about character. We make choices about morality; we make choices about integrity.

We live in a world that increasingly values tolerance. Our culture uses the word *tolerance* in a way that a Christian should not use it. We are expected to tolerate things that God does not tolerate. We have become not so much evangelicals but "evanjellyfish" in some ways. If we are going to be believers and followers of God, we must take a position—a position on social issues like abortion, a position on sexual perversion, a position on euthanasia and the cultural issues that face our world.

Moses took a position. How did he do it? It says in verse 26, "esteeming," or "considering." It is an accounting word. Considering Christ greater riches than the treasures in Egypt, because he looked to the reward. He looked at the end result. He looked away from the passing pleasures of sin and focused upon God. That is what repentance does. Repentance is not just about cleaning up your life and saying, "Oh, I am not going to do this, and I am not going to do that." That is morality. Genuine repentance is twofold. It is leaving the things that we should leave, and at the same time focusing on and embracing God. He chose the reproach, the suffering. We do not suffer for Christ like people of other ages have, or even as some in other places on our planet today. Sometimes, though, we are ridiculed intellectually or lampooned as anti-intellectuals. But think of Moses—he gave up the riches of Egypt.

Several decades ago, an archeologist named Carter broke into a tomb and discovered the remains of a grave that had not yet been robbed. The tomb was of one of the "lesser lights" of Egypt, a boy king by the name of Tut. Do you remember the wealth of that tomb? It was tens of millions of dollars. The treasure was displayed in museums around the world, and still is today. Think of the wealth of Egypt, yet Moses gave all that up to follow God!

There is born within every one of us a desire to hang on to stuff. If you do not believe that, then just look in your garage when you get home. We buy all this stuff that we think we just have to have. After a while, we put our stuff in the garage and we keep it for months, maybe years. Then one day we clean it out, have a garage sale, and someone comes along and says, "Oh, look at that stuff! I have got to have that stuff!" They buy it from us and keep it for a while in their house, and eventually it makes its way to their garage. Then they have a garage sale and mark it way down. Someone says, "Look! Fifty cents! I have got to have this stuff!" They buy it, and eventually it makes its way to a flea market or a swap meet. Someone else buys it, and then finally someone throws it away! Some day someone will be digging in the garbage heap, and they'll say, "Look at the stuff I found today."

We want to hang on to stuff. Moses chose between material things and following God. There is nothing wrong with stuff, but it should not be the ultimate priority, the ultimate ambition or the drive of anybody's life. Christianity is not, "Something good is about to happen to you." Sometimes your integrity may cost you a business deal; sometimes your faith or your convictions will cost you.

Faith Enables Us to Focus on the Invisible and the Spiritual.

Faith enables us to focus on the invisible and the spiritual. Look at verse 27: *"By faith he forsook Egypt, not fearing the wrath of the king; for he endured as seeing Him who is invisible. By faith he kept the Passover and the sprinkling of blood, lest he who destroyed the first born should touch them."*

In these verses, we see faith in action. It is not merely Moses believing. He's doing something. At some point, our faith should become active. Our culture is filled with people who say, "I have faith," because they believe that God exists. At some point our faith should be demonstrated in our actions of serving God. The Bible says that he kept the Passover. It is in the perfect tense, meaning literally he instituted the Passover. He did not keep it in the sense of keeping something that had been going on. He started the Passover. God sent one last plague against the Egyptians so that Pharaoh would let the people go. God told Moses, and Moses told Pharaoh, that on a certain night there would be the death of every firstborn throughout the entire land. God told Moses, and he instructed the people that the only way to be spared was to take a lamb, keep it in their house for fourteen days until it became like a little pet to the family. Then they were to slaughter that lamb as a sacrifice, dip a weed in its blood and put the blood over the doorpost of their house. When the death angel came, it would pass over them; and that is why it was called the Passover meal. It was a meal that was to commemorate their liberation from Egypt. The only problem is, they had not been liberated yet. That is like building a monument of victory before the war. That would be like Abraham Lincoln giving the Gettysburg address before the battle.

Moses instituted the Passover. By faith, they killed a lamb. Moses said they were supposed to cook the lamb and eat all of it, and any leftovers they were to burn—which personally is what I think should happen to leftovers! They were to eat it with their cloak tucked into their belt, their sandals on their feet and their staff in their hand, ready to go. Can you imagine the reaction of the people, saying, "Well, let me get this straight? You want us to get a little lamb, feed him for fourteen days, kill him and put blood over the doorpost?" The Hebrew people were slaves, but some of them were highly educated; they probably had graduate degrees and Ph.D.'s, maybe in Egyptian hieroglyphics. Yet by faith they kept the Passover. That night when the angel came, there was screaming and lamenting throughout the land.

Moses believed in Him who is invisible. He could not see God, and yet he believed. I can show you his humanity, you can see on occasion that he was weak and hot tempered, but he believed God. How did he do that? Because he focused upon the end, he focused on the invisible and the spiritual.

Let me give you a few points of application.

He Refused!

Some people would say that Moses was a fool for giving up those riches. Jim Elliott, the great missionary, said, "He is no fool who gives up what he cannot keep for what he cannot lose." There is an element of Christianity that is missing today, and that is repentance. Repentance is not just a one-time deal; it is a continual process. As God gives us light and understanding of things that are wrong in our life, we are under obligation to get rid of them. We meet Christians who even premeditate sin when they say:

- "I know we should not be living together, but God will forgive us."
- "I know we should not get a divorce; it is wrong, but God will forgive us."
- "I know that we should not get an abortion, but God is a God of love and He will forgive us."

What would you think of your children if they said, "Dad, I know I am not supposed to do this, but, you are my dad and you have got to forgive me." What kind of disrespect would that be to a father? Verse 24 says, *"he refused."* Verse 25 says, it was *"choosing."* Verse 26, *"it was esteeming, considering."* In my opinion, it is ineffective preaching and teaching to say, "Give up this, give up that, do not drink, do not do this, do not go there, do not watch that!" That is ineffective because it is merely morality. The message of Christ is not just repentance, it is, "Embrace God," at the same time. If you give all these things up in your life, you have emptiness, and God does not want us to be empty. He wants us to be full of His presence.

Repentance is twofold, it is turning from the world and sin, but at the same time it is turning to God. If a dog has a bone and you want to get the bone away from him, what are you going to do? You could wrestle the dog in a tug-of-war for the bone, and you might even get bitten. What is the wiser thing to do? Throw a big piece of meat down for him, and he will sniff at the meat. Then he will drop the bone and you can just pick it up. He is going for the meat because you offered him something better. That is what repentance is. Repentance is not about us trying harder, it is not about cleaning up our life. That is morality. It is not about trying to turn over a new leaf or reforming your life. It is about embracing God! It is about God becoming the focus of your life. Whenever you have habitual sin in your life, and you fall prey to the same thing over and over again, it is not because of the weakness of your will, it is a lack of focus upon God.

In 1949, Jim Voss worked for the mob, but he also worked for the L.A.P.D. He was a double agent, you might say. He stumbled into a tent meeting and gave his life to Christ. He said that he could no longer live with duplicity. In fact, he said, "I can no longer have both hands in different pots. If Jesus is Lord, He must be Lord of all." Jim Voss gave up his old lifestyle.

All of us come to the fork in the road and we must choose. William Booth started the great organization, the Salvation Army, ministering to poor people around the world. When he started it in England, he was not very well received by Christian people. He was particularly criticized by the clergy of his day. They thought it was beneath the dignity of a British preacher to be handing out soap, working the soup lines, and so forth. They had an ecclesiastical meeting to take him to task. They brought him into the auditorium, much like this auditorium, with a horseshoe balcony. There were hundreds of people there to see how he would respond to their accusations. He was on the platform, and they brought accusation after accusation against William Booth. They told him he should desist from what he was doing because he was shaming Christ with all the little ditties that they played on the drums. When they asked him if he would cease his activities, William Booth put his head in his hands for a long time as he was making the decision. In the balcony was his wife, Katherine. As the crowd was waiting in silence for William Booth's decision, Katherine stood and yelled as loud as she could, "William, tell them no. William, tell them no," and the Salvation Army was born! There is a point in the Christian life where you just have to say, "No, no, I will not live like that! I will not watch that movie, I will not dress that way and I will not let that in my mind. No! No! No!" That is faith!

Demonstration of Faith

Moses demonstrated his faith in action, forsaking Egypt, keeping the Passover. A few years ago, I received a jury summons, which as you know, is always a blessing for any citizen! I did not think anything about it because, being a pastor, I had never been kept on a jury. Usually, I am always the first one they let go. I am not sure why, but they do. I expected to be the first one to go but, for some reason, I fell through the cracks. I became a juror on a very complicated criminal case that lasted a couple of weeks, followed by three days of deliberation. There were twenty-seven different witnesses. It was purely a circumstantial case, so it was very complex. I ended up being the jury foreman, so it was my job to help lead the discussion. I think it was about the second day of deliberations, and I was trying to logically present all the evidence. Using a board to draw on, I explained the steps that we would need to take in order to make a conviction, which we eventually did. We needed to agree on eight different steps. If we agreed on those at the end, we would have a "guilty" verdict. If we did not, then we would have a "not guilty" verdict. I was laboring to present the logic of the case. We took a break some time about the second day, maybe about noon. During the break, it dawned on me—that old saying, "If it was a crime to be a Christian, would there be enough evidence to convict you?" I thought, "This is a circumstantial case. What if people were looking at my life, the circumstances of my life, and someone was writing it on a board. Would there be clear evidence that I am a person of faith?" Would there for you?

~ MARCH 24, 2004 ~

Karen Watson Memorial Service

Karen was a wonderful Christian lady, sent by Valley Baptist Church as a missionary to Iraq. She, along with three other missionaries, was murdered in the Mosul area by radical Islamic extremists on March 15, 2004.

Karen left a letter with Pastor Phil Neighbors and Pastor Roger Spradlin that was to be opened only on the occasion of her death. Following is her letter:

Dear Pastor Phil and Pastor Roger,

You should only be opening this letter in the event of death.

When God calls there are no regrets. I tried to share my heart with you as much as possible, my heart for the Nations. I wasn't called to a place, I was called to Him. To obey was my objective, to suffer was expected. His glory my reward, His glory my reward.

I thank you all so much for your prayers and support. Surely your reward in Heaven will be great. Thank you for investing in my life and spiritual well-being. Keep sending missionaries out, keep raising up fine young pastors.

In regards to any service, keep it small and simple. Yes simple, just preach the gospel. If Jason Buss is available, or his dad, have them sing a pretty song. Be bold and preach the life saving, life changing, forever eternal GOSPEL. Give glory and honor to our Father.

"The Missionary Heart"
Care more than some think is wise
Risk more than some think is safe
Dream more than some think is practical
Expect more than some think is possible.
I was called not to comfort or success, but to obedience.

There is no joy outside of knowing Jesus and serving Him. I love you two and my church family.

In His Care
Salaam, Karen

"Does it Pay to Serve God?" was preached at Karen Watson's Memorial service, held at Valley Baptist Church on March 24, 2004.

Does It Pay to Serve God?

MALACHI 3:13-18

"'Your words have been harsh against Me,' says the LORD. Yet you say, 'What have we spoken against You?' You have said, 'It is useless to serve God; What profit is it that we have kept His ordinance, And that we have walked as mourners Before the Lord of hosts? So now we call the proud blessed, For those who do wickedness are raised up; They even tempt God and go free.' Then those who fear the LORD spoke to one another, And the LORD listened and heard them; So a book of remembrance was written before Him For those who fear the LORD And who meditate on His name. 'They shall be Mine,' says the LORD of hosts, 'On the day that I make them My jewels; And I will spare them As a man spares his own son who serves him. Then you shall again discern Between the righteous and the wicked, Between one who serves God And one who does not serve Him.'"(NKJV)

To many of us, Karen's death is very personal, particularly for her family and friends. Even for those who only knew Karen casually, or perhaps did not know her at all, her death is a tragedy. It is a tragedy for someone so young and vibrant to be taken—especially someone who loved the Lord so much and had such compassion for other people. There are some in our culture for whom both her life and her death are perplexing. After talking to me about Karen's work in Iraq, a reporter asked me, "Would Karen say it was worth it?" Karen wrote a letter that was to be opened only on the occasion of her death. Karen began the letter by saying, "When you are called of God, there are no regrets." What the reporter really was asking is a question that all of us have wondered on occasion, and some have even dared to ask openly: "Does it really pay to serve God?" What is a quiet deliberation on the part of most of us had become an open and malignant question in the days of Malachi.

The people were asking, "Does it really pay to serve God?" Malachi brought an accusation against the people saying, *"Your words have been harsh against Me, says the LORD,"* and they looked at Malachi with incredulity and said, *"What have we ever spoken against the Lord? You have said that it is useless to serve God, and what profit is it that we have kept His ordinance?"* They continued, saying that it is vain, or hollow, or futile, or useless, it is like trying to catch the wind to serve God. What profit is it?

They gave four reasons why they did not think that it paid to serve God. Two reasons related to God's people and two to the ungodly. They said, "For God's people, there is no reward." They asked, "What profit is there in keeping the Lord's ordinance?" Also, there is no recognition for the godly—no recompense for the ungodly. The people declared that even those who are proud and do wickedness are raised up. The word *raised up* literally means to "prosper." They declared that the wicked are the ones who seem to prosper. So there is no reward or recognition for the righteous and no recompense or retaliation against the wicked.

The people said that even those who tempt God, those who shake their fist in the face of God, those who would murder missionaries, go free. And so the people of Malachi's time said that it does not really pay to serve God. By human observation, they were right! So much of the Christian world today says that prosperity is a mark of God's favor, that if you are a Christian, God wants you to never be sick or endure tragedy. The world today says that God wants your pockets to be lined with money. But that flies in the face of the reality of Scripture.

In Psalm 73, Asaph the psalmist said, *"Truly God is good to Israel, to such as are pure in heart."* That is a basic affirmation of faith that all of us would make—that God is good to those of a pure heart. But the psalmist said, *"My feet had almost slipped when I considered the suffering of the righteous and the prosperity of the wicked. It was too painful for me, and I could hardly grasp it until I went into the sanctuary of the Lord, and I understood their end."* He understood that there would be a payday some day—that God will some day reward the righteous and bring retribution against the wicked. But it is not now. It is in the future. The Bible says, *"Vengeance is Mine, I will repay, says the Lord."* We are not to harbor any idea of settling accounts; we are not to harbor bitterness. No one gets away with anything! Some day every human being will be accountable to God. But not today. There is an element of mercy in that. For those who reject Christ, this life— with all of its sorrows and all of its grief—is the very best that they will ever have in eternity. The Book of Romans says that the goodness of God leads men to repentance.

It Pays to Serve God if You Value the Attention of God More than the Approval of Men

So, does it pay to serve God? When you give your life in service to the Lord and love people half a world away, and a hail of bullets greets you, and your kindness is returned by murder, can we say it pays to serve God? Malachi speaks for

God and in essence says, "Yes, it does pay to serve God, if you value the attention of God more than the approval of men." Verse 16 says, *"Then those who feared the LORD spoke often to one another, And the LORD listened and heard them; So a book of remembrance was written before Him For those who fear the LORD And who meditate on His name."* The Lord listened. The word *listened* is the word used when a horse hears a loud noise and suddenly its ears perk up. For those who fear the Lord, God is paying attention! Not only is there divine observation, but also eternal preservation. Malachi says that God keeps a book of remembrance. The deeds of God's people are often forgotten. Not everyone in our culture approved of what Karen was doing, but I can tell you that she had God's attention. That is what the Scripture says.

There is not always a lot of recognition for those who serve the Lord. A century ago the greatest preacher in England was a man by the name of Charles Spurgeon, a powerful communicator of the gospel. He ministered at the Metropolitan Tabernacle in London, England. If you went to London today and asked people who Charles Spurgeon was, even scarcely a block from where he ministered, they would look at you dumbfounded and not be able to answer you. If you went to Chicago today and asked who Dwight Moody was, they would not be able to tell you. But God remembers. The Bible says there is a book of remembrance!

I love the story of an old missionary who served back in the days before extensive communication and travel. He had been on the mission field for decades and, in fact, his wife had died there. He was all alone, and it was time for him to come home and retire. He wrote that he was coming home by ship, arriving on a certain day by ship. As he was traveling, he wondered what kind of reception he would receive. He imagined that perhaps they would give him a parade. He was curious as to who would be at the dock to meet him. As he walked down the gangplank and the crowd began to dissipate, he realized that there was *no one* there to meet him. He began to grumble to the Lord as he picked up his meager belongings. Looking for a place to stay that night, he prayed, "Lord I have come home and no one cares. I have come home and there is no one here to meet me." He said that it was as if he heard a voice, not an audible voice, but deep in his soul a voice that said, "You are not home yet." Karen is home! It pays to serve God if you value the attention of God more than the approval of men!

It Pays to Serve God if You Value the Spiritual More than the Material

The second thing that Malachi declares is that it pays to serve God if you value the spiritual more than the material. Verse 16-17 says, *"For those who fear the LORD And who meditate upon His name. 'They shall be Mine,' says the LORD of hosts. 'On the day that I make them My jewels. And I will spare them As a man spares his own son who serves him. For those who meditate* [literally "put esteem or value upon the name of the Lord"], *there will be a day that I will make them My jewels.'"* In the ancient world, most kings were despots who owned everything. They owned the people, virtually, and all the wealth of the empire. How do you get your arms around such wealth? So when a visiting dignitary came and the king wanted to demonstrate his wealth, he would call for the king's special treasure or jewels. It was a chest: a trove of treasures of gems, rubies, diamonds and gold. You could run your hands through it and demonstrate your tangible wealth to a visiting dignitary. God says there is going to be a day when He will make the redeemed His special treasure or jewels. Some people have a treasure, and they are a treasure—like Barnabas, a wealthy man in the New Testament, or Joseph who gave Jesus the tomb in which to be buried. There are some today who say that if you are a Christian, it is God's will that you be affluent. We tend to Americanize Christianity. I love our political system and our economic system of free enterprise, where you are rewarded according to your work and ingenuity. But the fact is, much of the world lives in poverty. The Christian life is not about having a treasure. It is about *being* a treasure! The apostle Peter said that we are God's special people. The only thing in eternity that God is going to preserve is redeemed humanity. When the sun is burned out like a cinder, and the universe is rolled up like a scroll, the only thing that will be left will be the redeemed.

In 1923, the seven wealthiest men in the world met at the Edgewater Beach Hotel in Chicago to discuss world affairs and what seemed to be a coming financial crisis in the world. The net worth of these seven men was more than the treasury of the United States in 1923. Twenty-five years later after their meeting, a doctoral student researched what had happened to these seven men.

- Charles Schwab, who was the president of the largest steel manufactory, had died, having lost all of his wealth during the depression.
- Arthur Cutton, the great wheat speculator, had also died in poverty.
- Robert Whitney, who was the president of the New York Stock Exchange, had died after serving time in prison.
- Albert Fall, who had served in the President's cabinet, had been pardoned from prison to come home and die.
- Jessie Livermore, the bear of Wall Street, had taken his own life during the depression.
- Leon Frasier, the president of the Bank of International Settlement, had also ended his life in suicide.
- Ivan Kuger, the head of the world's greatest monopoly in 1923, in despair, had taken his own life.

Twenty-five years after these wealthy men met, even the hotel in Chicago where they met was gone. Jesus said, *"What shall it profit a man if he gains the whole world and yet he loses his soul?"* Karen did not have a treasure, but she was a treasure to the Lord.

It Pays to Serve God if You Value the Eternal More than the Temporal

Does it pay to serve God? It pays if you value the attention of God more than the approval of men; it pays if you value the spiritual more than the material, and it pays if you value the eternal more than the temporal. God says, *"In that day, I will spare them as a man spares his own son."* The verse is futuristic. I *will* spare them. We are not spared today as Christians. God does not always stop the speeding car. He does not always stop the terrorist bullet. In this world, there is sickness, tragedy and grief. On top of the normal issues of living in a sinful and fallen world are the abnormal difficulties of swimming against the tide of a decaying culture. Karen knew that life was about more than the "here and now." It is great to be a Christian—to have the fellowship of a spiritual family, the joy of the Lord and peace. Yet the apostle Paul said in that great passage on the resurrection, in 1 Corinthians 15, that if in this life only we have hope, we are of all men most miserable, because we would be deluded. The Christian life is not only about here and now; it is about eternity with God.

It Pays to Serve God if You Value Others More than Yourself

Does it pay to serve God? It pays if you value others more than yourself. Verse 18 talks about those who serve the Lord. How do we serve the Lord? We serve the Lord as we worship and through our obedience, but primarily we serve the Lord by investing in other people. The last thing Jesus said to His disciples as He ascended was, "Go into all the nations." Karen went! Was she afraid? She struggled with fear. She was apprehensive; she certainly calculated the risk. But courage is not so much the absence of fear as it is the disregard of fear.

Does it pay to serve God? Our culture looks at Karen's life and says, "No, it is useless, it is vain. Her life was a waste. It does not pay to serve God." In the day of Malachi, the people said, "No, it does not pay to serve God. There is no reward or recognition for the godly. There is no recompense or retaliation for the wicked." But God, when asked the question, "Does it pay?" says, "Yes!"

- If you value the attention of God more than the approval of men,
- If you value the spiritual more than the material,
- If you value the eternal more than the temporal,
- If you value others more than yourself.

Then *yes*, it pays to serve God! If we could ask Karen, "Karen, does it pay? Karen, does it pay? Did it pay to serve God?" I think Karen would say, "Oh, yes! Oh, yes!" For now she has heard those words, "*Well done, thou good and faithful servant, enter into the kingdom prepared for you.*"

*Do You Want
God
To Change Your
Life?*

An Invitation to Christ

The power of God to change lives begins with a personal relationship with God through Jesus Christ. Did you know that you were created by God for a relationship with Him? Colossians 1:16 says, *"All things were created through Him and for Him."* Our lives are changed as we realize the purpose for our existence, a relationship with Jesus Christ.

The path to a changed life comes as we recognize that our sin separates us from God. Romans 3:23 says, *"For all have sinned and fall short of the glory of God."* Romans 6:23 says, *"For the wages of sin is death…"* Sin keeps us from experiencing a relationship with God, and the Bible teaches that every one of us has sinned against God; God in His holiness must punish sin. The Bible also teaches us that God loves us so much that he sent His Son Jesus Christ to die for our sins upon the cross. God decided to take our punishment for sin upon Himself so that we could be saved from Hell, forgiven of our sins, and brought back into a relationship with Him. Jesus Christ died on the cross, was buried, and rose again to pay for the wages of sin.

We are forgiven of our sins by God's grace through faith in Jesus Christ. Ephesians 2:8-9 says, *"For by grace you have been saved through faith, and that not of yourselves; it is the gift of God, not of works, lest anyone should boast."* There is absolutely nothing we can do to earn our way to Heaven; salvation is an act of God's grace. There will be no bragging in heaven, because no one will be there because of his or her own merit. Salvation is by God's grace.

We are forgiven of our sins as we put our faith and trust in Jesus Christ to forgive us, based upon His sacrifice on the cross for our sins. The Bible teaches we must turn from our sins and turn to Christ, only then can God truly change our lives.

What about you? Have you ever confessed to God that you have sinned, and asked God to forgive you because of Jesus' death upon the cross for sin? If a changed life through faith in Jesus Christ is the desire of your heart, trust in Jesus today. Romans 10:13 teaches, *"For whoever calls on the name of the Lord shall be saved."* Experience the power of God to change your life through a personal relationship with God through faith in Jesus Christ!

Are you ready to give your life to Jesus? If that is the desire of your heart, go to God in prayer. Prayer is simply talking to God. Admit to God that you have sinned. Ask Him to have mercy on you and to forgive you of your sins. Thank Him for sending His Son, Jesus—whose life, death, and resurrection secure salvation for all who follow Him. Commit your life to Jesus. Tell Him that you repent of your sins and want to follow Him. Ask God to help you live for Him.

Dear friend:

If you have made this commitment to ask Jesus Christ to be your Savior, I want to encourage you to begin praying and reading your Bible every day. Ask God to help you to find a Bible-teaching Church where you will learn the Word of God and begin your spiritual journey.

We would love to hear from you if this book has changed *your* life! You may reach us at Valley Baptist Church, 4800 Fruitvale Avenue, Bakersfield, CA 93308, 661-393-5683 or www.valleybaptist.org.

Celebrating 20 Years of Changed Lives
Order Form

Postal orders: 4800 Fruitvale Avenure
Bakersfield, CA 93308

Telephone orders: 661-393-5683

Please send *Celebrating 20 Years of Changed Lives* to:

Name: _____

Address: _____

City: _____   State: _____

Zip: _____   Telephone: (_____) _____

Book Price: $19.95

Shipping: $3.00 for the first book and $1.00 for each additional book to
cover shipping and handling within US, Canada, and Mexico.
International orders add $6.00 for the first book and $2.00 for
each additional book.

Or order from:
ACW Press
1200 HWY 231 South #273
Ozark, AL 36360

(800) 931-BOOK

or contact your local bookstore